© 2008 The Little Bookroom
First published 2007 by Alastair Sawday Publishing Co. Ltd

© 2008 Alastair Sawday Publishing Co. Ltd
Photos © Rob Cousins
www.robcousins.com

Cover design (US): Louise Fili Ltd
Design concept (book interior): Company X, Bristol
Maps: Maidenhead Cartographic Services
Chicken photographs: Eshott Hall

Series editor: Alastair Sawday
Project editor: Jackie King
Assistant editor: Jo Boissevain
Writing and research: Alastair Sawday, Gail McKenzie
Regional guides: Kate Ball, Sarah Bolton, Melanie Harrison, Wendy Ogden
Production (UK): Tom Germain, Anny Mortada, Julia Richardson
Production (US): Adam Hess

Library of Congress Cataloging-in-Publication Data

Sawday, Alastair.
  Go slow England / by Alastair Sawday with Gail McKenzie ; photographs by Rob Cousins ; foreword by Nigel Slater.
     p. cm.
  ISBN 1-892145-66-9 (alk. paper)
  1. Ecotourism—Great Britain—Guidebooks. 2. Great Britain—Description and travel—Guidebooks. 3. Sustainable living—Great Britain—Guidebooks. 4. Ecology—Great Britain. 5. Great Britain—Guidebooks. I. McKenzie, Gail. II. Title.
  DA650.S39 2008
  914.204'86—dc22

                              2008016775

Published by The Little Bookroom
435 Hudson Street, 3rd floor
New York, NY 10014
www.littlebookroom.com
(212) 293-1643 Fax (212) 333-5374

Distributed in the United States by Random House.
Printed on 20% PCW recycled paper.

0 9 8 7 6 5 4 3 2 1

Go Slow England

Alastair Sawday

with Gail McKenzie

Photography by Rob Cousins

Foreword
by Nigel Slater

Special places to stay

Contents

Foreword by Nigel Slater

I like to know where I am when I stay away from home, not by looking at the masthead on the writing paper or by scrutinizing the logo on the absurdly copious bath towels, but by feeling part of the place. I don't want to stay in a room with a corporate "house style" that has been gently tweaked to reflect the area, but to stay somewhere that is rich with what I call a "sense of place." A place where everything feels right, from the floorboards to the bread to the flowers on the table. I suppose what I am after is a certain local distinctiveness and integrity.

When I choose somewhere to stay it means everything that the building is made of local stone or wood and brick, that it has a history and has been restored or repaired with sympathetic materials. It matters that the vegetables on my plate were grown in the owner's garden or allotment, that the lamb came from the farm over the hill and the proprietor had a hand in making my supper. Nothing could make me happier than knowing that the person who takes my booking is the one who also bakes the biscuits that come with my pot of tea or feeds the chickens that supply the egg for my breakfast.

I am not interested in a pretentious dinner. What appeals more is the idea of locally produced food that has been cooked simply and with respect. I like food to be what it is, food with an honesty and a heart and soul.

Yes, in the past I have liked it that room service answers my call in three rings, or that there's a fax on hand 24/7 but what really matters now goes much deeper than that. In the 21st century, I need to know the effect that my choice of accommodation will have on the local environment; how it enriches the community and the lives of those who work there, whether it cares about sustainability and the future of the area in which it stands. I value local color and flavor and the time in which to experience it. A sense that I am staying somewhere that brings good rather than harm or, worse, indifference to the place in which it stands.

That is why I welcome *Go Slow England*, and all who sail in it.

Nigel Slater

Introduction by Alastair Sawday

"Men travel faster now, but I do not know if they go to better things."
    Willa Cather, 1927

I write on a cliff top in Cornwall, gazing over a wide blue bay to a cluster of rocks and then beyond to the sea again. I have been coming here on holiday for a quarter of a century. The view has not changed one iota in those years, except where Nature has changed: sand bars, plants dying and others growing, rocks uncovered by tides, basking sharks basking more frequently. Nothing has eroded the distinctive character of the place. Knowing that what we love will still be there for us, year after year, has given our family a solid sense of self.

Back home in Bristol, I grow unfamiliar with my community. It has become less and less distinctive. Where once there was a convivial collection of grocers, corner stores and ironmongers there are now express supermarkets, hairdressers, minimalist cafés selling cappuccino and minimalist restaurants selling, inevitably, goat cheese salad, sea bass and rack of lamb. Or pizza. Few mom-and-pop operations can afford to stay here. Bit by bit the spirit of the community ebbs away, kept alive only by a few determined and visionary members of local community groups—bless them.

Every era creates its own agents of social change. Only time will tell which are the great movements of our age, but the Slow movement, born of a renewed regard for the simple pleasures of life, may well prove to be one of them. The Slow movement resists the homogenization of food and culture, and longs for the return to a sense of place. It will be a long battle.

Slow Food celebrates meals prepared with love and consumed at leisure, as in Italy, where life can still grind magnificently to a halt in the middle of the day. In 1986 a food journalist called Carlo Petrini was shocked to see that a McDonald's was planning to open an outlet in the heart of Rome—on the exquisite Piazza Navona, no less—and resolved to fight the invasion of fast food with Slow Food. It took off, and is still flying high. Now there are Slow Food "convivia," as groups of enthusiasts are called, all over the world. The movement was founded in the Piemonte town of Brà, and the town buzzes with slow activities—even a food academy.

Every November, in Turin, there is the Salone del Gusto, a Slow Food feast of global proportions when artisan growers come from all over the world to set out their tables. It is all part of the wider convention, Terra Madre, which brings together cooks, eco-gastronomists, small-scale producers and all those working to combat standardization and encourage biodiversity. I have known people to talk of the event with tears in their eyes. It is the world's greatest display of good food, they declare.

The Slow Food idea was such a good one that it had to go somewhere else, and this it has done—impressively—with Cittaslow. Slow Cities are urban reflections of the Slow Food concept: Thoughtful places which value peace and quiet, local production, pedestrians over cars, a dark night sky, artisan production, eco-friendly architecture, low energy consumption and, importantly, time to enjoy all these things as a community. Formed in Italy in 1999, the Slow City movement has spread to an international network of small towns. Slow Food, Cittaslow—this was just the beginning. The ideas are gaining pace.

There is an organization in Britain called Common Ground, devoted to the survival of what is best about the country. It has produced a superb leaflet called "Losing Your Place." Without once mentioning the word, it gloriously evokes the concept of "slow." Here is an edited passage:

We sometimes forget that ours is a cultural landscape, an invisible web. It is held together by stone walls and subsidies, ragas and Northumbrian pipes, Wensleydale sheep and halal butchers, whiskies of Islay and Fenland skies, bungalows and synagogues, round barrows and rapping, high streets and Ham stone, laver bread and Devon lanes, door details and dialect. Places are layer upon layer of our history and nature's history intertwined. They differ.

Common Ground argues for a renewed focus on locality, distinctiveness, detail, authenticity and patina. The French have made a profession out of it. *Appellation contrôlée* for wine carries important kudos; Identity, place and quality are intimately bound together. The place of origin and exact derivation are real and important. People can tell the difference.

This book talks much of people changing lifestyles, and places, in order to achieve a better life balance. The meat of the book is the celebration of forty-eight special places, here because they and their houses are especially beautiful, or slow, or inspiring, or all three. (And they are happy for you to read about them.) Here are people who have made choices that are available to most of us, if only we can gather up our courage.

A Slow life allows time to see the distinctiveness of things: the way bushes are swept shapely by the wind, trees interweave with one another, shadows hug the ground in winter's sun. Being slow is acknowledging what makes for a better, happier and more connected world. Good food and conversation, music and laughter, time

for family and friends—all will seem less elusive. So go and meet for yourself the people in this book, absorb their lives for a moment in time, and find inspiration.

CORNWALL & DEVON

Lundy

Bristol Channel

N

0   10   20   30   40 kilometres
0   5   10   15   20 miles

25

18
Woolacombe
72
Ilfracombe
Combe Martin
Lynton
Lynmouth
Berrynarbor
Parracombe

22

23
Barnstaple
Bratton Fleming
South Molton

24
Abbotsham
Clovelly
Bideford
Great Torrington
68
West Putford
Bradworthy

Bude

D E V O N

21

Okehampton
Drewsteignton
Exeter
15
Broad Clyst
Clyst St
64
17
Ottery St Mary
Beer

Tintagel

12
Launceston
Lydford Gorge
Lydford
Dartmoor Forest
Moretonhampstead
Kenton
16
East Budleigh
Budleigh Salterton
Sidmouth

Port Isaac
44
Trevone
Padstow
9
St Kew
10
Bolventor
Bodmin Moor
8
9
Dartmoor
National
Manaton
Widecombe-in-the-Moor
20
Bovey Tracy
Newton Abbot
19
A381
Exmouth
Dawlish
Teignmouth

Constantine Bay
Treyarnon
St Issey
6
Wadebridge
Bodmin
48
CORNWALL
13
Tavistock
Morwellham
14
Ashburton
14
Buckfastleigh
Staverton
Torquay
Totnes

Newquay
St Columb Major
7
8
Liskeard
11
A390
52
Plymouth
Saltash
Sparkwell
Plymstock
13
Ashprington
60
Dartmouth
Blackawton
Kingswear
Torbay
Paignton
18
Brixham
17

Holywell
Holywell Bay
Trerice
Lostwithiel
7
Looe
Torpoint
15
The Sound
Plymtree
12
Blackpool Sands
Bantham Bay

Perranporth
Summercourt
Goonhavern
St Austell
Polperro

St Agnes
St Ives Bay
3
Redruth
Truro
5
Feock
Pentewan
Mevagissey
Mevagissey Bay

36
2
St Ives
3
B3306
40
Hayle
A394
Penryn
Falmouth
10
11
Malborough
Kingsbridge
Stokenham
Salcombe
Sharpitor
Start Point
56

1
4
Marazion
A394
Helston
6
Mawnan Smith

Penzance
5
Land's End
2
Porthcurno

Grade
Kynance Cove
Lizard
Lizard Point

E N G L I S H   C H A N N E L

1 Slow travel   1 Slow food   1 Special places to stay

Slow travel

1. Minack Theatre
2. Walk St Ives to Zennor
3. St Ives School of Painting
4. Train from Penzance to St Ives
5. Penlee House, Gallery & Museum
6. The Potager Nursery
7. Bodmin & Wenford Steam Railway
8. Camel Trail Cycle Path

9. Port Quin Kayaking & Coasteering Tours
10. Rough Tor and Brown Willy
11. The Hurlers Stone Circle
12. Cowslip Workshops
13. Tavistock Farmers' Market
14. Canoe Tamar
15. Cremyll Ferry to Mt Edgecombe
16. Bantham Beach
17. Coleton Fishacre

18. Paignton & Dartmouth Steam Railway
19. House of Marbles
20. The Riverside Mill & Gallery
21. Tiverton Canal Company
22. Tarka Trail Cycle Track
23. Tapeley Park Gardens
24. Lavender Farm
25. Lundy Island

Slow food

1. Cookbook Café & Bookshop
2. Cove Cottage Tea Garden
3. Porthminster Café
4. Roskilly's Farm, Café & Ice Cream Parlour
5. Lemon Street Market
6. Camel Valley Vineyard

7. Cornish Orchards
8. The Mad Hatter's Tearoom
9. Countryman Cider
10. The Oyster Shack
11. Pig Finca Café
12. South Devon Chilli Farm

13. Sharpham Vineyard
14. Riverford Field Kitchen
15. Exeter Slow Food Market
16. Otterton Mill
17. River Cottage Farm Shop
18. Mortehoe Shellfish

Special places to stay

36. The Gurnard's Head
40. Primrose Valley Hotel
44. Cornish Tipi Holidays
48. Hornacott

52. Lantallack Farm
56. Lower Norton Farmhouse
60. Fingals
64. West Colwell Farm

68. Beara Farmhouse
72. Southcliffe Hall

Slow travel

1 Minack Theatre
Porthcurno (01736 810471)
Spectacular cliffside, open-air theater whose first performance —"The Tempest" in the summer of 1932—was lit by batteries and car headlamps. Explore by day, see a play at dusk.
www.minack.com

2 Walk St Ives to Zennor
Set off early on the coastal path via Zennor (six miles) with its characterful inn and on to The Gurnard's Head (three miles), then catch the bus back to St Ives (or vice-versa). Marvelous above-hedgerow views from the top deck.

3 St Ives School of Painting
(01736 797180)
Drop in for a Saturday life drawing class at 10am or 1.45pm; or Monday and Wednesday at 7.30pm: £8 for two hours. No booking, no equipment required, just enthusiasm!
www.stivesartschool.co.uk

4 Train from Penzance to St Ives
Passing the huge sand dunes of Hayle Towans and the sweep of Carbis Bay you avoid the parking madness of lovely St Ives. Buy a day ticket and hop on and off as you like, on one of the most scenic branch lines in the UK.

5 Penlee House, Gallery & Museum
Penzance (01736 363625)
Paintings from the Newlyn School and Lamorna Group hang in this Victorian house. If you're after a particular work of art, call in advance to check that it's showing. Peaceful gardens, good café in the orangery.
www.penleehouse.org.uk

6 The Potager Nursery
Constantine, nr Falmouth (01326 341258)
Stroll through this former garden nursery on a summer Sunday—for flowers, vegetables, fruit trees and a lush tangle that one day will become a thing of beauty. There's a glass canopied café for light lunches, homemade cakes; pick up a gardening book and stay awhile.
www.potagergardennursery.co.uk

7 Bodmin & Wenford Steam Railway
Bodmin (0845 1259678)
A thirteen-mile round trip that takes in a viaduct and Bodmin Moor. From the station at Bodmin you can walk to Lanhydrock House (01208 265950) for a touch of "Upstairs Downstairs" and spectacular magnolias.
www.bodminandwenfordrailway.co.uk
www.nationaltrust.org.uk

8 Camel Trail Cycle path
Bodmin to Padstow (01872 327310)
Call for route map, rent a bike at Bodmin or Wadebridge, then follow the disused railway line for a gentle seventeen miles through woodland and along the estuary to Padstow. Fish and chips await—or mussel soup at tiny, perfect Margot's Bistro up the hill.
www.sustrans.org.uk

9 Port Quin Kayaking & Coasteering Tours
Port Quin & Port Gaverne (01208 880280)
Join in a three-hour kayak tour: soak up the views and the wildlife, drop a mackerel line over the side, kayak surf at low tide.
www.cornishcoastadventures.com

10 Rough Tor and Brown Willy
Bodmin Moor (OS Exp 109).
Trek up to the two highest points in Cornwall and look to both coasts on a clear day. The remains of an iron age hill fort and bronze-age settlements reward you at the summit.

11 The Hurlers Stone Circle
Minions, Bodmin Moor (OS Exp 109)
"The inhabitants terme them Hurlers, as being by devout and godly error persuaded that they had been men sometime transformed into stones, for profaning the Lord's Day with hurling the ball." B3254 Liskeard to Upton Cross, left at crossroads for Minions; the stones are visible from the village car park.

12 Cowslip Workshops
Launceston (01566 772654)
Come for a course on patchwork, quilting, knitting and, for children, "Keepsake Fairies." There's a multitude of interesting fabrics to sift through

in the shop; tea and coffee, too.
www.cowslipworkshops.co.uk

**13 Tavistock Pannier &
Farmers' Market**
Undercover pannier market, built in
1850, a treasure trove of all sorts
(closed Sunday/Monday). There are
plenty of cafés in town for lunch
and a good farmers' market in
Bedford Square on the second and
fourth Saturday of the month.
www.tavistockpanniermarket.co.uk /
www.tavistockfarmersmarket.com

14 Canoe Tamar
Morwellham Quay (0845 4301208)
Paddle along the Tamar, three to
a Canadian canoe. From this
once-thriving copper port you
head past woodlands, old quays,
mines and chimneys for Cothele
House & Estate (managed by the
National Trust). Return transport
is included.
www.canoetamar.co.uk

**15 Cremyll Ferry to Mount
Edgecombe**
(01752 822105)
Follow in the wake of the Saxons:
from Plymouth's ancient waterfront
to Edgecombe House on the Rame
peninsula (01752 822236), with
Grade-I listed gardens and national
camellia collection. Take a picnic
or lunch in the 18th-century
orangery café.
www.tamarcruising.com
www.mountedgcumbe.gov.uk

16 Bantham Beach
Lovely sands, views to Burgh Island
and dog-welcoming in restricted

areas. Make for the beach at
neighboring Bigbury, then cross
the sands—or hop on the sea
tractor at high tide—to Burgh
Island, famous for its Art Deco hotel
and Pilchard Inn.

17 Coleton Fishacre
Kingswear (01803 752466)
Arts and Crafts house, designed in
1925 for the d'Oyly Carte family,
with exotic gardens that plunge
down the valley to the coastal path,
and great views. Fab cream teas in
the café.
www.nationaltrustorg.uk

**18 Paignton & Dartmouth
Steam Railway**
Paignton (01803 555872)
Chug along the Torbay coast to the
Dart estuary, hop on the ferry at
Kingswear to lovely Dartmouth, then
puff back again. Round trips also
include river cruises.
www.paignton-steamrailway.co.uk

19 House of Marbles
Bovey Tracey (01626 835285)
In an old pottery building is Snooki,
the biggest marble run in Britain.
Plus a museum of vintage toys;
glass-blowing demonstrations;
marbles and old-fashioned toys for
sale. There is a restaurant, too.
www.houseofmarbles.com

20 The Riverside Mill & Gallery Café
Bovey Tracey (01626 832223)
In an old stabling block (c.1850)
are jewelery, textiles, prints,
ceramics and furniture from the
Devon Guild of Craftsmen.

21 Tiverton Canal Company
Tiverton (01884 253345)
"The fastest way to slow down:" hop
on the barge as the horse tows you
along the canal path.
www.tivertoncanal.co.uk

22 Tarka Trail Cycle Track
Braunton (Cycle Hire: 01271 813339)
Head along the estuary, named after
Henry Williamson's otter, to Fremington
Quay Café (organic ciders, cream teas).

23 Tapeley Park Gardens
Bideford (01271 860897)
Crumbling splendor: a lovers'
evergreen tunnel and lily-dotted
lake. Tea and cakes in the old dairy
and occasional "Health and
Harmony" weekends.
www.tapeleypark.com

24 Lavender Farm
Cheristow (01237 440101)
Come to swoon over Eric's
120 varieties of lavender, farmed
under a countryside stewardship
scheme. Gifts and a tea room.
www.cheristow.co.uk

25 Lundy Island
(01271 863636)
Sail off from Bideford or Ilfracombe
to little Lundy. Join an organized
rocky shore ramble with the warden.
www.lundyisland.co.uk

Slow food

1 Cookbook Café & Bookshop
St Just (01736 787266)
Local smoked mackerel, soups, cakes and cream teas, plus 4,500 secondhand books to browse.
www.thecookbookstjust.co.uk

2 Cove Cottage Tea Garden
St Loy (01736 810010)
On the coastal path between Porthcurno and Lamorna (you walk here), a magical spot overlooking gardens that spill down to the sea. Clotted cream tea (tea from a local plantation, cream from the Lizard).

3 Porthminster Café
St Ives (01736 795352)
Linger over fresh oysters, bouillabaisse, local mackerel—worth every penny. Overlooking St Ives Bay.
www.porthminstercafe.co.uk

4 Roskilly's Farm, Café & Ice Cream Parlour
St Keverne (01326 280479)
Wend your way down to the Lizard and twenty-four flavors of ice cream. Café, craft shop, calves to watch, BBQ and live music in summer.
www.roskillys.co.uk

5 Lemon Street Market
Truro (01872 273031)
Cornwall's sole city, Truro, is a foodie hub. Visit the covered market for smoothies and chutneys and fairtrade goods. Farmers' market Wednesdays and Saturdays.

6 Camel Valley Vineyard
Nansallon (01208 77959)
Come for a late afternoon tour (April-October) or simply sample award-winning wine on the terrace. A deep and enthusiastic love of wine here.
www.camelvalley.com

7 Cornish Orchards
Westnorth Manor Farm, Duloe (01503 269007)
Take your pick from juices, ciders and punches.
www.cornishorchards.co.uk

8 The Mad Hatter's Tearoom
Launceston (01566 774634)
Novelty teapots surround you, Alice peers out from the wall. A big selection of teas, coffees, cakes, cream teas and salads.
www.the-madhatters.co.uk

9 Countryman Cider
Milton Abbot (01822 870226)
An apple mill and cider press in 15th-century stables; an orchard on the bank of the river Tamar. Bring your own containers and take some home.
www.crying-fox.com/cider1.htm

10 The Oyster Shack
Stakes Hill, between Kingsbridge and Bigbury (01548 843558)
Under tarpaulins and disused sails, simple, local produce and fresh fish. Bring your own wine.
www.oystershack.co.uk

11 Pig Finca Café
Kingsbridge (01548 855777)
On the Promenade, a Mediterranean menu, local and organic produce, good coffee and occasional live music. Open all day.
www.pigfinca.co.uk

12 South Devon Chilli Farm
Lodiswell (01548 550782)
One hundred types of chilies; fresh from June to November. Chili chocolate, too.
www.southdevonchillifarm.co.uk

13 Sharpham Vineyard
Totnes (01803 732203)
Wander sheltered slopes of the Dart, then taste the wine and cheese.
www.sharpham.com

14 Riverford Field Kitchen
Buckfastleigh (01803 762074)
Plonk yourself down at a communal table for a memorable organic meal (preceded by a tractor-trailer tour, or a walk at your own pace). Popular, must book. Closed November-March.
www.riverford.co.uk

15 Exeter Slow Food Market
(01297 442378) Third Saturday of the month, 10am-3pm.

16 Otterton Mill
Budleigh Salterton (01395 568521)
There's been a watermill here since 100AD. Artists' studios and cafe, too.
www.ottertonmill.com

17 The River Cottage Farm Shop
Axminster (01297 631715)
The latest addition to Hugh Fearnley-Whittingstall's food empire.

18 Mortehoe Shellfish
Mortehoe (01271 870633)
Stop for a perfect crab sandwich after a coastal walk from Lee to Mortehoe, or an evening lobster platter.

Pubs & inns

Tinner's Arms

Zennor, St Ives, Cornwall
One of Cornwall's most historic pubs with flagstones, fires, whitewashed walls and a fabulously long, well-stocked bar. The garden overlooks the sea, ales are from St Austell and menus change daily.
01736 796927 www.tinnersarms.com

The Star Inn

Fore Street, St Just, Cornwall
Locals chat in the low-beamed bar, old pub games thrive and the place is the hub of the local folk scene, with live music at least ten nights a month. In the bar, walls are littered with seafaring and mining artifacts. 01736 788767

Kings Head

Ruan Lanihorne, Truro, Cornwall
A pub with a heart. Niki and Andrew love what they do. Children are welcome in each of the dining rooms, dogs snooze in the bar. Find pine-backed stools, a comfy old sofa, a real fire. Behind is the Roseland countryside. 01872 501263

Duke of York

Iddesleigh, Winkleigh, Devon
The most genuine of locals: a big-hearted, generous place. It serves comforting food, real ale, Sams Cider from Winkleigh and a great welcome from farmer-pub landlord Jamie Stuart and his wife. Rustic and enchanting. 01837 810253

Rugglestone Inn

Widecombe-in-the-Moor, Devon
Head-ducking beams fill the parlor with its simple furnishings and wood-burner. Both rooms are free of modern intrusions, the locals preferring time-honored games such as cribbage, euchre and dominoes. Food is homey. 01364 621327

The Bridge Inn

Topsham, Exeter, Devon
Cut across the bridge too fast and you miss one of England's last traditional ale houses, the 16th-century Bridge. Ten real ales from the cask, gooseberry wine and homemade ham for the ploughman's.
01392 873862 www.cheffers.co.uk

Digger's Rest

Woodbury Salterton, Exeter, Devon
Arrive early to bag the sofa by the log fire. As well as the local Otter and guest ales, the good wines and the relaxing atmosphere, there's fine local produce, Gaggia coffee and soothing jazz.
01395 232375 www.diggersrest.co.uk

The Harris Arms

Portgate, Lewdown, Devon
The passion Andy and Rowena have for food and wine is infectious and the awards they are gathering is proof of their commitment to the Slow Food movement. Outside: rich rolling views.
01566 783331 www.theharrisarms.co.uk

Fortescue Arms

East Allington, Totnes, Devon
The dark panelled bar is where Tom and the bar girls hold court, the restaurant is inviting with terracotta walls, candles and great food, and the outdoor decked area is smartly spotlit at night.
01548 521215 www.fortescue-arms.co.uk

The Gurnard's Head

CORNWALL

Clinging to the toe of Cornwall, dipping into the wild Atlantic waters, the Gurnard's Head feels as though it lies at the very end of the earth. In the early morning, as cows meander to their milking shed, sea mists roll back to reveal the mellow ochre walls of this fine old "pub with rooms". (Charles disregards the term 'gastropub,' though the pub does serve fine modern food at laid-back tables.)

Charles and Edmund bought the Gurnard's a few years ago after creating the successful Felin Fach Griffin in Wales. They have quickly transformed this one too, with an intuitive sense of what people nowadays want. It was overhauled dramatically in a month. Out went the black-and-white décor and the horse brasses, in came a palette of earthy, lime-based colors and a contemporary informality. Small bedrooms upstairs were quickly upgraded—to warm and cozy, simple and spotless, with Vi-sprung mattresses, crisp white linen, Roberts radios and armchair throws, while the suite has gained a big tub—for a deep soak after a long day's walking.

One of the most impressive aspects of the conversion is that the locals remained loyal to the place throughout the process, and still are. And Charles and Edmund feel strongly that this is where their loyalties lie, whatever the demands of the "emmets," as the tourists are called (the word comes from an Old English word for "ant").

They were born in Wales, on a farm where they had to get up at five in the morning and stumble over to the dairy for fresh milk. "Mum had a stunning kitchen garden and we ate, of course, what was available in season." Their father had been a colonel in the Royal Welsh Fusiliers, then retired and took to farming and politics, famously keeping his deposit against Michael Foot in the Labour stronghold of Ebbw Vale.

"Home is where our understanding of taste, food and freshness stems from. We enjoyed it as children and we are enjoying it now. There were no supermarkets and we just walked into the garden to pick things." In Wales they have created an organic kitchen garden for the Felin Fach Griffin; they know that won't be so easy on a cliff top in Cornwall, but they are starting with a herb garden, and have already determined to source everything from within ten miles.

Edmund says: "As with the Griffin, the ethos that underlies what we do here can best be summed up as 'the simple things in life, done well'. This appears to suit the West Cornwall environment even better than the Welsh. And we have tried to put the Gurnard's once again at the center of its rural community. The beer is amazing value, drinkers are as welcome as stayers and eaters, and we try to give as much employment to local people as possible. Importantly, in high season, we don't betray our local trade for the lucre of the tourism trade."

The pub's reputation is riding high and that brings its own challenges—in July there can be a hundred food orders a day and the kitchens have to adapt. "The food then has to be faster but still as good," says Charles. "I am toying with the idea of building an outdoor clay pizza oven and a barbecue for fresh fish."

The head chef, Matt Williamson, is from New Zealand and revels in the output of the west country fields. He is obsessed with developing great flavors from simple ingredients, so all the bread is homemade, as are the jams, marmalades, relishes, terrines, pork pies, salamis and fruit jellies. Beef is salted on the premises, fish are smoked on a home-made smoker behind the kitchen. The very freshest fish has been known to go out as sushi. Salad leaves, fruit and vegetables are brought to the kitchen door by the farmer's wife (and anyone else who has spare homegrown produce they'd like to sell).

Matt is mastering the perfect Slow Sunday lunch using rib of beef cooked overnight and local potatoes roasted to perfection. The satisfaction of knowing that everything on the plate has come from within a ten-mile radius of the Gurnards is huge. Breakfast is held at a single large table—an old baker's table— looking out to the Atlantic. The mood is relaxed: newspapers, kippers, no rush. Checkout times are suggested rather than obligatory.

Charles and Edmund have also reintroduced the live Cornish Bluegrass music sessions that had been abandoned by the previous owners in spite of the Gurnard's being a famous old venue. These can be as simple and informal as one man singing at the bar for an hour or two. The pub was also renowned as a serious watering hole for St Ives' artists and once again art hangs on the walls—"we hope that the Gurnard's will become known for showcasing the amazing talent in the area"—books fill every shelf, too; if you pick one up and don't finish it, you can take it home and post it back or leave another to replace it.

This great little place is "about trying to make people feel as if they are in their own home, at the same time as keeping the standards of inn-keeping high. Importantly, we are not trying to make every last pound from each and every customer; a pot of afternoon tea will not be charged to a room, we don't

ask for supplements for dogs or for cots." And wine is priced fairly and in a way that would shame some London restaurants.

As for the greenness of the Gurnard's, Edmund says, "I am not going to make any extravagant claims. It is something that we are committed to taking a good look at and we want to get it right. For the moment, we are concentrating on doing things the right way in the kitchen, keeping our food miles down and observing basic common sense habits."

Years ago some Kentish farmers bought up a large swathe of West Penwith and merged several farms in order to introduce industrial farming; their efforts have not reached far. A little way down the coast road, Gilly Wyatt Smith, who once ran the Slad Gallery in Gloucestershire, grows herbs and Asian salad leaves that she delivers to the pub. Mackerel is easy to come by; strawberries can be bought at the small farm shops that are springing up all over Cornwall. Asparagus too. "It is all incredibly good value and fresh beyond belief," says Charles.

This is a lovely part of Cornwall, with countless exquisite bays and cliffs to enjoy. The flowers in spring are a delight, and the hedgerows and lanes are just as they were centuries ago.

Charles urges exploration of the area and the combination of the deep pleasures of walking, eating and sightseeing. He lures those staying in St Ives... "There's a wonderful walk here from the town. You can arrive for lunch and afterwards catch a bus back at 4pm from right outside the pub. If it's a double-decker, as it sometimes is, it's a scenic tour with breathtaking views from the top over the hedgerows to the sea."

Charles & Edmund Inkin

The Gurnard's Head, Treen, Zennor, St Ives, TR26 3DE
- 7 rooms.
- £80-£140. Singles from £60.
- Lunch from £4.50. Dinner, 3 courses, about £25.
- 01736 796928
- enquiries@gurnardshead.co.uk
- www.gurnardshead.co.uk

Primrose Valley Hotel

CORNWALL

"We want to be a positive force in St Ives." Andrew's words are music to our ears, a reminder that tourism can be more than it has largely become; so much of it involves little more than the open-cast mining of local resources and people. Andrew and Sue's determination to make a difference to their community as well as to the environment is an inspiration.

St Ives, of course, has for many years seduced the best-intentioned outsiders, including St Ia, around whose chapel houses began to cluster in the 6th century. The artistic focus of the town has always been remarkable, generating a special buzz. Whistler and Sickert came here in the 19th century, setting the tone for a 20th-century artistic invasion: Ben Nicholson, Barbara Hepworth and Bernard Leach among many others. In 1993 the Tate Gallery opened a new branch here—a giant artistic enterprise.

Today it is not only artists who nurture an affection for the gaily painted and clustered houses of the old part of town, the intimacy of the bay, the promenade, and St Ives's rare sense of isolation. It is far from the main roads and just on the edge of a strange and beautiful part of England around a village called Zennor (named after St Senara). You can walk there from

St Ives, straight into ancient England with stone walls laced close to each other around fields of medieval shape, a romantic, wild and brooding landscape, inhabited for at least 4,000 years. There is a fine pub there, the Tinner's Arms, built for the masons who built the church. It has a lovely garden and a fire inside for winter. The Coastal Path will carry you beyond to Land's End, along cliffs and land's edges as dramatically lovely as any. This is all part of the magic of St Ives.

Andrew and Sue were seduced by the same light that had seduced Whistler. "One crisp April morning we strolled down to Porthminster Café and on into town. It was simply stunning. We had to come and live here." Having persuaded Sue's parents to join them they bought a tired seaside hotel. Sue was six months pregnant and next door was a building site. "We couldn't do much at first but we did get rid of the plastic flowers."

They have been wonderfully clever with the limited spaces, creating a house that feels cool, contemporary and calm. It is delightfully fresh and unstuffy, with modern prints, pale wooden floors and bold wallpapers; where there were once swirly carpets there is open-mindedness and elegance; where

there were just two there are now "nine great staff, the vast majority full-time". They know, too, that they cannot sit still while the town changes around them. So they recently created an extravagant suite—red leather sofa, slipper bath, deluge shower (be quick if you are eco-minded), open brickwork, curved walls.

From the white wooden balconies you gaze upon the wide sea. Not the "sloe-black, slow black, crow black, fishing-boat bobbing sea" of Dylan Thomas, for most of the St Ives sea is kindly and more sparkling blue than black. You feel sheltered from both the sea and the outside world.

Cornwall may well become the first county in England wholly to embrace the new environmental mood. The hotel has built up an impressive list of Cornish food suppliers, and cheeses, charcuterie and smoked fish are always available. Hidden from view are other commitments: eco-friendly cleaning materials, a green energy supplier and an emphasis on recycling.

"We don't agree with guests having to be involved in the mechanics of recycling, though," says Sue, "and the last thing we want is to have notices everywhere dictating what they must and must not do. Our staff do all the sorting and our hope is simply that guests will absorb our approach throughout the hotel and take something of our ethos home."

Their sense of community has seen the beginnings of a fund-raising initiative for the Marine Conservation Society. Andrew says, "Three years ago we made a slightly brave move—we added £1 per room per night for the MCS, with an option to have it

> "It's only once you set off down the Slow road that you realize what a very long road it is"

removed. Few people have questioned it and only a handful have asked to have it removed. Over £5,000 has been raised and paid to the Society—all for very little effort."

It has been said that it's not easy being green and Andrew and Sue tussle daily with dilemmas. Some examples? Andrew was asked to talk on environmental issues at a conference in Northern Ireland—he was happy to accept but felt burdened by the fact that he could only do it if he flew. They want to use eco-friendly everything but the guest still wants to see snow white and fluffy towels; "grey towels aren't 'in' yet," jokes Andrew, so they continue to allow hot washes. Their door signs are made from recycled foamex and are printed in Cornwall— consequently they cost around £15 each, which doesn't appear to be a good business decision.

"But," says Andrew, "just as guests have come to expect the best mattresses, bedding and bathrooms, they increasingly expect excellent food and they want to know its provenance. That delights us.

"We hope that guests will appreciate what we are doing and not mind paying a little extra where we simply have to pass on the cost. We want to compete on quality and eco-friendliness, not on price."

So you will find beautiful organic soaps from Trevarno Gardens in the bathroom instead of small bars of paper-wrapped mass-produced soap; your breakfast sausage costs ten times as much as those that were served here when the Bisses took over... Guest satisfaction has shown these to be the right decisions, so it seems everyone is happy.

Another nice touch is the £2.50 discount per night offered to anyone who arrives without a car. St Ives, of course, is a perfect place for such gestures: you don't need a car. Walking can be all you do—along the coastal path in both directions, carrying a picnic made up for you by the hotel. Or take a bus to Penzance and stop off at St Michael's Mount, thirty minutes away; it is iconic, fascinating and less touristy than its French equivalent. With luck you will walk across the causeway and return by to the mainland by boat at a higher tide—or vice-versa. You leave with a sense of having shaken off this century.

Back in St Ives there is so much to do that these journeys may not appeal at all. The town is inevitably busy in summer, but gets more interesting by the year. There is now a Jazz Club, year round, on Tuesday nights, adding another touch to the cosmopolitan mood of a renewed St Ives.

The gradual process of shedding stress can start way before you arrive. The mainline train journey down to Cornwall is one of the loveliest in Britain. You then slip out of St Erth on the branch line and into St Ives station, moments away from the hotel.

"We have a reputation for being eco-friendly and we are determined to do better and better. It's not always easy," says Andrew, "and the dilemmas keep coming. It's only once you set off down the Slow road that you realize what a very long road it is."

Andrew Biss

Primrose Valley Hotel,
Porthminster Beach, St Ives, TR26 2ED
- 10 rooms. £90-£225.
- Platters available all year.
- 01736 794939
- info@primroseonline.co.uk
- www.primroseonline.co.uk

Cornish Tipi Holidays

CORNWALL

The layers of ingrained urban habit shed slowly but steadily here, and the first thing to go, once you've unloaded your gear, is your car. That, plus the fact that you're staying under canvas, means that your impact on the environment could hardly be lower and the stresses that occupy your mind dissolve away. Immediately there's a shift: without a car, a computer or a washing machine family dynamics change—everyone has to join in. Somehow though there seems to be more time for fun, too, as the rhythm of outdoor life washes over you. "Some people hardly leave the site—they don't have to if their children are happy making dens in the woods and exploring with new friends," says Lizzie.

Lizzie has four children of her own—the ninth generation in the family to be born in this parish—and she delights in seeing children enthusing about the wildlife and enjoying the freedom.

Lizzie's father farmed the old-fashioned way. As she explains "It was slower, less fraught. It didn't destroy the land and the livestock were treated in a humane way." Lizzie's sister now carries on the tradition. The land was quarried for fifty years and so is untouched by agro-chemicals. Indigo-blue dragonflies hover over lakes and ponds, butterflies flap through buttercups, spotted woodpeckers flit among the woods and tawny owls puncture the night's silence with their hooting.

After time away from her native Cornwall—university then journalism and PR in London—Lizzie came back to have her first child at thirty. "I didn't want to raise a family in London and there didn't seem much point in settling for life as a commuter."

Having made the decision to carve out a greener lifestyle and create the camp back on the family farm, they were surprised by resistance to their plans from locals and planners.

Most locals are convinced now that they are a force for good, the planners less so. There is an irony in their lack of support at a time when Cornwall is eagerly promoting itself in the sustainable tourism arena.

"A tipi pole doesn't even break the surface of the earth and we are facilitating carbon-free holidays yet we continue to struggle with them. We want to build an eco-structure with space for washing, drying and storage with a living turf roof, straw bale walls and a wind generator but again have met resistance. If I wanted to build a vile concrete bungalow, it seems there would be no objection."

The greatest irony is that the camp is not eligible for a Green Tourism Business Award simply because it has always been green. Lizzie explains: "I was told that as there was no evidence of 'consistent change and radical improvements'—i.e. because we have always been green—we don't count!"

Despite all that and the biblical rains of summer 2007, Lizzie is determined to keep on keeping on.

"I love seeing people experience the spiritual high of real camping. This is a world away from the

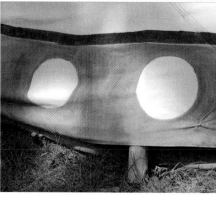

nylon'd nightmare of modern camping. Sleeping in a tipi is like sleeping in a living organic thing. The smell of the canvas and the twine, the gentle creek of the pole as it sways in the breeze—it's like sleeping on a boat. Your senses are assailed further by dew on your feet, birdsong, the smell of the campfire."

Lizzie sourced her American Indian-style tipis made of unbleached canvas from craftsmen in Cornwall, Devon and Wales; few road miles, no air miles. Other campsites have imitated her style and are awash with tipis, yurts and bell tents.

A stay here can be sociable if you want—in the "village field"—or private, tucked away in clearings. Everyone tends to congregate around the firepit under starlit, midnight blue skies; wine and stories are shared, children and grown-ups find new friends.

The tipis are scattered with patterned rugs, gas lanterns create a warm glow, the old primus stove keeps things toasty. Experienced campers know to

> "This is a world away from the nylon'd nightmare of modern camping. Sleeping in a tipi is like sleeping in a living organic thing"

bring from home the things that make the holiday more comfortable—padded rollmats, maybe airbeds, and favorite bedding (pillows recommended!).

There are showers now as an alternative to jumping in the lake, and flushing toilets instead of a trip to the bushes, but this still feels like getting back to basics. The lake that sits in the sixteen acres of wooded valley is perfect for cooling dips, rowing and trout fishing; there's a stream for toddlers and a warden on site all year round.

Being unprepared for observing nature at close quarters is a mistake. Lizzie tells tales of guests complaining about an influx of slugs and frogs—one damp summer—and of being upset by wasps one hot summer. "One woman was furious because a dormouse, one cold summer day, had retreated to her tipi for warmth, snuggled up in her very expensive cashmere sweater and nibbled a little hole."

But those who are not natural campers and who could afford to be in a waterfront cottage in nearby Rock continue to come because they want to feel something new. "If the sun is shining the experience can't be beat. Unsurprisingly," says Lizzie "there have been plenty of proposals."

Fathers have bonding holidays with their sons, too, groups of friends come to relax and know the children are being safely adventurous, couples come to simply be—together. There's the Camel Trail to be cycled, the Coastal Path to be walked, the beaches to be discovered (Polzeath for surfers, Daymer for small children) and pretty Port Isaac ten minutes away, where you can buy fish fresh off the boats.

A coracle builder at Falmouth College is keen to run courses on the water; Lizzie has plans for community and education work and is excited about the prospect of launching her proposal for sustainable eco-weddings and for yoga retreats.

The vagaries of nature can make or break your experience here, but you play your part, too. "Some people fall apart in bad weather, others determine to make the most of being here. A plumber and his family stayed last year—he had been declared bankrupt, lost his business and they hadn't had a holiday for four years. They arrived to torrential rain yet each day he and his four children and wife togged up and walked and swam and cooked. He even took it upon himself to keep everyone's spirits high—he inspired us all."

So bring your better self, come prepared and celebrate all that Lizzie has achieved.

"We've been beating the eco drum for ten years," she says. "At last people seem to understand the importance of what we've been doing. I feel now we are on the crest of a wave."

Ms Elizabeth Tom

Cornish Tipi Holidays,
Tregeare, Pendoggett, St Kew, PL30 3LW
- 40 tipis, 3 shower and loo blocks.
- £375-£555 p.w. Short breaks available.
- 01208 880781
- info@cornish-tipi-holidays.co.uk
- www.cornish-tipi-holidays.co.uk

Hornacott

CORNWALL

"Kind hearts, soft beds and great sausages!" wrote a visitor about Hornacott. But there is more—the unsung Tamar Valley being the real star.

This is a little-known part of Cornwall, just over the border from Devon, an area through which people pass on their way to the rest of the county. At the bottom of the steep lane that runs past the house is one of the oldest bridges in Cornwall, Trekelland Bridge on the river Inny. You are on the cusp of two counties—walk one way up the lane for views of Dartmoor and the other for views of Bodmin Moor, the closer of the two.

Mining in the Tamar Valley started in the 13th century and ruins of mines and mine stacks are bleak witness to the mineral wealth once found in the valley. From the 1800s there were three large mines here, producing copper, lead, tin, tungsten and... arsenic. The valley is now an AONB (Area of Outstanding Natural Beauty) with a rich wildlife and special beauty of its own. Before modern wheeled transport arrived the river was, of course, the main highway. The stone to build the great Cotehele House, a stupendous National Trust Tudor manor house overlooking the Tamar, came up the river by boat and was unloaded at Cotehele's little quay.

The Tamar valley was also famous for its fruit but now only a few Tamar cherry trees blossom in spring, where once there were thousands. Other fruit has fared a little better: apples, pears, strawberries, plums. There are some magnificent gardens in the area, such as Rosemoor, just over the border, and the Garden House, one of Mary-Anne's favorites.

Mary-Anne and Jos met in London and lived by Barnes Common for four years. "London is great fun for a young single person, a ball; I wouldn't have missed it for the world. But the trip to work got us in the end. One morning a bus got stuck on the bridge. I was there at 8:25am, and I got into work in Chelsea at 12:30—three miles in four hours! I looked at other commuters, white-knuckled and tearing their hair out, and I thought there must be a better way of life."

An undercurrent of dissatisfaction crept into their lives. "In London a lot of people just talked about schools and house extensions. Down here nobody cares whether you have a huge estate or a tiny cottage. They all seem to be friends with each other. Nobody gives a darn what car you drive, though a Lamborghini might get laughed at. A beaten up old Landrover has far more cachet."

"We had a friend who had bought an old place down here, knowing noone. We came to stay. After the third or fourth visit, we were heading back to London and we both went very quiet. Then we said, almost in unison, 'What on earth are we doing in London?'"

They moved down in 1994, with a family of Jack Russells, in search of a house that would, somehow,

"The funny thing is, we haven't downshifted: we never sit still!"

earn its own living. Doing B&B did not occur to them until they had moved in. They replaced the roof on the B&B section, once a grain store, and put skylights in. The office below had been a cow byre, with a beautiful—and unappreciated—view.

"We just got on with it," says Jos. "If we had thought about it we wouldn't have done it. We started doing B&B in 1996, giving guests plenty of their own space. They come into the main house for breakfast, which is a good way to meet up with us.

"We had a few friends when we moved down. Local people can be quite hard to get to know; it just takes time. But the neighbors would leave a bag of vegetables and I would bake them a fruitcake," says Mary-Anne. "You don't say 'thank you', you just

acknowledge it in some other way. Locals fear that people like us are bound to bring change. But Jos was brought up in Devon (his Dad was in the marines) and I had relatives here too, and we have no desire to change anything.

"Someone in London said to me, 'I'd like to downshift when I'm older, too.' The funny thing is, we haven't downshifted: we never sit still. We are far busier than in we would be in a nine-to-five job. Here you use every bit of your body to do something... cutting grass is physically exhausting! And having visitors is fun. They come to explore the Tamar Valley, Cothele House, the gardens, the art. People often stay and come back. They love what they find."

"On a quiet summer's evening, when you can sit out with a glass of wine—can you put a price on that? And there is some poor chap busting his guts in the city and earning a million—is he happy? No, because the chap next door is earning a million and a half!"

Hornacott's claim to be slow derives from the pace of life, the gradual learning about country ways, the enthusiasm for shopping carefully and for buying proper, locally produced food.

"I shop in Launceston. There is a wonderful butcher there who puts out big blackboards declaring which farm each bit of meat came from. But I heard something quite astounding one day: a customer

picked up a chicken and the butcher said 'it's free range.' To which she replied, 'Oh, I'm not having that, you don't know where it has been!' How's that for sophisticated shopping!"

They get their water from their own spring, too. Any attempt to be green is aided by North Cornwall's positive attitude to recycling: clothes, glass, bottles from the door, all with color-coded bags. Mary-Anne and Jos replace dead light bulbs with energy-saving ones and have a new and efficient boiler running on oil.

The only barrier to a slow life is the rabbit population. They compete for every vegetable—and tend to win. It can seem impossible to outwit them.

Jos's peaceful office is in the renovated cow byre. He has a kitchen design business, Templederry Designs. "I decided from the start that I wanted to create kitchens that fitted with people's lifestyles, rather than simply supplying a series of boxes that fit a space. It is very satisfying work."

Above his office is the guest suite, equally peaceful, wonderfully airy, beautifully self-contained with a lofty sitting room leading into a cool, blue bedroom, twin beds and a spotless little bathroom. You can sit as the sun goes down, admire the changing light and linger over the valley views.

A doorway leads, more prosaically, to an extra little bedroom and, then, to the main part of the

house for an enthusiastic welcome from the Jack Russells and a generous and, of course, local breakfast at the big dining table.

To a backdrop of grand old trees, the garden, loved and tended by Mary-Anne, tumbles down the slopes over one-and-a-half acres, with sunny lawns and shady spots and seats poised to catch the evening sun. A stream runs through after heavy rain and trickles quietly by in the summer months, its banks aglow with water-loving plants. A collection of old-fashioned English David Austin roses has been introduced—his are the only ones which seem to do well here, says Mary-Anne. It is a supremely peaceful setting. At the very bottom of the garden is their own hideaway, a Finnish barbecue hut.

"We don't have a lot of time to relax," says Mary-Anne "but we are so glad not to be office-bound. We are happy here."

Jos & Mary-Anne Otway-Ruthven

Hornacott,
South Petherwin, Launceston, PL15 7LH
- 1 twin-bedded suite. From £76. Singles £45.
- Dinner £18. BYO.
- 01566 782461
- stay@hornacott.co.uk
- www.hornacott.co.uk

Lantallack Farm

CORNWALL

Andrew came dressed as Heracles—and Nicky was beguiled. Amateur Dramatics has this reputation, and is obviously well deserved. Andrew was, at the time, a respectable solicitor and is now a district judge but much the same man underneath.

They once lived on Dartmoor but wanted more land and found this forty-acre farm in a part of Cornwall that has been relatively ignored in the frenzied rush to buy up the county. It is a beautiful corner of the world and they are still close to their beloved Dartmoor.

As for the farm, it was offered by the Duke of Bedfordshire in the 18th century to the Mount Edgecombe Estate as a dowry for his daughter. It is still intact. The Walkers have been here for twenty-one years and feel immensely privileged. The view from the terrace is breathtaking, sailing across the farm's valley and patchwork fields, carrying the eye to the hills beyond. The evening shadows create the effect of a sublime "pop-up" book. Sitting under the clematis and wisteria-clad pergola with a glass of wine, watching the swallows swoop low to catch flies over the pond and against the setting sun, one is drawn almost ineluctably to the slow life.

Nicky runs the farm with help from a variety of talented local people—dry-stone wallers, fencers, gardeners—and does so with a sensitivity to the land. It speaks to her in old tongues: Mushroom, Mine, Orchard, Pony Paddock and Hare's Leg, the old names for the old fields. She and Andrew have restored an orchard, planting seventy Cornish apple trees from which they make 650 liters of juice every year, organically, though not officially so. Old Cornish varieties include Lucombes Pine, American Mother and Cat's Head, and you will find them protected and revered here. So, too, are the bats, bees, birds and wildflowers.

Lantallack is a special place and the Walkers feel bound to share it with others. Under the Countryside Stewardship Scheme they have opened the farm to groups and schools; children come from all over the area. They walk the farm, dip the ponds, look at the old copper mine, study the wetland at the bottom of the orchard. Then they go back to Nicky's studio to do art-related projects. She is convinced that this is the way to ensure that they grow up respecting the land and its bounty. With luck they will also find it hard to bring themselves to buy and eat food that comes from factory farms.

Art plays a big role in Nicky's life. She creates "big spaces on little canvasses" and works with natural materials alongside paint: sand, wood, ash, straw, seeds, slate, brick, cast-iron, even horse dung. She takes her inspiration from the land and landscape. She has taught life drawing and landscape, print making and sculpture. Now she concentrates on doing it in her own big studio, but still does four weekly courses every year, taking special delight in working with beginners. "They come wanting technique and I get them to play.

They have to look, absorb, relax, feel what they want to say. I hate formulas in anything, even cooking!"

The Walkers are members of COAST, the very active Cornish sustainable tourism group. So there are solar panels hidden away in the vegetable patch, food waste for Polly the Gloucester Old Spot ("hers is the slowest life of all, nesting among the apple trees"), biodegradable bags for household waste, and

> "The view from the terrace is breathtaking, sailing across the valley and patchwork fields, carrying the eye to the hills beyond"

no miniature bottles in the bathrooms. Breakfast is of local sausages and bacon, homemade bread, Yeo Valley yogurt, their own organic eggs, fresh fruit salad and, when asked, smoked haddock baked with eggs and parmesan. Vegetarians can dive into croissants with creamy mushrooms and parsley.

Above the guests' sitting room—straw-yellow walls, duck-egg blue carpet, soft lighting, log fire—are two bedrooms with great beds and views. People who come here to stay are surprised by its loveliness, and often stay longer. "They arrive, chill and switch off, then head for the outdoor solar-heated pool. When people walk through the door we tell them they can go wherever they like, as if they were part of the family." That is generous, typical only of those who have found genuine happiness in their place.

"I do wish people had time to drift back here in all the changing seasons: our snowdrop wood in January, spring with its brilliant greens and young wheat, summer with the daisies and clover. I have had a charmed life and I don't take Lantallack for granted. That is why we share it. This place is a great healer."

The Walkers have two daughters, Lucy and Clare. Clare works with the BBC and Lucy, steeped in Cornwall, has come back as an actor/director and as recently worked with Wildworks, an international theater company based in Cornwall, that creates fresh and brilliant performances that work with the

landscape. This is all part of a Cornish renaissance inspired by Bill Mitchell, formerly of the Kneehigh Theatre Company, that is bringing new vitality to the cultural life of Cornwall.

Cornwall has always had its own ideas about many things. It once had a language, which is now being revived; has often fiercely resisted the Crown; and, so far from London, has had to fend for itself. It has produced people who are tough, a touch reticent, resilient and proud. With roads and railways reaching to the tip of the peninsula since the 19th century, the flow of outsiders has brought artistic vitality, a lot of cars, and fresh blood.

There is, too, a "real food" revolution. A walk down the high street of any town will raise the eyebrows of those used, until recently, to limited choice. There is much talk of Cornish food, with good reason; beach cafés that once battered and fried everything are now gastro inspired. The fish is as good as ever and Newlyn exports it all over Europe. For "the best crab baguette in Cornwall" head to The Rod & Line, across the fields at Tideford, where Sunday "lunch" starts at 5:30, perfect for surfers coming back from the beach.

For no other reason than that it is quaintly amusing, here is some doggerel by Sir Arthur Quiller Couch, prompted by a visit to the little harbor of Fowey and finding it pronounced "Foy".

> O the harbour of Fowey
> Is a beautiful spot
> And it's there I enjowey
> To sail in a yot
> Or to race in a yacht
> round a marker or buoy
> Such a beautiful spacht
> Is the harbour of Fuoy.

Nicky Walker

Lantallack Farm,
Landrake, Saltash, PL12 5LE
* 2 doubles.
* From £90.
* 01752 851281
* nickywalker44@tiscali.co.uk
* www.lantallack.co.uk

Lower Norton Farmhouse

DEVON

There is generosity of spirit here, visible in the easy way Peter and Glynis treat visitors and let them loaf about, sleep in, potter in the garden, do nothing. People are welcome to stay all day, even to have lunch and a cream tea. If they want to do more, there is far more to do.

Peter has a beautiful old Bermudan sloop and he will gaily sail you out to sea and along a coast memorable for its coves, green fields at the shore's edge, wooded valleys and villages that appear to be disconnected from the world beyond. Or he will amble up the Dart if the sea winds are too gusty. It is an enchanting river, with long stretches of green-clad bank giving way to villages like Dittisham, Stoke Gabriel, Tuckenhay—and even Totnes if the tide is high. You can stop off at them all; the yew tree outside Stoke Gabriel's church is as old as Christ, apparently.

Dittisham has a great pub or two, and a terrific buzz in the summer. Tuckenhay may even have jazz on the quay as you pull in for a drink at the Maltster's Arms. It is a gentle, deeply English river that begins high on the moor and ends with an historical flourish at Dartmouth.

It was also one of the first rivers to inspire Ted Hughes. More recently the poet Alice Oswald has written "the river's

story, from source to mouth," a remarkable homage to the Dart.

Two places I've seen eels,
  bright whips of flow
Like stopper waves the rivercurve
  slides through
Trampling around at first
  you just make out
The elver movement of the
  running sunlight
Three foot under the road-judder
  you hold
And breathe contracted
  to an eye-quiet world
While an old dandelion unpicks
  her shawl
And one by one the small spent
  oak flowers fall.

Dart, Alice Oswald, 2002

Peter can also take you off in his vintage 1935 Bentley. Cars are not usually part of the slow scene but this one can be forgiven for interloping. The narrow Devon lanes force an extra slowness, so it is stately.

The pace of life here gives people time to think about their own lives. Says Peter "When guests have been here for a while you can sense them reflecting on their life."

The house is an ancient stone farmhouse, secluded, at the bottom of a steep and narrow lane with banks covered, in spring, in wildflowers. The restoration by Peter and Glynis was done with panache and devotion, inspired by a surrounding countryside that has the serenity of an old painting, rich in memory and layers of meaning.

To depend too much on the outside world would be a betrayal of the fertility of this land, so there are eggs from here, homemade marmalade (with Sevillian help), vegetables, fruit and lamb from their own Devon fields. Their neighbor, Colin, helps with the lambing, his cousin Jill provides the dry cured bacon, and the organic apple juice is from another farmer nearby. Beef and sausages are from local farms, and bread is from the local baker. Best of all, the water is from their own spring.

Glynis's Plum Fudge Pudding

50g (2oz) unsalted butter
50g (2oz) honey
2 tablespoons double cream
2 tablespoons soft brown sugar
1 teaspoon mixed spice
75g (3oz) fresh breadcrumbs
3-4 ripe plums halved, stoned and thinly sliced
Clotted cream/creme fraiche to serve

• Melt butter, honey and cream, then divide between four ramekin dishes
• Mix sugar, spice and breadcrumbs in a bowl
• Top each dish with a layer of plums, then a layer of the breadcrumb mix, and repeat
• Bake at 200°C (400°F/Gas 6) for 20 minutes
• Cool for five minutes and carefully turn out

Mealtimes are as convivial as the sourcing of food, around one big table. Glynis loves this, and chatting while she cooks is part of it all. She cooks for vegetarians with all the enthusiasm one expects of her, and dinner is more like a party with friends than a formal experience laid on for guests. "Guests seem to like being part of life here, and we want them to feel at home. We like people," she says simply. "Some regular guests feel so at home they've offered to cut the grass."

Exuberant collectors of curios and antiques, Glynis and Peter created Italian, French and country

style bedrooms, refreshingly uncluttered and generous in size. Hard to believe the downstairs bedroom, with its seagrass floor and French walnut bed, was once a calving pen, and the chic bathroom a dairy.

Outside are nine acres, two of them now a mixture of soft fruit and vegetable plots, cottage gardens and a sunken fern-filled haven. Glynis is from farming stock and has taken easily to this new life, with her rare-breed curly-horned Wensleydale sheep, hens and competing rabbits.

One day they will create a secret garden, high up and with staggering views over the rolling Devon hills. "I remember the first time we came up here and, with that view before us, being astonished that we now lived here." The local hedgerow flowers—foxgloves, red campion and primroses—are encouraged to mingle with the imported ones. When battle has to be done with pests, natural soap is grated into some water and the lather is then a weapon—good advice from Glynis's grandfather. They love gardening and can get lost in it. Being almost self-sufficient in vegetables is satisfying, but so is a gentle dependency on locals who can provide what is missing.

Before coming here from Reading they sold shoes; a pair of children's hob-nailed boots hanging by the bread oven hints at the family trade. Peter had been to Brixham as a boy, on holiday with his parents, and the thought of returning to Devon had obsessed them both for years. When their daughter was twenty-two they finally abandoned resistance and told her that they were leaving. "Life was too short not to do it."

Quite so, and now, when the classical music wafts across the lawn and the sun sets over the glass-covered terrace you will admire their decision to change their lives.

Peter & Glynis Bidwell

Lower Norton Farmhouse,
Coles Cross, East Allington, Totnes, TQ9 7RL
* 3 rooms. From £70. Singles from £55.
* Dinner £20. Lunch £7.50. Packed lunch £6.
* 01548 521246
* peter@lowernortonfarmhouse.co.uk
* www.lowernortonfarmhouse.co.uk

Fingals

DEVON

Fingals is—dare we say it?—unique. It would be surprising to find other people running a hotel the way Richard and Sheila do. It is not so much a hotel, more the antithesis of a hotel: a big house with lots of bedrooms, run with a sense of fun and a rare informality.

Richard has strong views. "In some hotels I have been to you are given table Number 4 when you arrive and there you are stuck—on table Number 4—for breakfast and dinner. You have the same napkins, talk to noone and end up whispering to your partner over meals in a peculiarly English way. At Fingals everyone cross-fertilizes and joins in. We positively want people to use the place as a social melting pot. Thirty people who have never met before can find themselves sitting at one table and having a great time. It works brilliantly—hardly ever does it go wrong. If people want to eat on their own that is fine; there are two dining rooms and no kids at the big table. The result is something like an informal club."

Some people are uncomfortable with all this, of course—unhappy about the informality, the late meals, the touches of chaos, the quirky décor. That's what happens if you dare to be different. But for many people Fingals is a home-away-

from-home and they return like swallows, year after year.

"I was in London, burning out, running a restaurant (called Fingals, after my dog) for three years. I was an energetic amateur having a lot of fun, broke all the rules and was successful. One day I got out of bed and just froze. 'I have to get out of here', I said.

"I had seen a little black and white photo of this building and drove by, but thought 'no way.' I looked at lots of little hotels in Devon and Cornwall but didn't really like the feel they had. To be honest, I don't really like hotels with rules and regulations like breakfast between 8 and 9am and coming down for dinner at seven. The strangling restraint of them—there is nothing homey about that. This was years ago: we are coming up for the thirtieth anniversary of Fingals."

But Richard did come back and took a look around and thought, what a mess!

"It had been stripped of every ounce of character. Four flats, lino on the floor, shower in the corner of the room—that sort of thing. I had to strip it out and start again.

"My plan was to come down, start with the chef running the restaurant and cut myself off from London, slowly. I had one bedroom when I started in 1981,

and the hotel renovations are still going on now. It is a labor of love."

Every year the urge overtakes him to build something new. One year it's a barn, the next a folly or an eco cabin. This year it's an extension to the pool. And over the years much of the work Richard has done himself.

He is a driven man, pumping with restless energy. How can he possibly qualify to be Slow? Compared to his life in London, this is slow—and, of course, he pours his imagination and enthusiasm into providing opportunities for others to wind down. "I didn't come in here with all guns blazing, a big building plan and an architect in tow. It has been done bit by bit and grows organically. It has grown with personality and with an ethos—and it has taken twenty-seven years."

Fingals is undeniably beautiful, a handsome stone manor house in a tight little valley a mile or so from the Dart. It is dusted with art of all sorts, sculpture and painting by friends—in the garden and in all the rooms. The place bubbles with a mix of serenity and amused vitality. The Folly, a two-story hut on the banks of the stream, is a touch of delightful eccentricity.

Ducks quack across the lawn in the evening pursued by Sheila urging them to bed and getting in the way of tennis (ducks and Sheila both). Dogs roam everywhere; some of them belong to guests. Children run about the lovely garden playing tennis or ping-pong, or having a swim. Adults can be seen quietly reading behind a bush, on a near-hidden terrace or a private balcony. The evening is a time for conviviality, for drinks together in the tiny bar, for laughter and conversation that is rarely dull—for Richard and Sheila are often there enjoying it all. Sheila is a gem: sweet-natured, gentle, fun, patient and generous. She is the spirit in the machine, the cog that turns. Without her Richard would probably disappear into some Quixotic project never to emerge.

The place is far greener than most. "I came down from London with all the eco-books but found that running a hotel calls for a hundred compromises. But we are up for it now, putting in solar panels and building a second eco-hut for ourselves. The extension to the swimming pool will have zero emissions and a thermal-mass wall. We buy organic and local food, know our suppliers well and are wide open to new ideas. Walking is a big thing here; just step out of the door and Devon is yours: the Dart, the sea, the woods and miles and miles of green lanes. A little further is Dartmoor."

Fingals is not for the fastidious. The occasional spider may be overlooked; the bedrooms are an eclectic mix. Some are huge and open-plan, such as the green-oak barn where a whole family can stay. Others are smaller and simpler, even a touch traditional. All have antique beds, good mattresses and their own bathrooms. Dinner is served in the wood-panelled dining room at one long table. It is a mellow, lovely space that encourages conversation. The food is fresh, French and delicious. Éric the chef has been there ten years and clearly loves the place.

The generosity of Fingals reaches far. Richard often takes guests out on his old wooden speedboat, or on a launch. He is game for anything—showing you the Dart, lending you a bike and even pedalling with you—with his own brand of energy. Above all, he and Sheila really do want you to do your own thing. Come down to breakfast in your own time. (The quid pro quo is that you don't have to mind when dinner is a bit late.)

Perhaps the essence of Richard and Sheila's slow approach is treating every good moment like a fine wine—to be tasted, talked about and then drunk. In the bar is a Bakelite phone and a one-handed clock that declares "oneish, twoish, threeish..." Wry, real, and refreshing. Evelyn Waugh wrote in his diaries: "Punctuality is the virtue of the bored." Nobody should be bored here—so what does it matter?

Richard & Sheila Johnston

Fingals, Dittisham, Dartmouth, TQ6 0JA
- 10 rooms. Self-catering barn for 4.
- £75–£160. Barn £500–£800 per week.
- Dinner £30.
- 01803 722398
- richard@fingals.co.uk
- www.fingals.co.uk

West Colwell Farm

DEVON

"Slow is not 'slow.' It's alternative and humanistic, sensible and sustainable. It's country Prozac." These are words Carol Hayes could not have imagined herself saying in her old life, shaped by the London media. In the Eighties she and husband Frank were in the business of selling dreams through the programs they worked on. Their move to Devon at the end of that decade was a realization of their own dream.

After thirty-five years in broadcasting, and as confirmed urbanites, they shut the door on their central London penthouse for the last time, not without trepidation and doubt, for so many unknowns lay ahead. But there was great excitement, too, for they were headed for a new life in a "fally-down" 400-year-old East Devon farmhouse. West Colwell Farm—the footprint of which appears in the Domesday Book—and its deep valley setting had captured their imaginations.

Their purpose was to set up the sort of bed and breakfast that would give guests unusual peace and privacy. The old barn next to the farmhouse needed a huge amount of work but lent itself perfectly to the cause.

Their priority was to find local craftsmen to do much of the work with them. How on earth they found such a dedicated and talented building crew is a mystery to which many of us

would love the answer. All the old stone and beams were reclaimed and re-used and after months of sweat and toil a handsome Phoenix arose from the rubble, "strong enough," says Frank, "to support a cathedral. Two of the bedrooms are finished with a wooden deck that faces the untouched Offwell valley and catches the evening sun. The third is cozy and dramatic, tucked under the roof. "Guests head back here at four o'clock with wine and think it's heaven," says Carol. "Here you sense a greater awareness of where you are in the world."

The scene is even more bucolic now. Against the backdrop of that wooded valley, Frank's four friendly Devon "Ruby Red" cattle graze. "Deciding to buy them is the best thing I've ever done—there's something elemental about it." Frank didn't go into it lightly, but attended agricultural college in Dorchester to learn the theory of cattle rearing. Naturally reared and grass fed, his woolly breed can be left out all year and produce the finest beef. After slaughter, the meat hangs for three to four weeks before it's sold from the small shop in the farmyard. Frank's fondness for his cattle is tangible and he admits to indulging in a bit of discreet nose-rubbing. "It's fun for them and therapy for me."

He's pleased that he decided to farm the land himself. "When we first bought the farm I let the fields to farming neighbors. They were generous with their knowledge and happy to share their experience and that was the start of my learning curve."

The foot and mouth debacle followed. Oddly, some may think, Frank decided to choose that moment to enter the fray and try farming himself. "My farming neighbors were incredibly helpful and supportive and I learned a lot from them but I wanted to go beyond what an apprentice learns by being hands on. The course filled in the many blanks in my knowledge."

Most novice smallholders opt for sheep, hens or pigs but Frank has never regretted his decision to buy a small herd of cattle. "Devon Reds are a fantastic breed —raised to graze the rolling hills of Devon and the south-west climate suits them perfectly. I spend time with them every day, I talk to them and I know all their characteristics. It is one of my greatest pleasures.

"My relationship with them is profoundly rewarding and looking after them is genuinely enjoyable for me— in summer sun or winter gale. I find being with them grounding. The life and death aspect did take some getting used to but ultimately the aim is to eat great beef and supply something wonderful to guests and neighbors. The day animals leave for the butcher is not the greatest," he admits, "but then that balances with the joyful day that new calves arrive on the farm."

Sourcing local produce is easy in Devon. Honiton, three miles away, holds two weekly markets in its high street, plus a farmers' market; there are a great dairy and a bakery and thirty antique shops, too.

Cooking breakfast with local ingredients is something Frank takes on with enthusiasm. He adds exotic twists, such as serving his crispy bacon alongside pancakes made to a recipe learned in Massachusetts and drizzled with maple syrup (Frank gained distinction in "all the Pancake Arts" at the Pamela White Pancake Academy!).

Steve, the egg man, produces the best speckled eggs, each pencil-dated, polished and personally delivered. The eggs are served with a line-up of homemade sunflower-seed soldiers. There's also wheat-free honey-sweet granola, made on Dartmoor. For many guests the greatest indulgence is that all

this is served up at a time to suit them. Over the last of the coffee, guests plan their day with guidance from Frank who darts between table and kitchen in his white chef's apron. As he tells guests, at least one day here in this Area of Outstanding Natural Beauty should be car-free: a walk across Offwell Brook, a stroll in the bluebell woods, a mushroom hunt in autumn, a hike along the coastal path to Beer for crab sandwiches at the beach café.

"One of my greatest pleasures is meeting all the different characters that arrive at our farm. The work of running a B&B can be hard and relentless but that really is a perk. We have the most fascinating guests."

The village too is full of characters... Although the tiny neighboring hamlet of West Colwell has only four official residents, there are many friends who gather at the monthly Offwell Men's Breakfast Club. Frank and Carol edit the Offwell village newsletter and are gradually recording the personal stories of the locals. They also host the annual Christmas party for all those who live in the lane.

Frank and Carol know that many visitors come to them in a state of transition. On holiday in Massachusetts, Carol and Frank opened a secretaire in their hotel room to find "Secret Letter Society" headed paper and an "SLS" pen. Room 4 held thirty years' worth of letters secreted among books, all written anonymously by guests for others to discover and read.

Back home in Devon, in the "Farmer" room, they have encouraged their guests to do the same. People have joined in with enthusiasm. One note from a couple reads... "We are about to throw off the overcoat of responsibility and wear the swimsuit of freedom."

The writers have since told the Hayes that's exactly what they did.

Frank & Carol Hayes

West Colwell Farm,
Offwell, Honiton EX14 9SL
- 3 doubles.
- From £70. Singles £50.
- 01404 831130
- stay@westcolwell.co.uk
- www.westcolwell.co.uk

Beara Farmhouse

DEVON

From Essex to North Devon is—culturally—a very long journey. Richard and Ann once lived in Essex, where Richard's business was the restoration of old buildings. He did this for thirty-five years and then passed it all on to his sons. But the decision to move to Devon to slow down was profoundly wise, for they came to one of the sleepiest corners of a fairly sleepy county.

Richard needs "stuff" the way most of us need to get rid of it. Twenty-one tons of gathered "treasures" that he needed to continue his life as an accumulator came with them; he cannot resist anything unusual or interesting. But unlike many of us who collect odds and ends in the quaint hope of one day transforming them into something beautiful or useful, his skills are real. He is a carpenter and joiner, gifted with the imagination needed to create beauty and function out of discarded material.

For eighteen long months he and Ann labored to turn a run-down farmhouse into the rambling and lovely house it now is. They lived in boiler suits and boots, demolished walls, rescued cast-iron guttering from a hedge and turned the old oak from a tumbledown cowshed into a quaintly charming porch. The old stones from a cowshed have become the paving for the terrace.

Their magical touch with old material reaches into every corner of the place. The farmhouse had three old "shippons"—cowsheds. One is now Richard's second home and workshop, and he is in his element standing in a shallow pool of wood shavings, giving new life to old things.

Have you ever met anyone who has bought an old forge? One day Richard spotted one for sale in the local paper and felt he had to buy it. A retired blacksmith now comes by once or twice a week—heating, banging and coaxing raw metal into twisted candlesticks and bold chandeliers.

Those whose imaginations are happiest in the simpler ways of previous centuries would be happy here. There is a sense of right, timeless values at every corner. Indeed, Richard—faced with the task of restoring these ancient cob buildings—went on a course to learn how to do it authentically.

The money was spent before the restoration ended so they foraged for extra income—in a spirit of openness and fun rather than in worried desperation. They even took to "beating" on the local shoot, and discovered a deep delight in the area around their house. It is full of hidden combes, thickets and hollows, and of strutting pheasants and partridge.

The closeness of the North Devon coastline adds a powerful voice to the place and for many guests is the gilding on the lily. You can brave the choppy boat trip to Lundy island—a stupendous granite outcrop off the Devon coast, just three and a half miles long, and the place to spot rare Manx shearwaters, kittiwakes and those clowns of the air—puffins.

Another old barn, or shippon, has been turned upside-down to create a quiet place for four. Through an ancient archway and wooden latched doors are two cozy bedrooms and a cheerfully blue bathroom. Up the oak stairs is a living area with a wood-burning stove and views over the pond and the unsullied landscape beyond; settle in and you'll never want to leave.

The "Little Beara" is an engagingly eccentric stone playhouse for the grandchildren, where a tiny fire can toast both bread and feet. It was built by Ben, a young lad who came on work experience and who is now a fully-fledged stonemason. Other wry architectural gestures are the fully-tiled pig shed and the half-timbered house "for sale" by the fence, big enough to house half of one adult body or the free-ranging ducks and hens.

Part of the magic here is the clash of expectations. So deep is the rusticity of the life they lead that one expects a raw interior. But it is lovely, and in a sophisticated way. There is a subtle marriage of raw wood and old materials with modern ideas, all held together with a light ironic touch. It is homey, too: Ann has delicately stenciled bedroom walls and scattered her own needlepoint cushions across pastel bedspreads. The tone is intimate and tender, affectionate towards anything that has value, shape and beauty. It is "cottagey" rather than coy.

A slow rural life can only be slower and better with animals. There are enough of them here to make Richard look somewhat Noah-like at times, especially as they are so well housed. Reuben was the first Kune Kune pig, Reuben led to Ruby and then Parsley and Posy. Six Southdown sheep are growing fat in their easy role as lawnmowers along the farmhouse track.

It is easy to be here with Richard and Ann; they have not just accepted this life but are gaily immersed in it. There is no gulf between visitors and

them, just a seamless and immediate connection; witness the humor with which they greeted immaculately dressed guests one day as they themselves were wrestling in the mud with errant pigs. And they have turned ordinary things, like a pile of flower pots, into "objets d'amusement."

Given such a generous welcome, guests often become good friends, returning year after year, appreciating their hosts' place in the community and the unusual home that they have created. "We've made more friends here in two years than in twenty-five in Essex, and with the B&B we are never lonely. We don't have to go anywhere to find somewhere lovely to be; we just sit and look at the fields. Of course the pressures are still there—it's not some magic idyll where all your problems disappear. But we have chosen to be here and we don't have to work to the clock."

Compared to Essex, this corner of Devon is a hundred years in the past. "I went to hire some machinery," explains Richard. "In Essex, they would have taken my picture and demanded a deposit. Here they said 'Deposit? What do you mean?' That's trusting, and hugely refreshing."

"We do know people that have moved here, then moved back as they can't stand the slowness," Ann says. "You do have to wait to get work done." Both of them seem wary of technology. "Richard doesn't know how anything works unless you can hit it with a hammer!" Ann adds affectionately. But this attitude comes with having a great many other things to do. "Our time is spent doing, not sitting in front of a screen." When they have a spare hour or two they'd rather read or paint, potter in the garden, or hunt down that elusive chunk of wood. Sophisticated living comes more easily, perhaps, without much technology.

Ann & Richard Dorsett
Beara Farmhouse
Buckland Brewer, Bideford EX39 5EH

- 2 rooms.
- £65. Singles by arrangement.
- 01237 451666
- www.bearafarmhouse.co.uk

Southcliffe Hall

DEVON

In 1856 George Eliot came to Lee. She wrote in her journals, "Lee is a tiny hamlet which has lodged itself, like a colony of Aurora Actiniae, in the nick between two ranges of hills where the sea runs and makes a miniature bay."

Here she met the "sweet-natured" Reverend George Tugwell of Southcliffe Hall, a published authority on Actinia Aurora (sea anemones) and also on the fine North Devon scenery.

Lee remains a heavenly cove, perfect for rock pooling and clambering at low tide and awash with tales of smugglers. When Kate and Barry saw Southcliffe Hall for the first time on a misty January afternoon they had no idea it had such a wonderful view out to sea. By the time they'd reached this hidden corner of the West Country they had looked at 500 houses in their pursuit of peace.

"We are allergic to traffic noise," says Kate.

The only sounds the couple and their young son Benjamin now contend with are nightly owls and badgers, and the low-level chatter of birds in the day and the sound of the sea.

The house was an even bigger surprise. After the sweet-natured Rev. Tugwell died, the Hall was opened as a hotel in the 1920s, housed a school during the war, survived a fire to one wing, and then fell into the hands of a mildly eccentric Australian. A keen recycler, he had an ornate metal balustrade shipped over from Adelaide and a chandelier brought over from Buenos Aires after the Falklands War. He

reclaimed doors from a local chapel and fitted 18th-century French radiators. Kate and Barry have embraced his grandly idiosyncratic style and have undertaken a massive renovation. They have added their own exquisite treasures, too, collected while traveling the Far East and living in South Africa.

The bedrooms are vast, with big beds, antique flourishes and walnut furniture. The bathrooms are extraordinary one-offs—with roll-top baths and Victorian high-level cisterns. (They decided to heave out the red telephone-box shower and replaced it with a modern, roomier version.)

Each floor resounds with history. The bedrooms and the sea-view drawing room have mahogany floorboards, lifted from the dance floor in Ilfracombe's Victorian pavilion. The Rev. Tugwell's beautiful, and younger, bride Ethel loved to dance and for her delight he added a ballroom, with sprung floor and covered loggia. Kate and Barry have still to decide how to use this charming space: probably for weekend music and craft courses over the long winter months.

Smugglers loved this sheltered rocky cove and cut-off valley. The smuggler Hannibal Richards, six foot six with long black hair, arrived in Lee with his wife in 1789. He stayed until he died, fifty years later. Brandy and gin, Portuguese red wine and tea were his stock in trade.

Today, walkers and day-trippers rather than smugglers dot the cliff tops and bays. Rare orchids can be found among the long grasses, and shiny shells and those sea anemones—"flowers of the sea"— in crystal-clear pools. Barry and his friends often scrabble over to the next bay at low tide and hike three miles to the next village's pub. They choose a less hazardous route back in the dark.

Salmon Steaks Southcliffe Style

6 fresh salmon steaks (or tuna or sea bass)
2 tins organic coconut milk
1 dessertspoon peanut butter
1 dessertspoon red curry paste
Pinch of saffron
Juice of one lime
Bunch of chopped coriander
Fresh asparagus (in season late-April to mid-June)
Single cream

• Heat gently in open frying pan the coconut milk, peanut butter, saffron and red curry paste for 20 mins or until sauce has reduced by a third
• Reheat before serving but do not boil, stirring in the "skin"
• Add lime juice and half the coriander
• Steam asparagus, if using
• 15 minutes before serving, flash fry the steaks until just done (salmon should not be dry; tuna should still be pink)
• Pour over each steak two tablespoons of sauce, then garnish with coriander, two asparagus spears and a drizzle of cream

Barry was a city banker, who worked in South Africa for ten years. Kate's family is South African; she too worked in the corporate world. When Barry resigned he chose kitchen knives as his farewell present, and they traveled east for a year—to cook, explore and consider their futures. "The choice was to go back into corporate life or do something for ourselves. We were half thinking about having a family, so we came back to the UK—having bought our first Yorkshire house while in Kathmandu!"

Barry's dinners are special. In the oak-paneled dining room he ladles rich wild mushroom soup

(made from hand-picked funghi), followed by local roasted beef and bubbling gratin dauphinoise.

Bliss it is in the morning to stroll down through the gardens and take the path to the cove. Betty Boo (Boo) the Border terrier may join you for a while. Don't be misled by her unassuming manner; she's a Crufts champion and has many rosettes.

You could spend all week here without a car.

The Tarka cycle trail is over the hill and there are exceptional walks from the door. The six to eight-mile hike along the National Trust's South West Coastal Path introduces you to some of the most spectacular coastline in the country: rough and rugged cliffs, wild flowers in spring, steps down to secluded beaches, chance sightings of dolphins and seals. A treat, too, to return to afternoon cream tea on the terrace: a homemade scone lathered with Devon clotted cream and jam, and a stupendous view.

Kate reflects on their new life and loves the fact they have the time to spend with their son; she has also started a parent and toddler group in the village. Although bred in London, she loves those aspects of the countryside that contrast so starkly with city life; where the nearest supermarket is a trek and neighbors have time to share a cup of tea.

She and Barry genuinely want guests to relish their time here, relaxing, winding down, in winter as much as summer. You cannot help but do so, as you scour the rock pools of Lee Bay for crabs, anemones and prawns, surf some of Britain's best waves at Woolacombe and Croyde, or simply stroll along the miles of pale sands. On Barricane Beach you can eat fresh ciabatta sandwiches by day and feast on a Sri Lankan curry at night; if there are no seats, just settle on a rock and watch the sun go down.

Kate Seekings & Barry Jenkinson
Southcliffe Hall, Lee, EX34 8LW
- 3 rooms.
- £100.
- Dinner £25.
- 01271 867068
- stay@southcliffehall.co.uk
- www.southcliffehall.co.uk

SOMERSET, WILTSHIRE & DORSET

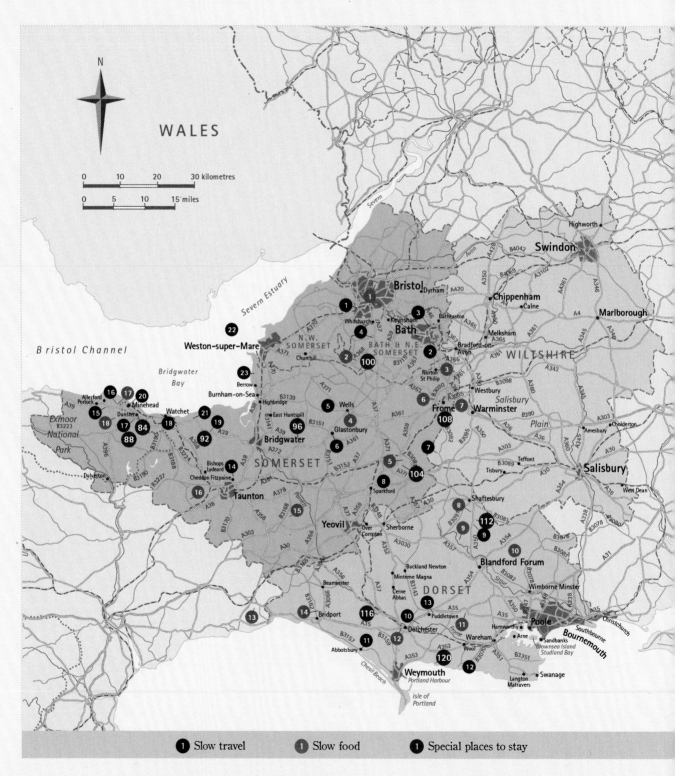

N

WALES

0   10   20   30 kilometres

0   5   10   15 miles

Bristol Channel

Severn Estuary

Bridgwater Bay

Exmoor National Park

N.W. SOMERSET

BATH & N.E. SOMERSET

SOMERSET

WILTSHIRE

Salisbury Plain

DORSET

Highworth

Swindon

Chippenham

Calne

Marlborough

Bristol

Dyrham

Whitchurch

Keynsham

Batheaston

Bath

Bradford-on-Avon

Melksham

Westbury

Norton St Philip

Frome

Warminster

Amesbury

Cholderton

Salisbury

West Dean

Teffont

Tisbury

Shaftesbury

Blandford Forum

Wimborne Minster

Poole

Bournemouth

Southbourne

Christchurch

Sandbanks

Brownsea Island

Studland Bay

Swanage

Langton Matravers

Weymouth

Portland Harbour

Isle of Portland

Chesil Beach

Abbotsbury

Wool

Wareham

Arne

Hamworthy

Puddletown

Dorchester

Bridport

Beaminster

Cerne Abbas

Minterne Magna

Buckland Newton

Yeovil

Sherborne

Over Compton

Sparkford

Taunton

Bishops Lydeard

Cheddon Fitzpaine

Bridgwater

Glastonbury

Wells

East Huntspill

Highbridge

Burnham-on-Sea

Berrow

Weston-super-Mare

Churchill

Watchet

Minehead

Dunster

Porlock

Allerford

Dulverton

Weston-super-Mare

Westbury

● Slow travel   ● Slow food   ● Special places to stay

SOMERSET, WILTSHIRE & DORSET

Slow travel

1. The Observatory
2. Prior Park Landscape Garden
3. Bath Boating Station
4. Stanton Drew
5. Priddy Sheep Fair
6. Glastonbury Tor
7. Stourhead House & Gardens
8. Cadbury Castle Hill
9. Fontmell Down
10. Hardy's Cottage
11. Abbotsbury Gardens
12. Ringstead Bay
13. Athelhampton House
14. Hestercombe Gardens
15. Selworthy Village
16. Periton Park Stables
17. Dunster Castle
18. Cleeve Abbey
19. Coleridge Cottage
20. West Somerset Railway
21. Kilve Beach
22. Steep Holm
23. Brean Down

Slow food

1. Bristol Slow Food Market
2. New Manor Farm Shop
3. Norwood Farm
4. Wells Farmers' Market
5. Godminster Farm
6. Frome Farmers' Market
7. Simpson's Seeds
8. Panary Co Ltd
9. Gold Hill Organic Farm
10. Long Crichel Bakery
11. Pampered Pigs Pantry
12. Dorchester Farmers' Market
13. River Cottage Courses
14. Washingpool Farm Shop
15. Julian Temperley
16. Gundenham Dairy
17. Hindon Organic Farm
18. Dunkery Vineyard

Special places to stay

84. No.7
88. Royal Oak at Luxborough
92. Parsonage Farm
96. Church Cottage
100. Harptree Court
104. Lower Farm
108. The Bath Arms
112. The Old Forge
116. Frampton House
120. Marren

Slow travel

① The Observatory
Bristol (0117 9241379)
The only "camera obscura" open to the public in England, housed in an 18th-century windmill on a green Clifton hill overlooking Brunel's iconic bridge.
www.about-bristol.co.uk

② Prior Park Landscape Garden
Bath (01225 833422)
Landscaped gardens with woodland walks, lakes, grottoes and Palladian bridge with 18th-century graffiti. No car park: come by bike, brave the hills.
www.nationaltrust.org.uk

③ Bath Boating Station
Forester Rd, Bathwick
(01225 312900)
Victorian boating station almost in the center of Bath. Punts (iffy), skiffs (romantic), can be hired by the hour or the day. Find a nettle-free bank, bring the sun hats and hamper.
www.bathboating.co.uk

④ Stanton Drew
The third largest collection of prehistoric standing stones in England. No kiosks, no coach parties, just three incomplete circles 100ft-360ft in diameter and fields of nonplussed sheep.

Thirsty types should know that three of the stones are in the garden of the village pub.
www.english-heritage.org.uk

⑤ Priddy Sheep Fair
Centuries-old sheep fair once held in Wells before the ravages of the Black Death saw it shifted to the windswept heights of Priddy. Held on the Wednesday that falls closest to August 21st.
www.priddysheepfair.co.uk

⑥ Glastonbury Tor
Puff your way up the magical Tor for a windswept view of the Somerset Levels, scamper down to New Age City for Abbey ruins, medieval monuments and shops selling carrot cake and crystals.

⑦ Stourhead House & Gardens
(01747 841152)
An 18th-century masterpiece of a garden, with lake, bridges, temples, grottoes, trees and a rather fine mansion to boot. Farm shop too, and civilized pub.
www.nationaltrust.org.uk

⑧ Cadbury Castle Hill
South Cadbury
The most interesting of the reputed

sites of Camelot, eighteen acres of tree-shrouded, bank-and-ditched hill towering 500ft above sea level. Views reach to Glastonbury Tor.

⑨ Fontmell Down
A short, easy walk up and over Fontmell Down gets the best of the views in the area and the finest displays of chalk downland flowers and butterflies, for a minimal amount of effort. Dogs like it too.
www.wildlifetrust.org.uk

⑩ Hardy's Cottage
Higher Bockhampton
(01297 561900)
Birthplace of Thomas Hardy who wrote *Far From the Madding Crowd* here. Small, delightful cob and thatch cottage sparsely and authentically furnished, with pretty cottage garden.
www.nationaltrust.org.uk

⑪ Abbotsbury Gardens
Abbotsbury (01305 871387)
Superb 18th-century walled coastal garden leading to a gentle coombe with camellias and magnolias in woodland, specimen trees and rare and exotic plants. Drop down to Chesil Beach with your hammer and chisel and dig out a fossil.
www.abbotsbury-tourism.co.uk

12 Ringstead Bay
Jurassic coast, west of horseshoe-shaped Lulmouth Cove. Pretty pebble beach with clean water perfect for swimming and snorkelling. Once used by smugglers, now frequented by fossil hunters.

13 Athelhampton House
nr Dorchester (01305 848363)
A glorious Tudor manor house with priests' holes and secret staircases, and a gallery in the attic devoted to the Russian cubist painter Maria Marevna. Wonderful Elizabethan-style gardens with topiary pyramids, beloved of Hardy.
www.athelhampton.co.uk

14 Hestercombe Gardens
Cheddon Fitzpaine, Taunton (01823 413923)
Acres and acres of gardens, from Georgian landscaped parkland to Arts & Crafts intimacy, designed by Lutyens and planted by Gertrude Jekyll.
www.hestercombe.com

15 Selworthy Village
Thatched model village on Exmoor's Holnicote Estate, that climbs the hill to a 15th-century church with gorgeous views to Dunkery Beacon, the highest hill in Somerset and the South West. Trot back down for a reviving tea in the National Trust cottage.
www.nationaltrust.org.uk

16 Periton Park Stables
Exmoor (01643 705970)
One-hour to full-day rides on glorious Exmoor.
www.peritonpark.co.uk

17 Dunster Castle
Dunster (01643 821314)
Subtropical gardens, historic, thriving village and magnificent 17th-century castle whose plasterwork ceilings are vacuumed only every fourth year to protect them.
www.nationaltrust.org.uk

18 Cleeve Abbey
nr Washford (01984 640377)
The most complete set of monastic cloister buildings in England.
www.english-heritage.org.uk

19 Coleridge Cottage
Nether Stowey (01278 732662)
Home of Coleridge, who lived in little Nether Stowey (and wrote "The Ancient Mariner" here), 1797–1800. The village is lovely and has a farm shop and tea room/bistro. The thirty-six-mile Coleridge Way opened in 2005 and marches you across the Quantock Hills, Bredon Hills and Exmoor—all the way to Porlock.
www.nationaltrust.org.uk

20 West Somerset Railway
(01643 707650)
Twenty miles of cherished narrow-gauge track from Bishops Lydeard to Minehead. Sit back and watch the Quantock Hills drift by; stop off for cream tea at Chives (01984 632038), a little deli in Watchet.
www.west-somerset-railway.

21 Kilve Beach
At low tide, this is a favorite haunt of geologists with spectacular rock formations and fossils. To the east, in the 15th-century remains of a chantry, is a pretty tea garden open all year.

22 Steep Holm
off Weston super Mare
Book the boat through the Kenneth Allsop Memorial Trust (01934 632307) for six windswept hours to roam the island's fifty acres, spot rare wild peonies, explore Victorian fortifications and send a postcard back home.
www.steepholm.org

23 Brean Down
Reached via 211 steps from the beach, this blustery National Trust peninsula is home to peregrines, kestrels and a bramble-smothered Roman temple. Picnic on the springy sheep-nibbled turf in the shelter of a hollow and take in stupendous views. Bring sweaters, dogs and toddlers on reins.

Slow food

1 Bristol Slow Food Market
Corn Street (0117 922 2646)
First Sunday of the month, first in
the UK. Line-caught Brixham
seafood, Devon beef, Glocestershire
perry: provenance is all. Links with
historic trading partners (Jerez,
Bordeaux) are in the pipeline, plus
educating children about food.
www.slowfood.com

2 New Manor Farm Shop
North Widcombe (01761 220067)
Tuck into the cakes and meals in the
Stable Tea Room before exploring
this wonderful farm shop.

3 Norwood Farm
Norton St Philip
Wind-powered working farm whose
Saddleback pigs and Wiltshire Horn
sheep are treated to a drug-and-
hormone free diet and fresh air.
Shop, café and play area.
www.norwoodfarm.co.uk

4 Wells Farmers' Market
Wells Town Hall
Wednesdays 2pm-5:30pm from late
May to early October.
www.wellsfarmersmarket.org

5 Godminster Farm
Bruton (01749 813733)
Bringing tradition up to date:
organic cheeses, specialist vodkas
(horseradish, cucumber, elderflower),
medicinal herbs.
www.godminster.com

6 Frome Farmers' Market
Cheese & Grain, Frome (01373 455420)
Every other Saturday. Fabulous.

7 Simpson's Seeds
Horningsham (01985 845004)
Specialists in capsicum seeds and
chili weekends.
www.simpsonsseeds.co.uk

8 Panary Co Ltd
Cann Mills (01722 341447)
Wood-fired Italian, French, British
and festive breads from working
watermill, and bread-making courses
for adults and children.
www.panary.co.uk

9 Gold Hill Organic Farm
Child Okeford (01258 863716)
Wide range of local and organic
food. Summer café.
www.thegreenhouse.biz

10 Long Crichel Bakery
Long Crichel (01258 863716)
Organic, wood-fired croissants and
breads from young artisan bakery;
master bakers from Scandanivia and
France drop by. Summer breakfasts
and lunches.
www.longcrichelbakery.co.uk

11 Pampered Pigs Pantry
nr Bere Regis (01929 472327)
Farm shop selling naturally reared
meat and local produce.
www.pamperedpigs.co.uk

12 Dorchester Farmers' Market
Poundbury (07932 637103)
First Saturday of the month.

13 River Cottage Courses
Trinity Hill (01297 630300)
Day and evening courses, feasts
and forages driven by the Hugh
Fearnley-Whittingstall philosophy
of self-sufficiency and passion for
real food.
www.rivercottage.net

14 Washingpool Farm Shop
North Allington (01308 425424)
North Devon beef cattle, Jacob
cross sheep, veg and soft fruit at
this family-run farm: fresh, tasty
and traceable. Restaurant too.
www.washingpool.co.uk

15 Julian Temperley
Kingsbury Episcopi, Martock
(01460 240782)
One hundred varieties of cider apple
fermented and distilled with passion
"and a certain amount of roguery."
An exceedingly fine cider brandy, too.
www.ciderbrandy.co.uk

16 Gundenham Dairy
North Gunderham (01823 662704)
BBC award-winning family farm
begun in the 1920s, specializing
in milk, cream, potatoes and
Christmas hampers.
www.gundenham-dairy.co.uk

17 Hindon Organic Farm
nr Selworthy (01643 705244)
"From the moor to your door":
superb pork, beef, lamb.
www.hindonfarm.co.uk

18 Dunkery Vineyard
nr Wootton Courtenay
(01643 841505)
Whites, reds and bubbly, produced
from seven gorgeous acres on Exmoor.
www.english-wine.com

Pubs & inns

Halfway House

Pitney Hill, Langport, Somerset
Local clubs gather for chess, music, hockey; real-pub-lovers return. In the two simple and homely rooms are log fires and a happy buzz. Soak up the alcohol with casserole and crusty bread.
01458 252513 www.thehalfwayhouse.co.uk

The Crown

The Batch, Churchill, Somerset
Modern makeovers have passed this gem by and beer reigns supreme, with up to ten ales tapped from the barrel. The rustic surroundings, jolly atmosphere and treacle pudding draw locals and walkers treading the Mendips hills. 01934 852995

Canal Inn

Wrantage, Taunton, Somerset
Bare boards, foaming pints and menus that proudly list suppliers, all within a five-mile radius. A farmers' market in the bar on the last Saturday of the month brings customers and suppliers together.
01823 480210 www.thecanalinn.com

The Malet Arms

Newton Tony, Salisbury, Wiltshire
Formerly a bakehouse for a long-lost manor, the old flintstone pub draws walkers and cyclists from miles around. Expect cracking ales, blazing log fires, robust country cooking and a cheerful welcome. 01980 629279

The Millstream

Marden, Devizes, Wiltshire
Pale beams, crisp colors and open fires give a fresh appeal to the open-plan space. Bags of character, a welcome for all, a superb modern menu and handpumped ales—we love this place.
01380 848308 www.the-millstream.net

The Flemish Weaver

High Street, Corsham, Wiltshire
A friendly local with a kitchen worth seeking out—and you'll find a framed roll-call of their food suppliers near the bar. Well-kept Bath Ales, stylish tables topped with fresh flowers, local artists' work on cream walls. 01249 701929

The Square & Compass

Worth Matravers, Swanage, Dorset
The name honors all those who cut stone from the nearby quarries. In the family for a hundred years, gloriously unchanged (two hatches still serve ale straight from the cask), it's high on the hill gazing out to sea. 01929 439229

The Museum Inn

Farnham, Blandford Forum, Dorset
Vicky, Mark and their (mostly) Aussie staff have created a blissfully warm and happy place to be, with cozy alcoves and a stylish dining room. The refit of the big 17th-century bar has kept the period feel.
01725 516261 www.museuminn.co.uk

Coventry Arms

Mill Street, Corfe Mullen, Dorset
A 15th-century riverside pub with its own island—the pub's freshly caught trout are sometimes reeled in by customers and may end up on your plate. Low beams, local ales and tables by the stream.
01258 857284 www.coventryarms.co.uk

No. 7

SOMERSET

"Whenever I hear men boast of hills, I will rise up in praise of the hills of North Somerset. They lie in wait for you round corners, they stand up in clusters, six or seven together, like domes of six or seven sunken St Pauls. They lift up to the sky fields which are among the loveliest in England. When the sun is over them... they bring a man very near to prayer."

That was H. V. Morton writing in 1937, but he would write the same now, for the northern part of Exmoor is little changed. Dunster is perhaps the loveliest of its villages, dominated by a once-Norman castle that has only ever had two owning families and with a wide main street of handsome medieval houses. The church is glorious, with the original rood screen still there in rare defiance of other churches' history. There are a tithe barn, once part of a priory, a dovecote, a water mill in working order, and a Gallox bridge used to carry pack animals across the river Anvill. It is on the very eastern edge of the Moor, happily distant from the less-seductive Minehead and only a quick bike ride from Mother Nature's best.

Jean-Christophe and Lucy can't quite believe their luck. Their house is right on the main street, yet on the edge of the grounds of the castle. Their steep terraced garden leads right up to them and you have a bird's eye view of the village from there too. The house, a 17th-century cottage, was owned by the castle and then the Crown. It is a listed building, beautifully restored by the recent builders with a stable door off the street, a big entrance hall and carved oak beams of the Stuart period. The staircase is of dark curved 17th-century oak and the windows are suitably mullioned. It is delightful.

Lucy tells their story. "It may seem a bit odd, starting a B&B from scratch at the ripe age of twenty-five, but we have both always been interested in "hospitality." We wanted to do a B&B that was different from the chintz-filled variety. Our love of the countryside and obsession with good local produce brought us to Dunster, where we have acres of moorland, miles of coast and beautiful forests in between.

"We have spent time perfecting the menu and scouring the local markets for the right raw materials. JC has been busy networking over numerous pints in the pub, meeting local characters and getting advice from farmers on where to fish and where to buy the best local meat. Even our chocolate is made in Minehead. High-quality meat is easy to get hold of here and the venison is good—as you might expect. Fresh fish is not so easy, so JC has taken to fishing for it himself off the pier at Minehead. (Editor's note: he abandoned that!). Food was always going to be one of the main features of our place. We wanted the ingredients to be good enough to speak for themselves."

Their food is simply delicious. JC was brought up in Normandy; his family spent their holidays exploring restaurants and his father, a hunter, taught him how to prepare and cook wild boar, venison and rabbit. He learned, too, about mushrooms and the sensitive approach they demand. He met Lucy at the University of St Andrews, where she was studying literature and he studied banking and finance. He resisted the lure of London, working instead in hotels and restaurants as beverage manager. The move to Dunster was to bring them closer to Lucy's mum, and they hoped to open a little restaurant. But that didn't work out, and here they are in a rather unusual "gastronomic" B&B.

The treat begins at breakfast, with JC's light and airy croissants and creamy smoked haddock and mushrooms. They will do you a picnic too: a flask of exquisite soup, *saucisson* and sandwiches, salads and

> "It is just a matter of time before JC hangs and dries meats in a nearby barn and makes his own pancetta for breakfast"

hard-boiled eggs. The cakes for tea are French: those "*petites madeleines*, short plump little cakes which look as though they have been moulded in the flute scallop of a pilgrim's shell," as Proust declared. The Auld Alliance with Scotland is celebrated with a grainy Scottish "tablet"—a "wee bit of heaven." Then the Taster dinner, for which you need to prime yourselves: five to seven little dishes designed to be "little bites of flavor and texture that leave time for wine and conversation in between.

"There are only two of us in the kitchen so we can't serve fast food; but we hope the food is worth the wait." It is, and how. Arugula soup with chorizo croutons; monkfish on cauliflower purée, with spinach and asparagus open ravioli; apple and calvados sorbet with Exmoor blue cheese, mango chutney and pine nuts; a tower of organic lamb with flageolet beans and asparagus; chocolate fondant and white chocolate parfait with raspberry coulis and chili chocolate; lavender ice cream and lavender crème brulée.

If you choose the set menu you may have to suffer awhile with food designed for mere mortals: asparagus

perhaps, and some venison from the Moor. It is just a matter of time before JC hangs and dries meats in a nearby barn, makes his own pancetta for breakfast—and re-shapes the food habits of a whole county.

A word on the delights of Dunster. The walking on the Moor may be superb, the riding unrivalled in southern England, the quiet almost unknown elsewhere in the country, the scenery soft and rugged all at once, but there is the Coastal Path too—and it leads you all the way round to Land's End.

"Running a B&B has been far harder than we thought—while our friends in London are speeding along in the rat race we are digging our allotment and baking biscuits." But JC and Lucy have a sure cultural touch, offering stylish quilts and goose down pillows, flowers from the garden and books to browse, soaps and bottled water from the Moor and a devotion to the area. The allotment revolution, however, is already well rooted and has swept them up. They spend long hours on their two allotments overlooking the village and the Bristol Channel. They do a bit every day, growing everything from garlic to tomatoes, arugula, raspberries, chilies and chocolate mint. There is no shortage of old men to advise them; there can be few sweeter pleasures than leaning on your spade and saying to younger gardeners: "Plant it the other way up or it will get the blight" and "I told you so. Mine are doing just fine."

It is a friendly village and they arrived at just the right time: to catch the annual Dunster by Candlelight festival in early December. They sold JC's little French cakes at the door. Dunster has acquired a pair of unusual and gifted inhabitants.

Lucy Paget-Tomlinson

No. 7, 7 West Street, Dunster, TA24 6SN
- 3 rooms. £60-£75. Singles from £45.
- Dinner £21. Afternoon tea from £5.
  Packed lunch from £5.50.
- 01643 821064
- info@no7weststreet.co.uk
- www.no7weststreet.co.uk

Royal Oak at Luxborough

SOMERSET

"We have no background music, no fruit machines and no pool table (I gave that to the village hall as the kids would get more use out of it there). There is no mobile phone reception," says James, "although we do have a dartboard and a quiz league."

James Waller knew nothing about pubs but was desperate to get out of London, where he worked in the frenzied money markets. Why a pub, when the work is even harder? Ah, but the work is rewarding and this pub is special. Pubs can play a major role in the life of a village, especially now that so many other aspects of village life have been taken from us. Their landlords are key figures.

"I was working in the City. Running a pub was the last thing on my mind. But my son Eddie was three and I was leaving home at 5:30am and getting back at eight. I entertained clients on Saturdays and spent Sundays exhausted.

"I came across a wonderful pub in Wales—we didn't buy that one but the seed was sown. We wanted to change direction and to be closer to our parents. I wanted to buy the type of place we like to go to: old world, quiet, atmospheric—this! Occasionally a cow or a tractor trundles past. It's perfect."

The Royal Oak, an old cider and perry pub, goes back 500

years. The Back Bar was at one time the local abattoir; meat hooks are still visible in the beams. The butcher also plied his trade here, with a small shop near the well (they still get water from their spring in the cellar) and, until the sixties, there was a bar for women only.

Even the local tailor, a Mr. Spiller, had workrooms in what are now bedrooms, and the village shop and post office were here until twelve years ago. "Progress" has removed them, though a new village hall has been built.

Two intimate low-beamed bars lead to a warren of dining rooms decked with polished tables and hunting prints on dark walls. A shelf heaves with walking books and maps, lent freely. "People come to walk, to sit by the fire, to do nothing. They go to bed early—the fresh air gets to them." (Bedrooms ramble around the first floor: individual, peaceful and homey.)

During the shooting season the bar hums with the sound of gamekeepers, beaters, drivers and picker-uppers from the nearby Chargot shoot. Shooting is a deep-rooted part of the local scene, and very convivial. "The shoot (pheasants and partridges) has been coming down for at least ten years. At lunchtime it's the beaters, picker-uppers and loaders. They all have their set

tables. It's a great atmosphere. They come in from the beginning of September until the end of January, and have their own back room to dine in.

"I'd never pulled a pint before we arrived. When we took over on the first day of January 2002, it was the last day of the shooting season and I had ninety in for lunch. In the first three months of being here my feet hardly touched the ground. I lost two stone!"

The spirit of the place has worked its magic on the once-overwrought James.

"My wife Sîan goes up to London to work, but spends as much time here as she can. She does the breakfasts, and the flowers. It is the most wonderful place to bring up children. Ed is nine now and goes off on his bike with his friends. Everyone in the village knows him. The school bus picks him up from the door.

"We have kept the basic format. The village is small but people have been coming here all their lives. People play cribbage, backgammon, scrabble. The locals talk and drink. The dogs doze by the fire."

James's commitment to local life is shown by his attitude to the regulars: there's one big table right by the fire, reserved every evening of the year just for them. One seat in particular is reserved for Dennis, who has been drinking amiably here for eighteen years and has his portrait on the wall.

James inherited Tim Sandy as head chef. He was trained in London and later worked at Bentley's, the seafood restaurant, hence the Royal Oak's emphasis on fish, alongside game. The menu changes seasonally, with daily specials too. The beef, lamb and venison almost walk off the hills into the kitchen. "When I have the roast lamb on a Sunday I can point out to our diners the chap who grew their lamb."

The fish comes from St Mawes in Cornwall. Soups and puddings are homemade. In the inter-connecting Green and Red Rooms diners are encouraged to take their time, and have the table for the whole evening, an unusual touch.

The beer is as local as possible and so are the two scrumpy ciders: Thatcher's Cheddar Valley and Rich's. "If I change the beer there is widespread outcry! And you have to have cider in a Somerset pub."

It is marvelous to stay and eat at an inn whose landlord is so contented with his lot. "I'm hands on,

and have Anita, who is a godsend. I'm my own man here, setting my own agenda. I enjoy meeting people and everyone has time to talk. We've made more friends in six years here than we did in twenty in London. Within two days of arriving we knew the postman's name. The hours are long, but I'm not answerable to anyone. And the staff are so friendly; everyone helps each other."

A folk group plays at the back, in the "Blazing Stump Bar". Rumor has it that in the sixties the parsimonious landlord would put a single log on the fire; if you wanted another, you brought your own.

It's competitive, village life: fetes, mouse racing in the village hall, plastic duck racing on the stream. There's a shared horse, too, owned by The Royal Oak Syndicate. "He's called Mr. Chatterbox, and now and then we pile into a bus and go off to Taunton or Newton Abbot to see him run. My father was a jockey in the 10th Hussars so I feel I have a some racing spirit in my blood."

Luxborough is in the Exmoor National Park, in a green, sheltered valley between the Brendon and Croydon Hills, close to rugged moorland and woodland. The village is right on the Coleridge Way that runs from Nether Stowey to Porlock on the coast. The inn is twenty-two miles from the start and a perfect overnight stopping point.

In the next year or so the Coleridge bridleway will be complete. There are stables near the Royal Oak and James is putting up tethering posts to the side so that thirsty riders can pop in for a drink.

Exmoor is stunning at all times of the year. It is almost as wild and beautiful as England can get. The Royal Oak gilds the lily—magnificently.

James & Sîan Waller

Royal Oak at Luxborough,
Luxborough, Dunster, TA23 0SH
- 11 rooms. £75–£100.
- Main courses £11.95–£15.95. Bar meals from £4.95.
- 01984 640319
- info@theroyaloakinnluxborough.co.uk
- www.theroyaloakinnluxborough.co.uk

Parsonage Farm

SOMERSET

Samuel Taylor Coleridge lived in the Quantocks and was a terrific walker. In a surge of literary energy he is said to have stridden from his little cottage in Nether Stowey to Bristol and back, just to change his library books. During the three years he lived here with his wife and sons he was inspired to write some of his greatest poems: "The Rime of the Ancient Mariner," "Kubla Khan" and "The Nightingale;" he lured his friends the Wordsworths here too, grew vegetables, kept pigs, ducks and geese and had an apple orchard. Yet he was more a poet than a smallholder.

> Now, my friends emerge
> Beneath the wide wide Heaven—and view again
> The many-steepled tract magnificent
> Of hilly fields and meadows, and the sea,
> With some fair bark, perhaps, whose sails light up
> The slip of smooth clear blue betwixt two isles
> Of purple shadow!

"This Lime-Tree Bower My Prison"
S. T. Coleridge, 1797

These close-fielded, valley-tucked, tree-dappled Quantock Hills are a lure. The footpaths criss-cross the hills, meander through the wooded coombs and down to the sea, barely changed since those times when the poets spent their days walking the hills. The Coleridge Way, thirty-six miles of unspoiled walking, starts down the lane and runs, or walks, all the way to Porlock on the coast; Suki will lend you the maps.

She and Rich are modern-day smallholders, inspired by their own experiences as much as by the romantic poets. Suki, who trained as a primary teacher, is, among other things, a potter and has created her own studio in the old stable, with a kiln and two wheels, where she holds classes. She is originally from Vermont, one the greenest and most rural states in America, and with a rich modern culture of self-sufficiency. (Ben and Jerry's ice cream began there, with milk at guaranteed prices from family farms.) She always wanted to run a bed and breakfast and the idea grew when she met her husband Rich, who was born in Somerset but living and working in Vermont as a forester.

Fifteen years ago they made the move back to Somerset with their two-year-old daughter, bought Parsonage Farm and began the B&B. They have been slowly creating a center of rural delight ever since.

To their existing enthusiasms they have added slow travel, using bicycles to get around whenever possible and encouraging their guests to walk the hills or cycle the lanes as well; there are bikes to borrow. Rich is a part-time cycle warden for the national cycling charity Sustrans. Their personal idea of a holiday or break is to wander off for a few days walking the wonderful coastal path or cycling a Sustrans route. They also offer visitors a 5% discount for arriving by public transport, foot or bicycle.

Their smallholding is of three acres, rich with vegetables, fruits, a scattering of hens and two hives. There's a beautiful large walled garden with flower borders, a natural spring and a vegetable patch full of globe artichokes, asparagus, potatoes, peas and soft fruit. Suki lets the garden "tell" her what to cook for dinner. "I don't really plan meals. I just go into the garden and see what's there to inspire me." It might turn out to be butternut squash risotto and a salad with nasturtium flowers, of a freshness that city dwellers can only dream about.

Twelve years ago they planted an apple orchard, for this was once apple country and many farmers have grubbed out their old orchards—succumbing to the relentless pressure to conform and grow for the mass market. In the autumn, with guests often joining in, they press their own apples (old Somerset varieties) using a wooden press from Devon and making a hundred bottles of pasteurized apple juice each year.

The quality of life here is rich. That notion of "exclusivity," familiar to those drawn to five-star hotels, is countered here by a profound inclusiveness. You are invited in, embraced by it all, and the sense of community is palpable. Rich volunteers as the village footpath officer, Suki helps edit the village magazine. Strawberries are picked at the neighbor's organic farm and the jam is swapped for the produce. Rich lends the same farm his tractor in exchange for organic bacon and sausage for the breakfasts; barter is alive and well. Artwork of local scenes created by artist friends is displayed on the walls, and can be purchased.

There is even a wooden lodge in the garden for WWOOFers. These are Willing Workers on Organic Farms: a wonderful source of intelligent and motivated workers on one hand, and an unusual and rewarding way, on the other, of finding work all over the world.

The sense of community flows into food buying too. "The balance between organic and local is a continuing subject of conversation in the house," Suki says. "When we are running low on something such as milk or fruit, do we support the local village shop or drive off in a car to buy organic? We are constantly weighing and balancing these issues."

The idea of community, of course, reaches beyond Nether Stowey. Rich is involved in a community-based forestry project in Malawi and other parts of Africa encouraging the development of community-based tree nurseries, and setting up a charity there, InterSilva. The colorful shop set up in the dining room sells jams, marmalades, local honey, pottery and Exmoor soaps alongside socks from Vermont and woven stars and other crafts from Malawi.

There are many commitments to all things slow. Porridge cooked overnight on the Aga with pinhead oats can supplement a traditional English breakfast—or a "Vermont" one of redcurrant pancakes with pure maple syrup. It helps to have an Aga, no doubt, but this is typical of the overall mood. Rich provides the logs for the wood-fired boiler that heats the house and for the fire that is lit for you at breakfast, or in the evening for dinner. This is a place that encourages you to unwind—garden seats, hammocks, a terrace for tea, log fires in winter—and you don't have to check out straight after breakfast as you do in many B&Bs.

For this 17th-century rectory farmhouse, right next to Over Stowey Church, the restoration has been authentic and true. As one guest wrote: "We have felt soothed by the undemanding comfort of your home and by the beauty of the landscape."

The delight in being here comes from many sources—the family, their house, the garden, their values, the sheer beauty of it all—but perhaps most directly from their palpable ease with themselves. A guest coming back covered in mud would never be a problem here. And a long soak before dinner in one of the big old roll-top tubs would be the final treat.

Susan Lilienthal

Parsonage Farm, Over Stowey, Bridgwater, TA5 1HA
- 3 rooms. £55-£65. Extra beds available.
  Singles £35-£50.
- Supper £10. Dinner, 2-3 courses, £20-£25.
- 01278 733237
- suki@parsonfarm.co.uk
- www.parsonfarm.co.uk

Church Cottage

SOMERSET

It is surely the best turned-out Potting Shed in England. At the bottom of Caroline Hanbury Bateman's garden is a bolthole for two, from whose warmly dressed bedroom window a 14th-century church tower is framed.

Have your Aga-cooked breakfast brought to you here—there's a little round table for two—or wander over to the 400-year-old cottage and pull up a chair by the big pine table. Caroline is a fantastic cook and is happy to rustle up anything from kedgeree and Welsh rarebit to Spanish omelette, however the mood takes you. What is not to be missed is her earthy, moist soda bread with its bubbly crust. The dough is deliciously elastic, "a doddle to make."

Caroline discovered Church Cottage six years ago, then decided to start a B&B. It's a brilliant spot, a great stopping off point for the South West, lying in the Somerset Levels where the unforgettable Glastonbury Tor rises out of the morning mist. It's also right on the cycle route from John O' Groats to Land's End—though it would be a shame not to linger here, walking the lanes and wetlands.

A lifetime of adventures began when Caroline and her mother headed for Africa on a troop ship just after the war. Spending her childhood on an isolated farm in Kenya, electricity-

free, life was simple. "My Mother was rather ahead of her time and believed in the power of fresh food. She said the only household items she bought were loo paper and sugar. As we lived forty miles from the nearest township, and the roads to that were impassable in the rains, it was just as well she was practical." In Somerset, Caroline nurtures that ethos. "Our food is local wherever possible, and organic. I make my own bread, grow a lot of vegetables in the garden among the flowers, and always have fresh flowers in the house."

Caroline's past life has turned her into her own "mother of invention". Returning to England her life took yet more turns. She trained as a cook, learned the wine trade, went gardening, raised four boys. "Skills start at home and they're instinctively in you," and the family always sat down together to eat. "Breakfast was a bit rushed, packed lunch was at school, but supper was sharing and chatting time. I feel sorry for families that, for whatever reason, don't—it only takes one hour of the day and possibly less if everyone joins in the preparation."

No processed food was bought, no microwaves used, everything was fresh and cooked daily. "We grew our own vegetables, had hens for eggs,

and made bread. Because I'm a hopeless and disinterested pudding maker, puddings rarely appeared. I did feel slightly chastened when some of the boys' friends came home for supper, and to show willing I'd made a milk jelly. This was the height of excitement for them, but sniffed at by their friends!"

All the boys are good, imaginative cooks now, great believers in the power of fresh and "real" food. One has his own pie business, The Square Pie Company, in London, selling at Spitalfields and Selfridges.

A stint in West Cork heightened Caroline's foodie passion, where the Slow Food movement is in full force. But her version is slightly more "hands on and everyday"—a more English approach. She prides herself on being quite possibly the only woman in England to have never been to a takeaway.

"The idea of going to a restaurant and taking a meal away doesn't appeal to me," she says, "you miss out on the conviviality of eating and the atmosphere. Added to that I do like to know what is going into my food and wonder if you can trust a restaurant that is trying to serve those inside and those wanting to take food away."

Her "slow" style spills over into the quiet country garden, where there's a pleasing mix of flowers and vegetables on show. Climbing French beans stand to attention among the flowerbeds—they work harder than runner beans, as they crop time and again and can withstand a drought. And the first freesias she's ever grown outdoors suggest warmer summers to come.

"Once you've got wild rocket [arugula] in the ground you never need another packet," says Caroline. And here it's left to spread its bounty among the other plants, creating easy ground cover and a brilliant green manure—as well as being exceptionally tasty.

"Most shop-bought cosmetics contain cheap fillers to give bulk and the impression of value"

The cottage, with its polished old flagstones and chunky beams, has a history. Not so very long ago, ten children would have been raised in one part and the rest given over to peat. Now the house is warm, countrified and cozy—a whiff of wood smoke in autumn, floppy roses in June. There is an exotic "out of Africa" touch, with carvings, paintings and a bronze sculpture of a cheetah peering out over his savanna. Bedrooms, two of which have en suite bathrooms, are small and simple—pine furniture, cool colors—while the Potting Shed is a peacefully private nest for two.

The new oak staircase was constructed by a village builder; the odd sloping floor and wonky wall add to the charm; the vintage "Vacant" sign on the downstairs bathroom door gives a quirky touch. In simple restful bathrooms, azure bottles reveal another of Caroline's talents. Forty years ago she started making natural skin potions, more for herself than anyone else; cosmetics were costly. Now "making cream is like making mayonnaise" and something that was driven by necessity has become a cottage industry. From rosewater, beeswax and the oils of lavender, frankincense, witch hazel and rosemary Caroline makes creams and tonics that are fragrant and soothing.

"With shop-bought products, much of what you are paying for is packaging rather than good quality ingredients. I like using my own range for the same reason I like eating my own food—I know what has gone into it. I guess I like to be in control.

"Commercial creams will be made in huge vats which will need chemicals to sterilize them and then stabilizers added to the finished potion to give it a long shelf life. I am pretty sure, too, that most shop-bought cosmetics have cheap fillers in them to give volume and, thus, the impression of value."

Caroline can keep her prices down because she doesn't sell commercially—if she did, all ingredients would need a certification under EU law that has to be renewed each year. This can amount to more than £1,000 per ingredient.

She is delighted that her sons appreciate the principles behind her range. "They are actually quite keen on it all. Modern men are, although men of my age are a bit more iffy about the benefits!"

Caroline has many traditional skills to pass on. Her youngest son tells her she should write it all down—day to day, what she does and how. For now... relish her house and garden, accept her lightly chilled rosé as the sun goes down, wander off to the lichen-dusted bench at the end of the garden, and raise a glass to a simple life in the slow lane.

Caroline Hanbury Bateman

Church Cottage, Station Road, Shapwick, Bridgwater, TA7 9NH
- 2 doubles. £60-£85. Singles £50-£75.
- Packed lunch.
- 01458 210904
- caroline@shapwick.fsnet.co.uk
- www.profileskincare.co.uk/bnb/bnb.html

Harptree Court

SOMERSET

If you haven't heard of the East Harptree Orchestra you will be forgiven—just. It is fondly referred to locally as the EHO, is 150-strong and has just celebrated its 20th anniversary with yet another concert on the lawns of Harptree Court. The audience was most of the village and lots of friends, over 1,000 of them.

David Pitts, a local deputy head teacher-turned-conductor, started it all with three families around the kitchen table. He accepts anyone who can play one bar of music, adults and children alike. There are nineteen flutes, twenty-six clarinets, one French horn, three trombones, thirty violins, four cellos, fifteen recorders and fourteen saxophones. But this is no musical frivolity; one of their number joined a German orchestra, one drummed for the Mary Poppins musical, and one plays the keyboard for the Scissor Sisters. Any profits go to buy instruments to lend out free to young people.

Harptree Court, in the same family for three generations, is at the center of many of the village events and takes its duties seriously. There's the Village Fete—of course—and the Women's Institute, both grateful recipients of the Court's homemade cake and home-grown raspberries. The Chew Valley Monday Club tea happens here, as well as the playgroup's autumn leaf ramble, the National Gardens Scheme openings, church suppers and school balls.

Linda and Charles feel that ownership of such a huge house carries serious responsibilities, but they seem to enjoy these events as much as anybody. One imaginative and unusual project is the sharing of the big walled kitchen garden with a group of villagers who are allowed to use half of the garden for free, thus increasing the amount of organic fruit, flowers and vegetables available locally. The walled garden is also the source of most of the fresh food served to B&B visitors. Jo and Andrea set up a table and sell bunches of sweet williams, sweet peas, red potatoes, asparagus, zucchini, beans and onions. It is a new project, and is growing apace in this walled space that keeps out rabbits and raises the temperature a couple of degrees. The concept of "slow" is entirely familiar here, though perhaps under the more familiar heading of "country life."

Charles's grandfather bought the house in 1920, with money made from shipbuilding in Bristol. All Bristolians knew of the Charles Hill shipyard, just across the water from the cathedral and very much part of the Bristol tradition. Its slow demise was a cause of much sadness—the slow end of Bristol's long and proud history as a working harbor. But shipping did well after the First War and the Hill family lived in style. There were two grass tennis courts where the lily pond now is and grandfather would invite the Australian tennis team to stay in the house and play with him when they were in Britain.

The house was also once a sort of local Hellfire Club, with gambling parties and frighteningly high

stakes. It was not unknown for people to lose their houses but after one or two were seen searching the house for guns with which to shoot themselves after such losses, the gambling stopped. The twenties and thirties brought hard times; Charles's father and the family lived in one room, the Hall, with an open fire and no other heating. Five children and the parents learned to co-exist.

Perhaps the experience reinforced a broader sense of community too. As well as providing green space for most of East Harptree's institutions, the Hills are active in the village—Charles has been a church warden and Linda was a Chairman of the school's PTA. The three children are not far away: Katie is a marine biologist, Emily is doing an engineering degree at Bristol and Matthew will leave school in Wells in 2008.

The house itself is a classic of its kind, a big old Georgian manor house filled with fine furniture. From 1802 to 1875 the Waldegrave family owned it, but Lady Francis Waldegrave, who was fond of partying, sold it as not grand enough for her purposes. It remains unchanged: un-grand, full of bonhomie and generosity, without a trace of pretension.

Much of this atmosphere must come from the fact that three generations live here; Charles's mother is here, still a determined gardener and planter. She came from another Bristol trading family so she brought her own furniture with her, gilding an already handsome lily. You will find old rugs, candles, dark wooden floors made of purple heart wood from Trinidad, bells at the bottom of the stairs to ring when you are in need, flowers from the garden everywhere and a blazing open fire in winter.

As the Hills were shipbuilders they were able to bring those skills to the house; witness the brass screws in the floorboards. Upstairs there is a cozy sitting room for visitors, overlooking the croquet lawn. There are four splendid bedrooms for guests— Rust, Lavender, Blue and Yellow—all with fine, quiet views, heavy old family furniture and paintings. (The umbrella, flashlight and map in each wardrobe are there to encourage you to walk to the village for a drink or dinner in the excellent pub.) The

bathrooms, two en suite, are conventionally modern, and larger than they need be. The one belonging to the Rust Room has the views, so you may be forgiven for lingering long in the bath.

The garden is seventeen-acres huge, with a folly, underground passage, ice house, croquet lawn, waterfall, ha-ha, lake, clapper bridge and an old swimming pool that is now a lily pond filled with

> "One unusual and imaginative project is the sharing of the big walled kitchen garden with a group of villagers"

goldfish, a few carp, dragonflies and damselflies. This is a place for dreaming, for playing croquet and tennis, for taking cream teas under a great tree on the lawn. The garden and woodland teem with wildlife; deer and woodpeckers are frequent visitors, a fox might trot past the window.

This is how a slice of English society lived right up to the First World War and beyond, a gentle life in a not-so-gentle age. For most people there was no choice between fast and slow, though "fast" for the privileged few would have meant hectic partying, gambling, traveling up and down to London.

What you find here now are conviviality and community, local food generously served, the encouragement to "be" rather than to rush, and a nourishing sense of connection with the past. In the words of one Irish visitor: "This is the best place we have ever stayed."

Linda Hill

Harptree Court, East Harptree, Bristol, BS40 6AA
- 3 rooms.
- £90-£100. Singles from £70.
- Dinner £17.50-£25.
- 01761 221729
- location.harptree@tiscali.co.uk
- www.harptreecourt.co.uk

Lower Farm

SOMERSET

Four generations of Charles's family have cared for and worked this land. Some years ago he and Susie fell in love with, and restored, Lower Farm, and they've spun a little magic, conjuring up a gentle yet hard-working way of life in tune with everything around them. Apricots soak up the sun on old farmyard walls, Sweet Heart melons lie heavy in the hand, chickens strut in the orchard, children and pets roam free. There is something of France about Lower Farm, for Charles and Susie did the whole self-sufficiency thing there before being drawn back home with the children. There they had pigs, goats and vines, and totally immersed themselves in the life.

Reminders of their French days are here and there: massive wine barrels that contained their 1997 vintage, and a well-worn sign (fashioned out of old wallpaper using children's marker pens) now displayed in the guests' kitchen, gaily touting "Les Produits Biologiques du Monsieur 'Anglais' Charles Dowding."

Charles is a pioneering organic grower. He has practiced the no-dig method for twenty-five years, started one of the first vegetable box schemes in England and has written two books, *Organic Gardening—the Natural No-Dig Way* and *Salad Leaves all Year Round*. More "gardener" than "farmer" these days, he also

runs courses at home on how to grow vegetables, so you can learn about the advantages of mulching over digging, the influences of the moon, how to choose the right seeds and how to lessen slugs. His daily work revolves around growing award-winning salad leaves—Rouge Grenobloise, Bijou, Chartwell—creating a rich, glossy palette of greenish-purple plants on the compost-rich land, set against a backdrop of spelt wheat (using polytunnels in winter). November's leaves alone include radicchios, sugarloaf chicory, mixed endives, lettuce, lambs lettuce, chard, spinach and parsley.

As dawn breaks, Charles starts plucking his tender leaves and Susie prepares herself for breakfast. She's the artist in this partnership, applying imagination and talent to everything she does. As breakfast approaches, the table in the self-contained guest barn gathers homemade produce: pressed apple juice, thick strawberry jam, bittersweet marmalade, Susie's homemade cereal and Charles's wholesome bread. Their cooked breakfast is not resistible for a moment: eggs running gold from the Black Rock chickens that you can watch from the huge gallery window, thick, sweet, succulent bacon from Bill the local butcher. The day has only just begun.

Public Footpath
Bratton Seymour 1½

As the sun warms the lime-pointed walls and a slight breeze stirs the washing on the line (no tumble dryer, of course), Charles embarks on his "patented" salad-spinning technique—involving a swinging crate and lots of muscle power. This charming man has a fine organic pedigree, and his pioneering vegetable box business grew from just six boxes in 1983 to ninety just seven years later, all traveling no further than five miles from the farm.

> "Charles's daily work revolves around growing award-winning salad leaves—Rouge Grenobloise, Bijou, Chartwell—creating a rich, glossy palette"

Charles's current main output is bags of mixed salad leaves; you'll find them at the Montague Inn down the road and in local shops and restaurants. He sees growing vegetables as a "dying art," but is finally gaining the recognition he deserves, spreading the word as a writer and lecturer for the Royal Horticultural Society. (Even Raymond Blanc has applauded his salad leaves.) He enthuses about the new UK varieties that allow him to grow such good apricots and melons, reminding him of days in France.

Everything they learned in France has been put to good use here. Horse manure and compost from the local recycling center enrich the clay soil. Spent corncobs and vegetables from the garden are fed to the chickens. It's a near-perfect cycle. Charles and Susie also keep alive the Somerset tradition of making cider and apple juice, in their case from fruit collected around the village. The day passes in a quiet, productive way: tending plants, making preserves to stack up in the original cheese room, sorting out the family and greeting and looking after guests. As the day draws to a close, Charles retires to what was once the old dairy to do something that distinguishes him from most of us: making flour by grinding wheat, ready to make another batch of bread.

When they came to this pretty, ramshackle 18th-century farm they determined to restore it with consideration for the environment. They insulated the ceilings with recycled paper and sheep's wool and installed a wood-burning stove. Guests are gently encouraged to recycle; there are a compost bin and a recycling box behind check curtains in the kitchen; and, in the bathrooms, Great Elm Physick Garden's herbal cleanser and Susie's own bath salts, organically made with English herbs and plants.

The Dowdings have converted the first floor of the old stone granary barn into a wonderful space for guests. Bedrooms are blessed with comfortable beds, views reach across the garden to fields, and the oak-floored, high-raftered sitting room, with wood-burner and extra beds, has a large collection of delicate artworks scattered across its limewashed walls. Susie spent a lot of time in the London art world and worked with and sat for John Ward CBE. These are mainly his works, even down to the specially commissioned image on their B&B card and her own cereal label.

Not far from Lower Farm are the gardens, follies and exotic trees of the Stourhead Estate, owned by the National Trust; you could spend a glorious morning strolling around the mansion and lake. Or, more vigorously, join the Leland Trail that runs from Alfred's Tower. Descend through forest, woodland and pastureland (dropping off for lunch and a real ale at the Bull at Hardway) before striding steeply back up to the tower, one of the finest follies in England.

You can return to the big, quiet barn and wish yourself into this life. There are chickens clucking below, swooping swallows, nodding sunflowers, golden fields of wheat and food straight from the field. It is an enviable life, but they have worked harder than we can imagine to create it.

Susie & Charles Dowding

Lower Farm,
Shepton Montague, Wincanton, BA9 8JG
- 2 rooms. Extra beds in sitting room.
- From £90.
- 01749 812253
- enquiries@lowerfarm.org.uk
- www.lowerfarm.org.uk

The Bath Arms

WILTSHIRE

There's something deliciously English and slightly eccentric about The Bath Arms... Lord Bath portrayed as a maharaja in rich traditional costume, local game and smoked meats on the menu, skittles and ale, exotic Peacock and Karma Sutra bedrooms. But then you are within the extensive grounds of the Longleat Estate. This "boutique" hotel is also a million miles away from its urban counterparts—and it's more country pub than hotel.

Christoph Brooke leases this 17th-century coaching house in the sleepy village of Horningsham from Lord Bath. "I'd be delighted if someone came in here and thought it was owned or run by him."

He believes that any good estate hotel should take as much influence as possible from any slight eccentricity of the individuals involved, the family, the history or the house.

Flashman, English Eccentric, Geisha, Oriental... each of the fifteen bedrooms lives up to its name, some in the main house, some in the converted barn. East subtly meets West: heavy inlaid furniture, silk bed throws, generous mounds of cushions, apothecary potions to soothe the senses. The Karma Sutra room is heavily influenced by Lord Bath's own series of murals. In the sixties he and some young art students continued to muralize the walls of his apartments at Longleat. Bathrooms are bedecked with tasteful collages—including "eccentrics" of our times: Noel Coward, 1920s bathing belles and a dog at the wheel in driving goggles.

"When I go away I always want to go somewhere where I don't feel a stranger," says Christoph. His philosophy is clearly at work here. Locals regularly pop in for a pint of fine Horningsham Pride—brewed specially for the hotel by a local microbrewery. Villagers are also free to use the skittle alley for their hotly contested tournaments and children's parties; they show movies, too. When it came to naming the beer there was a local competition. The shortlisted names went to Lord Bath for his casting vote and "Horningsham Pride" it was (beating "Oh Elegant Soul"—a pleasing anagram of "Longleat House"—that the present Marquess's father had inscribed on the back of his Bentley).

Christoph started in the trade as a breakfast waiter at Claridges, before being promoted to running the dessert cart; "it was all very heady." From here he quickly moved on within the Savoy Group, and then ran his own successful London restaurants and juice bars. Now he has several projects on the go, so friendly manager Sara Elston runs the show.

Christoph's passion for local, seasonal food came about through a business he runs with his uncle that looks at rural diversification through farm shops and other ventures. Suppliers to the Bath Arms are local: cheese from Longmans in Wincanton, beef from the Stourhead Estate, eggs from the Egg Company in Trowbridge, pork from the Cranbourne Estate. "We are not xenophobic but we believe in our local suppliers. I prefer to pay my money to businesses within fifty miles," says Christoph. Frank Bailey the chef, too, is local.

Caesar Salad for Two

1 clove garlic
25ml (1fl oz) white wine vinegar
1 egg and 3 yolks
100g (4oz) parmesan, grated
300ml (1/2 pint) vegetable oil and 75ml (3fl oz) olive oil
2 Little Gem lettuces and 2 heads of chicory
1 chicken breast
1 slice of bread for croutons
8 anchovy fillets

• Cover base of roasting tin with oak chippings and one teaspoon of Earl Grey tea leaves. Place on hob until chippings are smoking (but do not flame); place chicken breast on wire rack to smoke for 4 minutes
• Cover with tin foil and place in pre-heated oven (180°C/350°F/Gas 4) for 20 minutes
• Whisk the egg, yolks, garlic and white wine vinegar in blender, then slowly drizzle the oils into the mix, taking care it does not separate
• Add parmesan, seasoning and 80ml (3fl oz) water
• Dress the salad leaves
• Add chicken slices, anchovies, croutons and decorate with parmesan shavings

In the restaurant Lord Bath's "Indian" portrait hangs on the far wall, against shimmering Cole & Son wallpaper and with exotic glass "peacock" lights in full display. In good weather you can eat outside on the impressive stone terrace at the back; for a relaxed lunch or barbecue you can tuck yourself in the shade of the Twelve Apostles—a dozen pollarded limes— at the front. In the evening the restaurant has an especially local menu. "We don't do towers and drizzles and we don't do fusion." There is, instead, an emphasis on traditional preserving methods— smoking, curing, potting and pickling—and on the use of game, fish, rare breed and offal.

It's a happy set-up here, though sometimes wildly busy, the sort of place where everyone turns their hand

to whatever is needed. Sara's father is now in charge of the young but burgeoning vegetable garden at the back. Produce makes its short way to the kitchen and there may be a little vegetable selection for young guests to take home. The plot also houses four rare-breed pigs.

If you wander down the drive down past the hotel, through the little village of Horningsham, the breathtaking parkland of the Longleat Estate—landscaped by Capability Brown—swings into view, with the Elizabethan splendor of the house looming in the distance. And part of the way down is one of the inn's latest retreats—a three-story, self-catering lodge (that holds two plus two kids), with direct views of the house and a great little chill-out room at the top in Christoph's favorite purple. The lodge is nowhere near as entertaining as the inn's rooms but the privacy it gives is appreciated by guests.

There shouldn't be a reason in the world to feel tense, but just in case you do, there's The Hip Bath off the courtyard. Here, beauty treatments and massages can be smoothly arranged, as pure and as organic as can be. If you stay, you also get discounted tickets to Longleat and all its glories so you can get within stroking distance of the lions and have monkeys climb on the roof of your car. (And there's a safari bus for the nervous.)

"I care about the area, the locals, the suppliers, the food chain," says Christoph. "And I support everything I possibly can in the village."

A poster on the bar wall pretty much says it all: "Open Acoustic Session—It will be very informal and disorganized, sitting around the bar making a noise... if you've never played in public before, this could be the place to start. We all started somewhere."

Christoph Brooke

The Bath Arms, Longleat Estate, Horningsham, Warminster, BA12 7LY
- 15 rooms. Lodge for 2-4. £80-£145. Singles £60.
- Lunch & dinner £5-£30.
- 01985 844308
- enquiries@batharms.co.uk
- www.batharms.co.uk

The Old Forge

DORSET

Sailing sedately down Dorset lanes in a 1929 Morris Minor, sunlight dancing on the shiny blue bonnet, a picnic hamper resting on the front seat... the prospect of smoked mackerel pâté, lemon drizzle cake, ginger ale and homemade elderflower cordial moments away. This happy adventure is not lifted from the pages of *The Wind in the Willows*—this is the Kerridges on a grand day out. And the picnic is one they can rustle up for you—accompanied by Tim and the Morris Minor.

Tim Kerridge takes pride in his cars—old, lovingly recycled cars. His father had raced his 1930s Lagonda at Silverstone, and handed down both the car and the passion, so vintage cars are in the blood. Now Tim runs a post-war car restoration business from home.

When he and Lucy discovered The Old Forge twenty years ago they had no jobs, no money and two small children. The site originally housed a wheelwright's workshop and a blacksmith's forge; the history went back 300 years. The moment they stepped into the yard, they fell in love with it.

The place was a ruin. Tim salvaged what he could, from massive elm beams to black-smith's bellows, and brought it all slowly back to life. It came

with an antiques business up and running, which Lucy decided to take on while also setting up a small museum on site. Sharing resources—Tim's engineering skills, Lucy's optimism, their combined love of recycling of old materials—they found a way to make it work. Lucy was a nurse, and had spent a season on Iona immersing herself in the organic way of life. She'd done everything, from catching lobsters to making beds.

Gradually The Old Forge has evolved into a charming B&B. The exteriors are smothered in wisteria and "Rambling Rector," fragrant from April to July. Cozy attic bedrooms, reached by steep stairs, have homemade quilts and country antiques; bathrooms are scattered with seashells; Pears soaps sit on basins in nostalgic fifties style. Warm peaceful corners full of books invite readers and the Smithy has a honeysuckle-entwined pergola where you may sit on hot days. Children love it here; there's even a willow tunnel for them to explore. Walkers love it too, but this is one of those B&Bs where, if you want to, you can stay in all day.

Which would be a shame, for much of the scenery is breathtaking. This area of the English countryside is perfect for cycle rides, the North Dorset Cycleway taking you through the hills and vales of Cranborne Chase, the Blackmore Vale and the Dorset Downs. Then there's Shaftesbury to visit, home of the steep and cobbled hill immortalized by the Hovis ads—and the Georgian market town of Blandford Forum.

Tim and Lucy have raised a delightful family, too—Millie, Lottie, Sophie and Jack. They have never had much money yet no one seems bothered. "The children remember nothing else," says Tim. All the money they make is ploughed straight back into the

"A more recent project has been the restoration of a 1934 gypsy caravan, meticulously painted in Romany style"

enterprise. Hard to believe that before he met Lucy Tim was, in his view, "an utter failure." Harsh words from someone who has so successfully made engineering skills his tools for life.

Each year sees a new project. One year it was the restoration of the old blacksmith's forge into The Smithy: a cozy self-catering house with a galleried bedroom, a wood-burning stove and a sense of history —along with sweeping views of Fontmell Down. A more recent project has been the restoration of a 1934 gypsy caravan. Once a showman's wagon built for itinerant fairground workers and performers, it has been meticulously painted in Romany style and is now planted on the edge of a field full of buttercups and daisies where horses and hens roam (its shower and toilet in a converted outhouse thirty yards away). Clamber out of the small but perfectly formed bed— three foot seven inches wide, surprisingly popular with Americans—brew some tea on the old brass electric kettle, fling open the "stable" door and the world is yours. The views are spectacular.

Their passion for recycling shines through. In the B&B, an iron bedstead, wonderful old typewriters, dolls' houses and a rocking horse; in the yard, old enamel advertising signs and petrol pumps. Cabbage green and ointment pink... the mellow shades washing the walls and furniture are in complete harmony with the place.

It's worth getting Tim going on about recycling; he has an unusual perspective on it. His contribution lies in persuading people not to dispose lightly of their vehicles; after all, disposal requires tremendous heat energy. One solution is not to produce quite so many new cars; another is to make existing ones less environmentally damaging and longer-lived.

As well as the car workshop and Smithy there are two acres of land behind the house, creating a paddock for the horses and a village green, to which guests have their own entrance. Lucy and her daughter Sophie have a passion for long-distance riding and are often on horseback in this rolling Hardy country and out along the Jurassic coast.

From the orchard planted in 1993 come old apple varieties such as Newton Wonder and Peasgood Nonesuch, which Lucy presses into sweet, cloudy juice for the breakfast table. For breakfast, the Marran and Black Rock hens deliver speckled brown eggs with rich golden yolks—it seems that Black Rocks just keep laying.

Trusted local butchers supply rare-breed sausages and bacon, and Lucy makes jams from hedgerow fruits and marmalade when the Sevilles come in. Delicious coffee is served in vast blue china cups. For dinner, the pub is a mile away, and serves good food.

As well as the hens and the horses (two Arabs: Jasmine and Ariel) there are Molly and Willow the labradors, Daisy the westie and Pudding the labradoodle. The restoration is superb—and continues. Life is lived to the full. "It's a great place—it always helps us, and finds a solution," says Tim. "We plan to live and die here."

Tim & Lucy Kerridge

The Old Forge, Fanners Yard,
Compton Abbas, Shaftesbury SP7 0NQ
- 2 rooms & 1 double in gypsy caravan. From £70.
- Vintage picnics available.
- 01747 811881
- theoldforge@hotmail.com
- www.theoldforgedorset.co.uk

Frampton House

DORSET

The Romans built a fort in the valley and the Benedictines built a monastery there in the 11th century—Frampton Priory. It is beautiful, rich English countryside of the most irresistible kind, with deep valleys, ancient woodland, heathland and chalk downland and beech trees. The tourist brochures call it Hardy country, and it is: he was born nearby. As a child he would have seen deer, and glow worms (you can still see glow worms at his house). Of the deer coming to the windows in winter he wrote:

From the sheet of glistening white
One without looks in tonight
As we sit and think
By the fender brink.

This is the countryside of Toller Fratrum, Long Bredy and Little Bredy, Sydling St Nicholas and Up Sydling, not to mention Cerne Abbas and its ruder neighbor, Up Cerne or, even more seductively, Piddletrenthide. Why Dorset has produced such a rich crop of fanciful names— many belonging to little streams —is a mystery, but they all tell a story as names should. Only a few miles to the south is the extraordinary Chesil Beach, a long shingly ribbon that unrolls between Portland and Lyme Regis, longer and more surprising than you can possibly expect of

a country that usually deals in small marvels.

Frampton House is all that is left of a once vast 18th-century house of fifty to sixty bedrooms. It belonged to the Sheridan family (of "School for Scandal" fame) during its last splendid days but the family train hit the buffers with the Great Crash of 1931 and the house was largely demolished in 1932. Many others were too, and another great slice of English architectural history was destroyed after the war when the owning families simply couldn't afford them. Even so, what remains of Frampton is impressive: the laundry, stable block, kitchen gardens and outbuildings. There are some fine old mahogany doors and the original stone fireplace in the drawing room, and ten of the original 10,000 acres. The great house was a classic of its kind: a Capability Brown park and a Palladian style stone bridge by Sir Christopher Wren. What a loss! England was once rich in these houses, rivaling even the châteaux of France.

The choices that brought Nick and Georgie here were serious ones. Nick comes from a Somerset family and ran the family food manufacturing business, the sixth generation to do so. His great, great grand-father generously provided the food for a free lunch for the population of Yeovil

celebrating Queen Victoria's Golden Jubilee—160 people carving joints in two vast tents. Nick's was a secure life but not without its problems. He used to drive about 40,000 miles a year—a transport odyssey not untypical of our times. But he gave it all up and now works from home, delightedly helping with the B&B, running a local business, enjoying the animals—Potter and Dumble the black labradors, Dudley the Tibetan terrier, Poppy the ex-hunter.

Georgie's family is from Leicestershire, where one ancestor was bodyguard to Elizabeth I—a sort of Tudor Bouncer Royal. Frampton is full of family portraits, lending extra credibility to this classically country house. But Georgie moved off the beaten track into drama college and eventually to Brussels where she acted and modeled and had an antiques business. Back in England, she took to writing about antiques too. Upon marrying Nick her family joined his (making two sons, a daughter and stepchildren) and once they left home she decided, bravely, to take a Fine Art degree. She now paints portraits, of people and animals.

They both enjoy running a B&B, and it shows. Says Georgie: "It's a bit like being a duck—on the surface it's all going swimmingly but under the surface you are having to paddle like crazy. Always the experience must be special for guests.

"We organize personalized weekends for groups of friends, too—we can take them on a wine-tasting tour or to gardens not normally open to the public."

It is a house for all seasons: summer on the terrace with a glass of pink wine; autumn shoots and winter breaks with hot baths and English tea, roaring fires and fine food. Not everyone loves cooking but Nick and Georgie revel in it, offering a choice of starters and then a single *plat du jour*, and whatever vegetables are in season—a great idea, so you can really focus on getting one dish right. (A few restaurants are known to do this, including the much-loved Riverford Kitchen in Devon.) The coast is nearby so the fish is fresh. The olive oil and the wines are from Provence while most of the other ingredients are sourced locally.

Dorset food is renowned for its quality and diversity; nature dealt the county a winning hand and it is too tightly rumpled to be farmed industrially.

In fact, the travel writer H. V. Morton wrote a charming passage about Dorset food. While wandering in Christchurch Priory he was met by a "maiden" who asked him if he wanted a lobster. Bemused, he found himself saying yes. Out it came, and was followed by an invitation to have tea. By the time he finished he had stuffed himself with both lobster and Dorsetshire cream tea. "Lobster and cream tea are not for pilgrims," he wrote. "I believe that the Crusades could have been stopped by a Dorsetshire cream tea."

Dorset is one of the few English counties to be free of motorway intrusion; perhaps it lends itself to slow living. It has been marginal to English history, even its ports giving way to the larger ones elsewhere as ships became bigger. Lyme, Poole and Weymouth traded well with Newfoundland for a while, but that didn't last for long. The crafts and industries that have flourished here have been slow ones; rope, twine and netting were big in Bridport until recently. Marble from Purbeck graces buildings all over England and the white stone of Portland is a building block of the nation. There is an unhurried feel to Dorset. Long may it be so.

How, one wonders, did a couple like Nick and Georgie, both from very conventional backgrounds, get into B&B? Georgie was idly reading a copy of *Country Living* magazine while having her hair done and spotted a competition demanding a written passage extolling the virtues of the B&B life. She secretly entered, and won. The die was cast and they now actually had to do it. The magazine's clandestine inspectors gave them a top rating and they resolved to continue, to the benefit of us all.

Georgina & Nicholas Maynard

Frampton House,
Frampton, Dorchester, DT2 9NH

- 3 rooms. £85.
- Dinner £22.50.
- 01300 320308
- maynardryder@btconnect.com
- www.frampton-house.co.uk

Marren

DORSET

Take the adventurous track to the edge of the cliff and join Peter, Wendy and Mambo (the black Labrador) for the best antidote to stress within three hours of London.

Peter says "it's balm to the soul, living here." They are an ideally complementary couple of designers, generous and easy, and they delight in sharing their haven, a lovingly decorated thirties house in six acres of garden and woodland, all set about with National Trust land. Wherever you stand you hear the sea. Wherever you look you see beauty.

Peter, a master of slow living and a natural contemplative, declares that he spends his whole life "drawing, mowing, gazing out to sea and going down to the beach." He forgets to mention the bread he bakes, the breakfasts he takes such care over, his artistic gifts and his fossil-hunting eye. (Founded on 400 million years of geology, this is fossil country and the house is a showcase for some remarkable specimens.) Peter also does what he calls "innovation," meaning he is an inventor, which roundly calls on all the skills he acquired during his previous careers in the army, advertising and manufacturing (yacht masts were his mainstay). He looks and he sees.

Wendy, a gentle dynamo whose loves are plants and people, designs gardens. "What I really like are vicarage-type gardens: wild and formal side by side." Judging by her own, she has a sure sense of the right and fitting: it's wonderful. And she's a qualified tree surgeon. You may spot her one day in full surgeon's regalia, looking half her age half way up a tree, "crown raising" to create more views of the sea. They have a chipper and make their own mulch: not a whiff of a chemical rises from these borders.

Both love learning new arts, new skills. Wendy was a professional cook for twenty years—directors' lunches, factory openings—before converting to garden design. Then she felt tree surgery would be a good ticket to add to her diploma in landscape artistry, so she sallied forth and got it. And she is ever eager to learn more about plants. Meanwhile Peter, who still considers himself an artist manqué despite ample proof to the contrary (his Janus-in-a-tree-trunk outside, his exquisite little bronzes inside), is starting a degree in graphic design, an idea gleaned from a recent guest.

In 1999 they left their old house in Hampshire, regretting only the friendships they had forged there. Peter remembered Dorset and its beauty from a childhood holiday, the Marren offer fell onto their doormat after months of fruitless searching, the site seduced them instantly and Wendy knew as soon as she set foot in the little wooden church on the cliff that she was the person they needed to do the flowers. So they set to work.

Marren was in need of major works, the house hadn't been touched for forty years and the little wood was a jungle of bramble and nettles. They cleared and felled and dug the land. Now a carpet of

happy bluebells can be seen in May, Wendy cooks cauldrons of bramble jelly and damson jam for the breakfast table, the giant Greek oil jars on the terrace provide a Mediterranean-like focus between inner eye and sweeping horizon, winding pathways reveal secret retreats, and 150 prettily pebbled steps take you up and down the terraces. Another sixty-four—the "stairway to heaven"—lead from the wood to the top of the garden and a breathtaking view.

When at Easter a cross is planted out on the cliff edge by the little church it feels like a place "where Heaven meets Earth."

Considering the house to be a blank canvas and too small, they moved walls, added a kitchen, placed their fine family furniture just so—neither too classic nor too unexpected—and filled the drawing room with Grandmother's mementos and their own modern pieces. It now breathes understated luxury and sea light: the interiors sing with good taste, antique pine floors are softened with kilims, colors and fabrics are quietly contemporary.

Step from that glorious garden into your airy room (one has its own entrance), deep-mattressed bed and luxurious bathroom. Early in the morning

"Now the bluebells can be seen in May, and Wendy cooks cauldrons of bramble jelly and damson jam for the breakfast table"

the sweet smell of baking wholemeal bread drifts through as you wake. And Peter will soon be at the Aga, squeezing oranges, delicately chopping fruit into a salad, turning his local eggs and high-class sausages—perhaps, even, a morning harvest of wild mushrooms—into the most scrumptious breakfast. He skimps on nothing; together, they take B&B into another league.

The house is right on the coastal path with uninterrupted views of the sea over to the Isle of Portland that juts four and a half miles into the Channel. Portland is also renowned for "attitude:" deep superstition holds that pronouncing the name of

the long-eared furry animal that digs burrows will bring the workings down on the workers. Hardy called it the Isle of Slingers because the inhabitants used to throw stones at unwelcome strangers. Today you will find a welcoming little café overlooking the Channel.

Those who need to work off some early-morning energy will love the scramble down the steep 300-foot slope to the beach, the dip in the bay, and the walk back up. Sometimes the water is crystal clear and you can see shoals of bass. This is the Jurassic Coast, a UNESCO World Heritage Site that stretches ninety-five miles from Exmouth to Swanage. Visit it by bus or by boat, or walk the four miles to Lulworth Cove, one of the purest examples of cove formations ever, and its associated Lulworth crumple where the rock looks as if a giant has washed it and forgotten to iron out the creases. Nearby is the endlessly photographed Durdle Door. Then catch the ferry back to the cove below Marren, have a swim and stroll home for tea.

Wildlife is happy here too. The owls will hoot you to sleep, one knowledgeable guest spotted twenty-seven bird species, another played with the badgers and fawns. But however slow and remote it may be, Marren will be overtaken by Olympic fever for a few glorious days in 2012. Weymouth and Portland have been appointed the official venue for the Olympic sailing events and the Cartwrights' house and garden will have a birds'-eye view of some very exciting racing.

Come and bask in the gentle welcome and take the time to get to know your hosts. They say that guests can "arrive looking quite grey, and leave revived"—literally "resuscitated."

Peter Cartwright

Marren
Holworth, Dorchester, DT2 8NJ

- 2 doubles. £85.
- 01305 851503
- marren@lineone.net
- www.marren.info

[LONDON, SURREY, SUSSEX & KENT]

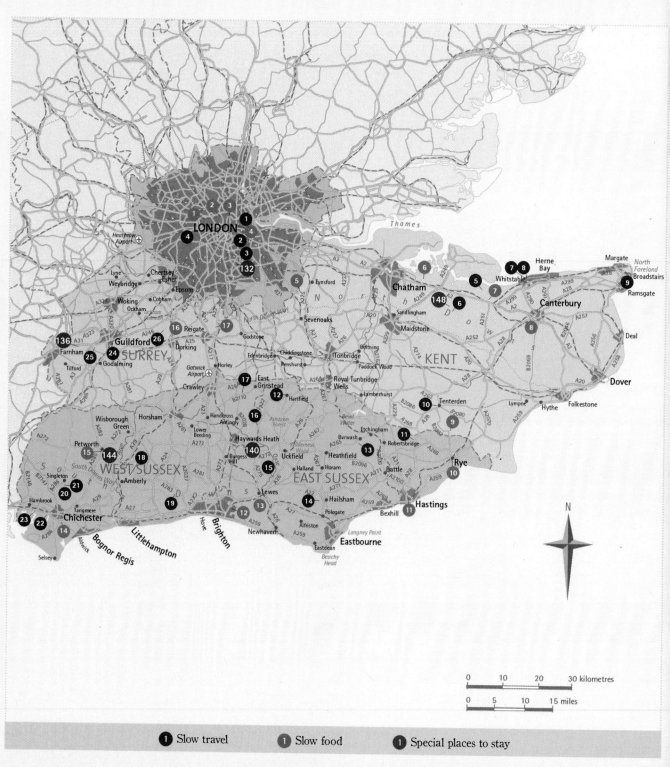

Slow travel · Slow food · Special places to stay

LONDON, SURREY, SUSSEX & KENT

Slow travel

1. Dennis Severs' House
2. Dulwich Picture Gallery
3. Horniman Museum
4. Chelsea Physic Garden
5. Saxon Shore Way
6. Doddington Place Gardens
7. Whitstable
8. Thames Barges
9. Broadstairs
10. Kent & East Sussex Railway
11. Great Dixter
12. Ashdown Forest
13. Bateman's
14. Michelham Priory
15. Boating on the Ouse
16. Bluebell Railway
17. Bushcraft
18. Parham House & Gardens
19. St Mary's House & Gardens
20. West Dean Gardens
21. Weald & Downland Open Air Museum
22. Fishbourne Roman Palace
23. Bosham Church
24. Guildford Lido
25. Loseley Park
26. Polesden Lacy

Slow food

1. Mr Christian's Delicatessen
2. Kennards Good Foods
3. St John's Bar & Restaurant
4. Borough Market
5. The Hop Shop
6. The Barn Yard
7. Shepherd Neame
8. The Goods Shed
9. Chapel Down Vineyards
10. Rye Farmers' Market
11. Maggie's Café
12. The Tea Cosy
13. Breaky Bottom Vineyard
14. Montezuma
15. Cates Deli
16. Denbies Wines
17. Fanny's Farm Shop

Special places to stay

Slow travel

5 Saxon Shore Way
On the long-distance footpath leading to the white cliffs of Dover is a flat, wildlife-rich stretch (four nature reserves): Conver Creek, Harty Ferry, the village of Oare, Faversham.
www.faversham.org

10 Kent & East Sussex Railway
The line wends its way from Tenterden—"the jewel of the Weald"—for ten miles via Northiam to Bodiam. Great views from Bodiam to the battlements of the National Trust-owned castle.
www.kesr.org.uk

1 Dennis Severs' House
(020 7207 4013)
In spruced-up Spitalfields in London's East End, an 18th-century house as it would have been at the time of the Huguenot weavers. Hushed, atmospheric and (once a week) candlelit.
www.dennissevershouse.co.uk

6 Doddington Place Gardens
Sittingbourne (01795 886101)
Open Easter to end of June for spectacular azaleas and rhododendrons—plus Edwardian rock garden, herbaceous borders, fine trees, clipped yews.
Lunches and teas.
www.doddingtonplacegardens.co.uk

11 Great Dixter
Northiam (01797 252878)
Flagstones, wicket gates, long grasses spangled with flowers and sub-tropical exotics in the gardens of the late, great Christopher Lloyd.
www.greatdixter.co.uk

2 Dulwich Picture Gallery
(020 8693 5254)
In lovely, leafy Dulwich, the first purpose-built art gallery in the country. Canalettos, Rembrandts, Watteaus, Gainsboroughs—a gem.
www.dulwichpicturegallery.org.uk

7 Whitstable
The amusements arcades have given way to fish restaurants, galleries and windsurfers but the fish market remains—along with the seafront cottages, pebbles crunching underfoot, beach huts, cockle stalls and superb oysters.

12 Ashdown Forest
Once a royal hunting ground, later home to Pooh Bear's Hundred Acre Wood. Two lengthy circular walks start at Hartfield (two pubs), culminating in a crossing of the Pooh Sticks Bridge.
www.walkingworld.com

3 Horniman Museum
Forest Hill (020 8699 1872)
The wonderfully eccentric collection of a rich London tea merchant: where else would you find a 1937 jazz drum kit and an old stuffed walrus? Hilltop park boasts rabbits, goats and great views. Entry is free.
www.horniman.ac.uk

8 Thames Barges
Whitstable (01795 534541)
Set sail on the beautiful 1892 barge *Greta* for a close-up view of the eerie WWII forts off the Kentish Flats.
www.thamesbarges.co.uk

4 Chelsea Physic Garden
(020 7352 5646)
Near the Chelsea Embankment, a walled, secret and serene botanists' garden. The first greenhouse was built here in 1681.
www.chelseaphysicgarden.co.uk

9 Broadstairs
Seven golden beaches on a bay, a tidal paddling pool for little ones, a boathouse for the harbormaster, the oldest working lighthouse in England and Morelli's for scrumptious ice cream. John Buchan's novel *The 39 Steps* was set here.

13 Bateman's
Burwash (01435 882302)
Beautiful Jacobean home of Rudyard Kipling. Oriental rugs, Jungle Book etchings, 1928 Rolls Royce and book-lined study with pens, typewriter and pipe. Gardens run down to river and mill.
www.nationaltrust.org.uk

14 Michelham Priory
Upper Dicker (01323 844224)
On its own moated island, an Augustinian priory that evolved into a country house. Furnished Tudor rooms, a working watermill, an Elizabethan great barn, tea rooms, tranquil gardens and play area.
www.sussexpast.co.uk

15 Boating on the Ouse
Barcombe (01273 400414)
The Anchor Inn has boating rights over a gorgeous stretch of the river, down to the weir at Sutton Hall. Set aside two hours for a paddle upstream and back—plus hamper.
www.anchorinnandboating.co.uk

16 Bluebell Railway
Sheffield Park to Horsted Keynes (01825 720825)
Eighteen miles of all-steam standard gauge track, gleamingly preserved stations and several circular walks.
www.bluebellrailway.co.uk
www.walkscene.co.uk

17 Bushcraft
Turners Hill (01444 482619)
Hone your survival skills, from friction firelighting and making shelters to snaring and cooking game. "Serious but fun" courses for adults and families last one to four days.
www.wildwoodbushcraft.com

18 Parham House & Gardens
Storrington (01903 742021)
Enchanting Elizabethan house with walled gardens to match: orchard, flower borders, greenhouses, 1920s Wendy house.
www.parhaminsussex.co.uk

19 St Mary's House & Gardens
Bramber (01903 816205)
Charming 15th-century timber-frame house with a panelled, furnished interior. Ivy-clad Monk's Walk and topiary snail in the gardens, romantic ruins in the lovely village.
www.stmarybramber.co.uk

20 West Dean Gardens
West Dean (01243 811301)
Tranquillity in the rolling South Downs: walled kitchen gardens, Victorian glasshouses, Edwardian pergola, rustic summerhouses, arboretum walks, restaurant, shop and chili fiesta in August.
www.westdean.org.uk

21 Weald & Downland Open Air Museum
Singleton (01243 811475)
In a serene setting, fifty historic buildings rebuilt to their original form, many furnished, some with period gardens. Hens, sheep, shire horses, working flour mill and Tudor kitchen, where you can tuck into tasty spinach and oat pottage!
www.wealddown.co.uk

22 Fishbourne Roman Palace
Fishbourne (01243 785859)
What began as a military base

became a sumptuous palace... The remains of one wing of the largest domestic Roman building in Britain are now under cover. Handle artifacts on behind-the-scenes tours.
www.visitsussex.org

23 Bosham Church
Beautiful Saxon church, a saunter from the boats and the quay. Creek and village are loved by both yachties and artists, the church is depicted in the Bayeux Tapestry and the front road floods at high tide. Enjoy estuary views from the terrace of the Anchor Bleu.

24 Guildford Lido
(01483 444888)
Next to Guildford College in the heart of town, an Olympic-size pool in gardens that have kept their 1930s charm. Picnic lawns, paddling pools, café and crazy golf. Open April to mid-Sept.

25 Loseley Park
Guildford (01483 304440)
Moat, ancient wisteria, vine walk, wildflower meadow and walled garden based on Gertrude Jekyll's "rooms." Tea room serves Loseley ice cream and cakes. Tours of the Tudor house, too.
www.loseley-park.com

26 Polesden Lacy
Great Bookham (01372 452048)
Gracious home of the legendary Edwardian hostess the Hon Mrs Greville, in landscaped gardens with sweeping downland views. Lunches and teas in the stable block.
www.nationaltrust.org.uk

Slow food

1 Mr Christian's Delicatessen
11 Elgin Crescent (020 7229 0501)
In yummy Notting Hill: the
cinnamon croissants outside hint
at the scrumptiousness within.
www.mrchristians.co.uk

2 Kennards Good Foods
57 Lambs Conduit St (020 7404 4030)
A gorgeous deli on a car-free street
in literary Bloomsbury, with tiny
café attached.
www.kennardsgoodfoods.com

3 St John's Bar & Restaurant
26 St John St (020 7251 4090)
Near Smithfield's fine old meat
market, a place of pilgrimage for
lovers of gutsy British food.
Utilitarian-chic in burgeoning
Clerkenwell. Not for vegetarians.
www.stjohnrestaurant.co.uk

4 Borough Market
Foodie haven in Southwark (southeast of Tate Modern) where celebrity
foodies mix with city bankers and
trendy East Enders. Open Thurs-Sat.
www.boroughmarket.org.uk

5 The Hop Shop
Shoreham (01959 523219)
Pick your own apples, treat yourself
to lovely Chelsea Gold-winning hop
bines and dried lavender, essential
oils and traceable farm foods. Special.
www.hopshop.co.uk

6 The Barn Yard
Upchurch (01634 235059)
On Gore Farm, gooseberries,
blackberries, plums for the picking.
Plus farm shops and café, woodland
trails, ducks to feed and maize maze.
www.the-barnyard.co.uk

7 Shepherd Neame
Faversham (01795 542016)
Britain's oldest brewer. Gaze into
the mash tuns, learn how Spitfire
and Bishop's Finger are made.
Tutored tastings.
www.shepherdneame.co.uk

8 The Goods Shed
Canterbury (01227 459153)
In a lovely old railway building,
wild pheasants, organic sausages,
artisan cheeses. Tuck into a market-
produce lunch in the bustling
gallery restaurant.

9 Chapel Down Vineyards
Small Hythe (01580 766111)
The Chapel Down English rosé
outsold all other rosés at Selfridges
last year. Tastings and tours, shop,
wine bar and bistro.
www.chapeldownwines.co.uk

10 Rye Farmers' Market
Strand Quay
A step away from some of the most
beautiful town streets (Mermaid St,
Watchbell St, Church Sq) in the
country. Wednesday mornings.
www.ryemarket.org.uk

11 Maggie's Café
Hastings (01424 430205)
Opposite the beach, above the fish
market and world-class smokery,
crab sandwiches and brilliant fish
and chips. The café keeps fisherman-
friendly opening hours—from 5am
to 3pm.

12 The Tea Cosy
107 Southover St, Brighton.
A high-camp décor, crumpets to
Duchies Cream Teas, and house-rules
that wisely ban 1980s leggings.
www.theteacosy.co.uk

13 Breaky Bottom Vineyard
Rodmell (01273 476427)
The 2003 Cuvée Alex Mercier is the
sparkling wine of choice at the
British Embassy in Paris. "Sussex is
the new Champagne."
www.breakybottom.co.uk

14 Montezuma
Chichester (01243 537385)
From the finest organically grown
beans flow white buttons, milk
turtles and truffles. Fabulous.
www.montezumas.co.uk

15 Cates Deli
Petworth (01798 343634)
Olives and quiches, organic
chocolates and *batteries de cuisine*
in market town known for its
antiques and girly boutiques.
www.catesdelicatessan.com

16 Denbies Wines
Dorking (01306 876616)
Largest vineyard in England with
two restaurants and winery tours.
October grape picking includes
vineyard-workers' lunch.
www.denbiesvineyard.co.uk

17 Fanny's Farm Shop
Merstham (01737 554444)
Eccentric, with picnic tables in the
garden and teas in the treehouse.
www.fannysfarm.com

Pubs & inns

Greenwich Union

56 Royal Hill, Greenwich, London
The interior hues reflect the glorious ales that Alastair Hook creates at his brewery; his Red, White, Amber and Chocolate beers slip down easily. Food from French chef too. 020 8692 6258 www.meantimebrewing.com

The King William IV

Byttom Hill, Dorking, Surrey
Take an OS map to locate this rural treat tucked down single-track lanes. Super-snug interior, Brakspear ales, homemade pies, grassy front garden with views—super after a hike. 01372 372590 www.king-williamiv.com

The Parrot

Forest Green, Dorking, Surrey
The Gottos are passionate about food and the pub showcases meats reared on their farm on the short, imaginative menu. Beams, settles, log fires—and an imaginative farm shop inside. 01306 621339 www.theparrot.co.uk

The Fountain Inn

Ashunt, Steyning, Sussex
Be transported back centuries. In the flagstoned and candlelit bar, awash with aromatic woodsmoke, is wholesome food along with a great selection of wines and four real ales. A firm favorite among locals. 01403 710219

Royal Oak

Wineham, Henfield, Sussex
A rural survivor, the pub almost lost down a country road is six centuries old and has been refreshing locals for the last two. Low beams, picnic tables on the grass, sandwiches and soups. 01444 881252

Anglesey Arms at Halnaker

Halnaker, Chichester, Sussex
Laid back, refreshingly free of airs and graces, a cracking good local run by people committed to keeping its charm. Moules and boules in the garden in summer. Perfect. 01243 773474 www.angleseyarms.co.uk

The Sportsman

Seasalter, Whitstable, Kent
Slip off to Seasalter for a meal you won't forget, a gastronomic haven amid marshland. Light-filled rooms, chunky wooden tables, a log fire and fabulous fresh fish. 01227 273370 www.thesportsmanseasalter.co.uk

Shipwright's Arms

Hollowshore, Faversham, Kent
Surrounded by salt marshes, the below-sea-level building and boatyard are protected by a dyke from the tidal creek above. Three tiny bars are warmed by open fires; food sustains sailors. 01795 590088

George & Dragon

Speldhurst Hill, Tonbridge, Kent
"We try to buy from people not companies," says Julian Leefe-Griffiths. Beams and flagstones, a lovely, easy atmosphere and chef Max Leonard's gutsy food is the biggest treat. 01892 863125 www.speldhurst.com

24 Fox Hill

LONDON

"We live in a sort of human advent calendar—we never know who will be coming through the door. It's wonderful. Of everyone who comes I think, "there is going to be something delicious about you, and I am going to find it."

That heart-warming expression of warmth speaks volumes about staying here and reflects the biblical sentiment: "Be not forgetful to entertain strangers: for thereby some have entertained angels unawares." The house throbs with family atmosphere and vitality—here live Shreddie the dog and Hudson the cat—and it has a countrified feel, too, rare in the city.

Sue's deep-rooted conviviality was nurtured by a nomadic childhood with a Navy father who met her Canadian mother during the war. She was hauled from one country to another, attending thirteen schools and meeting people from every corner of the world.

"I absolutely love doing B&B. I like a rich diet of people. Given a little time here, most people fold into the life of the family."

Tim was also brought up in many different countries. His father was a military scientist, part of the team that invented radar. Tim has inherited his energy and after a career in IT is now Chairman of the Depaul Trust that rescues children from the streets in fifty-two projects all over the

UK. He travels a lot and makes the breakfasts when at home.

Fox Hill is a leafy oasis in South London, a red-brick 1880s semi-detached house, its big rooms stuffed with treasures from around the world and Sue's art. "We both love technology, but my creative side is slow." Sue started quilting quite late in life, once the children had flown. The quilts are beautiful, influenced by her stay in America but mainly the product of time spent at Chelsea Art College. She quilts by hand and by machine, doing commissions and presents for friends. All the beds have classic quilts on them and the bedrooms are stunning; more designs hang on the walls. "When I am making a quilt it can take me up to three years. I tell Tim that my quilt could last for over 200 years while his computer may last for only five!"

The stairway is perfect for hanging textiles as there is little light to fade them. Sue hangs some of her best works there, including an exquisite hand-sewn silk work from her end-of-degree show. She is interested in colors, the patterns in plants, felt (which she also makes), dyes and batik. You can see it all here, some with a Latin American influence, others African or Indian (her father was born in India). It gives the house a rare vitality.

Damson Fool

• Stew 450g (1lb) damsons with 4+ tablespoons water till soft and pulpy
• Sieve to get purée and sweeten to taste
• Whip 284ml (1/2 pint) double cream till softly peaking, fold in gently and chill

Almond Biscuits

100g (4oz) butter
100g (4oz) sugar
1 egg yolk
1/2 teaspoon almond essence
150g (6oz) plain flour
1 teaspoon baking powder
pinch salt
slivered almonds

• Mix all the ingredients and roll into walnut-sized balls
• Place on a greased baking tray and press an almond sliver onto each one, flattening the ball at the same time
• Bake in a pre-heated oven at 180°C (350°F/Gas 4) for 20-25 minutes, until golden brown

There is a garden too, bigger and more peaceful than most city gardens, with a shady, jasmine-scented terrace and a raised pond with lilies and goldfish and gurgling water. It is long and lovely, lush with tree ferns and exotic acers and arums. An attempt to raise chickens came to grief in the mouth of a fox; no surprise for the area teems with them. There is, suitably, a fox-shaped brass doorknocker on the front door. Foxes have their own way of dividing modern urban communities; some people feed them, chicken fanciers hate them, others—like Sue—have a sneaking admiration for them.

Sue leads the family in its search for a slower life. The things she loves doing take time: cooking, gardening, painting, textiles—and foraging for wood for the sitting room's fabulous Swedish stove. With quilts that take up to three years to make, and garden plants that take time to grow ("as I say to my American friends, it is not very American: it doesn't come up tomorrow") there is little point in hurrying. She makes her own bread and jams and is getting to grips with composting and recycling in an area whose council is not very supportive. She happily admits that there is much more they could do but they are well on the way and need no convincing that a slow life is a healthier and happier one.

Pissarro painted this street in 1870 and the painting, one of a dozen surviving from this period, hangs in the National Portrait Gallery: *Fox Hill at Norwood*. From one of the windows one used to be able to see the tree he painted; sadly it came down in 2007. Both he and Emile Zola took refuge here from France during the war with Prussia; Pissarro returned in 1871 to discover that only forty of the 1,500 canvasses that he had stored there remained.

Crystal Palace Park is only seven minutes' walk away, home to a Grade I-listed monument and national treasure: the dinosaurs. These sculptures were commissioned in 1852 for the opening of the Park, a Victorian theme park of 200 acres, which received the reconstructed Crystal Palace. It burned down, tragically, in 1936, but the dinosaurs lived on. They caused a national sensation when unveiled; now two million visitors came to see them every year. The park hums with activity—athletics, concerts, conferences—and all the excitement of the impending Olympics. Plans are also afoot to turn the park into one of the most spectacular green spaces in Europe.

A poster from the Twenties hangs in the front bathroom and reads: "Upper Norwood and Crystal Palace—Exceptionally healthy because of prevailing wind from the coast—eighty feet above Thames therefore out of valley fogs." Fox Hill is an unusual and inspiring place to stay when visiting the capital: the views from the top of the road are huge, reaching, on a fine day, to the Home Counties. Central London is twenty minutes away by train, yet frogs sing and owls hoot at night, and woodpeckers wake you in the morning. The wildlife is surprising. The area is rich in restaurants and museums: the country's oldest public gallery, the Dulwich Picture Gallery, is close, as is the Horniman Museum. Sue or Tim will take you to Crystal Palace station from where you can catch frequent trains to Victoria, while the No 3 bus to Oxford Circus is a sightseeing trip in its own right.

"What a place to plunder!" said Marshall Blucher, the Prussian General at Waterloo, as he gazed upon London. He hadn't even been to Fox Hill.

Sue & Tim Haigh
24 Fox Hill, Crystal Palace, SE19 2XE
- 3 rooms.
- £85–£100. Singles £50.
- Dinner £30–£35.
- 020 8768 0059
- suehaigh@hotmail.co.uk
- www.foxhill-bandb.co.uk

Shoelands House

SURREY

Behind the beautiful brickwork façade there is an engagingly haphazard interior—loved, lived-in, practical, and strikingly un-suburban for Surrey. Those who stay here experience a family home with a palpable sense of history and without a burdensome awareness of the latest style: family photos and ecclesiastical portraits, tapestry rugs and embroidered sofas. Nothing matches—but why would you care when there are carved wooden panels, creaking stairs (pure Jacobean), oak doors, great wooden beams and those wonderful old-fashioned radiators against which you can lean nostalgically? Even the bathrooms are old-fashioned, with wallpaper—almost unheard of in these stylized times.

Shoelands is a strange name. But it goes back to the 1200s and is derived from Solands, Shuland, Shewland and Shooland. The earliest record of the name was a moated manor house at 'Solands' close to the present house. The house was rebuilt in 1616, the date carved over the main door; later rebuilding by the Victorians replaced what was destroyed by fire. It is now part of the Hampton Estate, owned by four sisters of whom Sarah is one.

This is an Area of Outstanding Natural Beauty and the estate farms along traditional lines. Hampton Lodge, lived in by another sister, is at its center—the Lodge is a registered Georgian house set in rolling parkland designed by Repton. Shoelands House itself is in a beautiful valley bordering the southern slope of the Hog's Back and some of the old Pilgrims' Way from Winchester to Canterbury.

All this in Surrey—one of the most densely inhabited areas of England.

It is a tribute to the UK's planning laws that so much of this county is still wooded and peaceful, with great swathes of common land and sandy heath. Even the towns and villages have managed to hang on to much of their old-world charm, if they are not too close to London.

Guildford has a handsome high street, a castle keep and a modern cathedral, and marries past and present with good sense. Farnham is one of Surrey's least spoiled towns and the proud possessor of a castle. It has been through the usual historical mill: Kings and Queens, from Edward I to Victoria, have slept in it, Cromwell besieged it and right now it is a training center. Farnham is lovely in parts, with gabled 17th-century almshouses and some fine Georgian and Tudor houses.

Londoners who love old places can hardly believe their luck when they discover an unpretentious house overlooking a small lake, in a beautiful estate within a quick rail journey. Once inside, they are charmed by the Great Hall's church-like paneling, the sitting room's carved stone fireplace and wooden mantle, and the very lovely wide, low, dark-oak door that leads to the stairs and the bedrooms, one of which (the twin) has an en suite bathroom. The bedrooms are huge, with old prints on wallpapered walls—unashamedly old-fashioned. Breakfast may be taken in that grand hall, at a long table with leather-backed chairs. If you want to sit and read you can use the sitting room with its inglenook fire, books, comfortable sofas and family photos.

Sarah and Clive get most of their vegetables from the impressive walled garden behind Hampton Lodge, a short drive away, where Sarah's sister Bridget and her family live and manage the farm. The young German gardener, Cornelia, came from the RHS

"Many visitors come to see the gardens of Surrey, and there is a rich supply of them"

garden at Wisley seven years ago and does the garden proud: rows of nodding sunflowers, dahlias and all manner of chemical-free fruit and vegetable.

The garden of Shoelands is wild and rambling. There is a painting from 1793 that reveals how the original front gardens once looked and the four flowerbeds around a small terracotta urn are a recreation of this. The beds to the side of the front path have been planted with David Austin roses and lavender, the back garden is divided by a mellow brick wall against which a contoured bed has been planted. There are more beds, paths, willow, a stream and bridge and old box hedge and some flowering trees and shrubs.

The small medieval lake has been revived and filled with water lilies and edged with bulrushes; ducks may follow. Beyond, the hens lay the eggs for your breakfast in the luxurious surroundings, for a hen, of the old greenhouses.

Meat from the estate is sold locally in boxes: beef, wild venison, pheasant, Hampton Herby sausages and beef pies. Sarah's grandfather introduced a herd of Guernsey cows in the thirties; sadly they had to be sold in 2004 because of the milk price.

The ups and downs of the milk price have carved swathes through the British dairy industry; farmers are still selling their cows while Britain can't get

enough of the stuff, and the prices to farmers barely reflect the cost of production. The herd here is, more safely, of beef cattle kept partly to eat the grass in the park. There are hops too, the last ones to be grown in the county. They are sold to the Hog's Back Brewery, to Adnams in Suffolk and to Harveys in Lewes, and have won many prizes.

This is a big place to keep going, and the B&B brings in useful income. Clive also runs his own business, representing fruit producers worldwide. Sarah, once a guide at the art collection of Sutton Place, did a degree in History and Archaeology and has wide-ranging interests.

Light bulbs at Shoelands have been low-energy from the moment it was possible, they have kept the original underground sewage system (charmingly called Tinkerbelle), and heating comes from a new bio-mass system using woodchip from the estate. The garden hardly needs water, because the alluvial soil is so good; the valley is green even in drought. Rainwater from the new offices goes to the lake.

Many visitors come to see the gardens of Surrey, and there is a rich supply of them. The RHS says:

"A Martian could be excused for thinking that Surrey was the center of the horticultural universe." Gertrude Jekyll devotees are in their element here. There is her own garden at Munstead Wood, its house designed by Lutyens, Loseley Park, an Elizabethan mansion with a walled garden, Hatchlands Park with a magical bluebell wood and Wisley, home of the Royal Horticultural Society.

Surrey comes into its own as a marvelous county for gentle exploring, and Shoelands as a harbor of traditional values. It is as easy to go slow here as in the wilder reaches of England.

Sarah Webster
Shoelands House,
Seale, Farnham, GU10 1HL

- 2 twins/doubles.
- From £80. Singles from £50.
- 01483 810213
- clive@clivewebster.co.uk

Griffin Inn

SUSSEX

The Griffin is a 16th-century inn overlooking the Ouse Valley in Fletching, a village with a lovely Norman church and old beamed buildings. Simon de Montfort prayed for victory in the church before the Battle of Lewes in 1264. He won. The countryside is gently undulating, the South Downs just to the south and Pooh Bear's favorite places right here in Ashdown Forest. In fact, you can play Pooh Sticks from the bridge where Christopher Robin played the game. Traditions are faithfully adhered to in Sussex—as they are at the Griffin.

Cricket, for example, has its roots deep in Sussex soil. From the 1860s-1950s, the Australian cricket team would stay with the Earl of Sheffield nearby.

The Griffin has long views across to Sheffield Park and the Pullan family are cricket-mad, supporting the Fletching village team, sponsoring nets and hosting dinners after the games. The Griffin also has its own teams, one of which is the Dotties (Dear Old Things) Cricket Club, set up by Nigel in 1998. To join you have to be fifty or over, or "dotty" by nature. Nigel was captain, James is now, and the team is largely made up of Griffin regulars. They also get involved with the Bonfire Society; all the villages around Lewes have a bonfire in the weeks before November 5th,

with a procession and fireworks.

The Griffin is a family business. Says Nigel: "We have lived in the same village, Nutley, three miles from here, for over thirty years now. I had been running restaurants and wine bars and working for large companies. When we bought the pub we thought that our four sons might at some stage need work, and that has duly happened. It has been family-run for the last seventeen."

Once a coaching house on the smugglers' route from Newhaven to London it is a very old building, some of it going back 600 years. They have done a tremendous amount of work without undermining the rustic mood. The clientele has changed over the years but they have kept the village atmosphere in the sofa-relaxed Club Bar. There are open fires and warm paneling, red carpets and settles, fine prints on the walls. As for the bedrooms, those in the inn have an uncluttered elegance: uneven floors, soft colored walls, country furniture, free-standing baths. Those in the Coach House are quieter; swish new rooms in next-door Griffin House are quieter still.

Like all good pub owners, they support their local breweries, of which two are organic: Hepworths and Kings, both of Horsham. Food too is as local as

Roasted Squash & Red Onion Risotto

1 medium squash, chopped in quarters and deseeded
1 teaspoon chopped red chili
1 tin chopped tomatoes
1 tablespoon honey
olive oil
1 teaspoon cumin
1 teaspoon garam masala
2 red onions, finely chopped
3 cloves garlic, finely chopped
250g (8oz) Arborio rice
1 liter (2 pints) vegetarian stock

• Pre-heat oven to 200°C (400°F/Gas 6)
• Drizzle oil over squash and place in oven-proof dish with chili, tomatoes, honey, cumin and garam masala. Roast for 1 hour. Remove and leave to cool
• Remove skin from the squash and chop into bite-size pieces
• Fry the onions and garlic in oil until transparent, then stir in rice
• Add stock, a ladle at a time and stir until absorbed
• Keep stirring and adding stock for about 20 minutes or until all liquid is absorbed
• Mix in the squash with all its juices and serve

possible, with a large market garden run (organically) by Ian and Nicola Setford half a mile away. "We can even say what we would like them to grow for us. We get all our asparagus, peas, squash, salad leaves and flowers from there. They rely on us and we on them.

"We discovered a brilliant fisherman in Rye, Paul Hodges. He now comes five times a week with fresh fish and shellfish, from lobsters to cockles. We have organic veal from a farmer up the road and all the lamb from Romney Marsh. There are a lot of good growers and producers round here."

James went to university in London, worked at the Blue Water Grill in Sydney, then came back to the London bar and restaurant scene.

"The Griffin changed organically but the rot stopped when my brother David came and managed the place. My mother had had live-in managers, which didn't work too well. David came in and made it look good—he then moved on and the buck passed to me. I came down from London thirteen years ago. We grew the kitchen, put bedrooms in the Coach House, did up the garden and bought the house next door. We put in barbecues and won the Best Barbecue in Britain award four years ago. Fish cooking on open drums—food as cabaret!

"I now run the business. It's Slow—we make everything here, even the ice cream and bread. The

kitchen is making foccacia bread now. Virtually nothing is bought ready-made."

Suppliers are critically important for James. "They grow for us and we buy everything they produce. Paul Hodges, the fisherman, was just a man with a boat when we met him. There is something about the seashells in Rye Bay; you get a fantastic spectrum of fish. We did a deal with him: everything he landed twice a week we'd buy. Now he supplies all the restaurants round here.

"Having seven chefs speaks volumes about what we are trying to achieve—and we like running the bar and restaurant menus side by side. We appeal to quite a broad church. People can have a great meal in the restaurant then come round to the bar for a drink to finish the evening. That's how it works: dyed-in-the-wool Sussex locals may be best friends with the estate owner down the road.

"Things are constantly evolving. We do wine tastings on Tuesday evenings in winter, and gourmet dinners. There's live jazz on Friday and some Saturday nights, and Sunday lunchtimes. There's cricket in summer and lots of different groups of locals meet together here in the evenings, too. We could turn it into a "restaurant in the country," but that would distract from the fact that we are the oldest licensed premises in the south of England. We've had a

continuous license for 500 years! There is no pressure in the bar to eat and people feel comfortable popping in for just a chat and a drink. But you cannot survive solely as a drinking pub—drink-drive legislation has started killing the old kind of country pub.

"Rural businesses need more help from us all. Some people moving to the country from cities don't use their local shops—they shop in supermarkets, then tear their hair out at the inconvenience when the local shops close. They're living a Marie-Antoinette existence!"

One of James's favorite words is "scrudging," an invented word to mean "recycling something, and giving it another life." It could be something from a skip or a river, it could be a 600-year-old pub. It is an honorable activity. The combination here of passion with success is powerful, and this Sussex community is enriched by the Pullan family's commitment.

Nigel & James Pullan

The Griffin Inn, Fletching, Uckfield, TN22 3SS
- 13 rooms.
- £80-£140. Singles £60-£80.
- Bar lunch & dinner £10-£20. Restaurant £22-£30.
- 01825 722890
- info@thegriffininn.co.uk
- www.thegriffininn.co.uk

Castle Cottage

SUSSEX

Castle Cottage is almost too pretty to believe, standing within the grounds of Coates Castle, an 18th-century Strawberry Hill gothic mansion. Ancient woodland is the backdrop on every side, a land as quiet as a woodland valley. Here are trees, trees and grassland—a magical sight for city eyes. Alison and Ron have created something unusual and beautiful out of very little, as you will learn.

The treehouse, of course, is the great attraction, appealing to the child in us all. It is cradled in the open arms of a huge chestnut tree, with the trunk and main branches piercing the house and forming a natural four-poster to the double bed.

It has a glass ceiling in the shower, a stitched thatch roof and a safari feel: a leopard-print bedspread, African artifacts, animal skins. An entry in the visitor's book sighs: "I long to be aloft in a tree/ Its lean, strong limbs gently cradling me." You share the tree with squirrels and birds, buckeyes bouncing off the roof in autumn. It is a very special place to sleep; one couple who had just met decided to get married after two nights up there.

Says Alison: "that tree was crying out to be 'tree-housed.' We had seen one at the Chelsea Flower Show. Ours was originally going to face into the woods, but

the view into the garden is so nice. Originally we built it for ourselves; now we can barely keep up with the demand!" Ron teamed up with an ex-Trappist monk who had learned his building skills in India and who proved to have a rare and delicate touch with materials. They built the treehouse together after building the barn, using felled trees from the estate down the road as much as possible. "He has a good empathy," says Alison admiringly of her Trappist builder. "I was taught conservation from the age of five, in the middle of Africa, and have lived my life like that. We learned how to live with shortages."

The barn, attached to the cottage, is equally lovely but in a different way. The bedroom and bathroom have pitched roofs with enough glass to give you the feeling of being right up among the trees. The room in the main house has French doors leading onto a small balcony overlooking the garden. The attention to color and texture is exceptional; Alison's design talents are the perfect match for Ron's recycling and building skills.

When they bought the house in 1995 it was an "old forge for development," very run down, little more than an old agricultural shed, no tracings of

a forge. It simply housed bits of tractor to service the castle. "We did a lot of the work ourselves and, as a result, can afford to live in this area, surrounded by mature trees. Alison is a designer and has an architectural eye—we've been able to make the most of every opportunity."

They had both lived in South Africa, Ron, a Londoner by birth, and Alison after a childhood in Zimbabwe. They worked for a textile company in Durban but returned to the UK independently before

> "You share the tree with squirrels and birds, buckeyes bouncing off the roof in autumn"

meeting up again. They rented a house for three years nearby and kept an eye out for the perfect place.

"I was coming up towards retirement," Ron says. "The inspiration for the treehouse is that we both love Africa. I'm also a bit of a collector, and I hate spending money! We made the kitchen from scratch—the economics decide what you must do.

"We are gypsies first and foremost, and scrap merchants! We have spent a lot of time in France, and when I see something unusual I have to have it, however apparently useless it may be. I've got a shed full of locks and doors, door furniture, all sorts of things. Alison can see something and know it's going to work. There is no real styling: it's a bit eclectic. It gives the place a certain presence when it's not all brand new. Everything has history to it."

Alison bubbles with the delight she has in living here. "We are extremely happy here—it's bliss. When you retire there is almost a deafening silence, and you could feel you are not part of the world anymore. But here, doing B&B, we meet so many different people. And it allows us to do things we fully enjoy that we couldn't normally afford."

Ron is astonished, in retrospect, that he allowed himself to be so confined by his previous life. "For forty years I worked for three weeks' holiday a year. My background is in advertising and marketing, and I worked under a lot of pressure. In the seventies I went to South Africa and worked for textile

manufacturing organizations there." Now they are here, and admit that it is hard work. Ron says he's never known his life whiz past at such a rate. "Working together could have been a conflict—but it's not. We get on very well. I'm the front person and Alison is a brilliant cook."

Breakfast is served at a massive table in the conservatory, among the antiques and dripping ferns. (Ron has a passion for large exotic plants.) Sausages and bacon come from a butcher in nearby Storrington, seasonal produce from local smallholdings, milk from a local dairy. "The dairy man had had it with the supermarkets so he decided to go direct; now he has 300 customers. We go to the farm shop to collect the milk and cream. The milk is so sweet. The cows have a state-of-the-art barn."

This is a richly rewarding area for explorers and culture-seekers, with the South Downs Way close by: one hundred miles of footpath, cyclepath and bridleway. Petworth House is close too. Turner was fond of Petworth, inspired by the beauty of the landscape and the relationship he forged with the third Earl of Egremont. He was given the freedom to come and go as he wished and did some fine paintings here. Now the house is run by the National Trust and puts on frequent musical events.

But it is, above all, the wilder element that draws people here. The garden is alive with owls, deer, bats, woodpeckers, rabbits and moles ("more moles than anything"). They are a mere forty minutes from Gatwick yet surrounded by estate land and the river—all open access.

Alison is clear about her feelings for the place: "I expect we shall stay here until we die."

Alison Wyatt
Castle Cottage,
Coates Castle, Fittleworth, RH20 1EU
- 1 double, 1 family suite in barn, 1 double in treehouse. £90–£125.
- 01798 865001
- alison@castlecottage.info
- www.castlecottage.info

Dadmans

KENT

Once the world's first passenger railway line, the Crab and Winkle, ran close by. It carried oysters from Whitstable to Canterbury; now it is a path for cyclists and walkers. Whitstable's oysters are known as Royal Natives, with exceptionally white shells and a reputation that reached as far as Rome, where they weighed down the tables of rich Romans at the time of Christ.

The Roman historian Salus wrote: "The poor Britons, there is some good in them after all: they produce an oyster." Whitstable lives on, famous for its oysters, hosting a festival in their honor in July.

North Kent is an intriguing part of England, close to London yet very much itself. It features little in tourist brochures, perhaps a stroke of luck. Come to Lynsted for cherry-orchard country and a deep sense of peace.

The house, Dadmans, "laden with history but not remotely spooky," was once two 16th-century cottages which were joined together in the 18th century. The curious name comes from the Dodmanny family that once lived here. In 1910 the house was a school, which explains the bell still hanging on the eastern elevation. It is now in very different hands but is still surrounded by pastoral fields of sheep and cattle and apple orchards.

It has become the sort of house of which any glossy magazine would be proud: comfortable, in immensely good taste, full of books and splashes of color. Bedrooms have patterned fabrics, fresh flowers and good bathrooms, one heavily beamed with a claw-foot bath. Amanda read History of Art while doing up the house yet managed to continue making jams and compotes on her Aga—and forage for sloes for delicious sloe gin.

Amanda and Pip's parents were neighbors living not far from here. They were unlikely not to get together, and indeed met up later, on a sailing boat off the Cornish coast. Why the B&B? "Pip is semi-retired—a surveyor. We have spare rooms, spare energy, and we enjoy entertaining people." They now do everything themselves, gardening and cooking, keeping the place going. But there is no sense of strain: they have bundles of energy and this is what they love.

The Slow aspects come naturally: a refusal to use a microwave or to join the consume-and-discard society, an enjoyment of real food, convivial meals and good company. Both their mothers were homemakers; Amanda makes her own bread. The meat comes from Mr. S.W. Doughty who is still licensed to slaughter; the beef comes from the fields next door. Fish comes from Herman's Plaice, and there are farmers' markets in Whitstable and Canterbury.

"One of the reasons people come here is because they like the personal touch, to come and meet the owners. We do eat with people—only a few times we don't. People expect to be part of the whole country-house feel—to be entertained. We keep it quite small-scale to keep it fun—treating strangers as friends. And, because this is often the first or last port of call for foreign visitors, we experience a rewarding mix of languages and cultures round the dining table."

Having a fine garden is a great help if you want to be happily Slow. Amanda and Pip have poured energy and imagination into theirs. They bought the

"They have Peasgood Nonesuch apples and Morello cherries, walnuts, hazelnuts and conference pears, and a greenhouse bursting with tomatoes"

house because of the trees, and have planted many more. Kent is widely known as the "Garden of England" and the soil is perfect for fruit. They have Peasgood Nonesuch apples and Morello cherries, walnuts, hazels (grown both for hazelnuts and sticks for the garden) and conference pears, blueberries, loganberries and a greenhouse bursting with yellow and red tomatoes.

Composting is important here; there is an impressive row of compost bins. The vegetable garden is fenced against rabbits and includes wonderful stands of sweet peas. The flowers find their way into the house in summer, casting their fragrance into bedrooms and dining room.

It was John Keats who coined the name:

Here are sweet peas, on tiptoe for a flight,
With wings of gentle flush o'er delicate white.

The hens are all rare breeds; some lay blue eggs, others have hugely impressive pompoms on their heads.

The country's oldest independent brewer Shepherd Neame is down the road in Faversham and you can smell the sweet barley and malt on the air on "mashing" days. Kent was also England's main producer of hops for the brewing industry—a few hop fields remain—and Londoners in the thousands would migrate down to the fields for hop-picking work.

Perhaps that was in Dickens's mind when he wrote The Pickwick Papers: "Kent, sir, everyone knows Kent—apples, cherries, hops and women."

There is an especially rich concentration of things to do and see in Kent. You can walk the Saxon Shore Way from Conyer Creek to Faversham, and watch birds (now that is seriously slow) on the RSPB reserve. You can borrow a bike and follow a cycle route. You can visit Canterbury and re-boot your long-forgotten store of historical memories. A short drive away are Deal Castle, all battlements and dark passageways, and Leeds Castle, which has seen more of England's history than most places and is set on two islands in the heart of Kent. And you can walk to the sublime gardens of Doddington Place.

It would be a shame not to taste the local ale. There is a wonderfully isolated little pub on the shore near Faversham called the Shipwright Arms. Surrounded by salt marshes it draws its own water and uses propane gas for cooking. Best of all, it serves Kentish beer, Goachers and Hopdaemon. Further along the coast is the Sportsman pub at Seasalter, serving beer from Shepherd Neame and terrific food.

Back at Dadmans—after a strenuous day of pottering from village to shore to castle to pub—you will be glad to be free from the roar of modern life.

What is it that roareth thus?
Can it be a Motor Bus?
Yes, the smell and hideous hum
Indicat Motorem Bum.

Thus wrote A.D. Godley, almost a century ago.

Amanda Strevens

Dadmans, Lynsted, Sittingbourne, ME9 0JJ
- 1 twin, 1 double.
- £80.
- Dinner £12.50–£25.
- 01795 521293
- amanda.strevens@btopenworld.com
- www.dadmans.co.uk

[SUFFOLK, NORFOLK & NORTHAMPTONSHIRE]

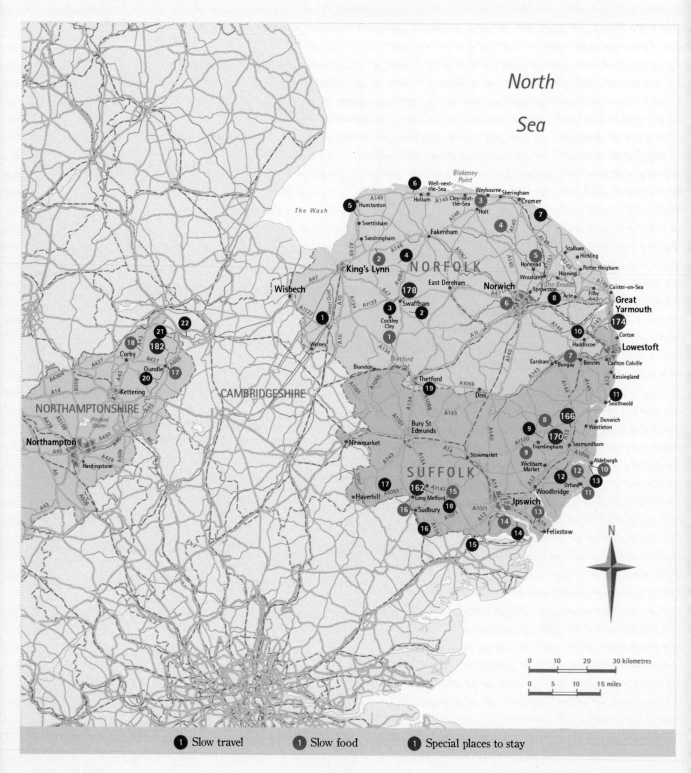

North

Sea

The Wash

Blakeney Point

NORFOLK

SUFFOLK

CAMBRIDGESHIRE

NORTHAMPTONSHIRE

King's Lynn
Wisbech
Norwich
Great Yarmouth
Lowestoft
Northampton
Corby
Oundle
Kettering
Newmarket
Bury St Edmunds
Stowmarket
Ipswich
Haverhill
Sudbury
Felixstow
Woodbridge
Aldeburgh
Southwold
Dunwich
Westleton
Orford
Framlingham
Saxmundham
Wickham Market
Carlton Colville
Kessingland
Beccles
Bungay
Earsham
Diss
Thetford
Brandon
Long Melford
Swaffham
Cockley Cley
Welney
East Dereham
Fakenham
Sandringham
Snettisham
Hunstanton
Well-next-the-Sea
Holkam
Cley-next-the-Sea
Weybourne
Sheringham
Cromer
Holt
Horstead
Wroxham
Sprowston
Acle
Caister-on-Sea
Filby
Haddiscoe
Corton
Stalham
Hickling
Potter Heigham
Horning
The Broads
Thetford
Stour
Hardingstone
Pitsford Water

0   10   20   30 kilometres

0   5   10   15 miles

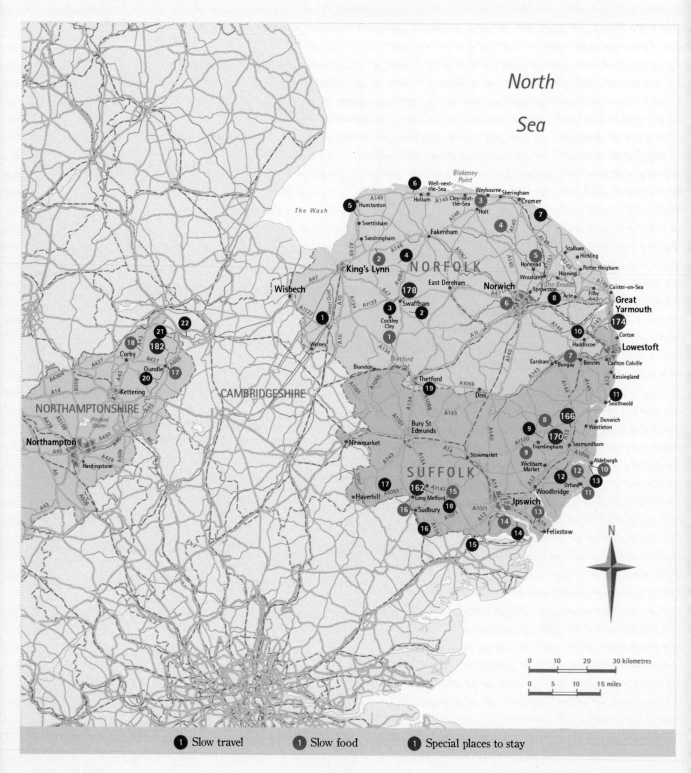 Slow travel   Slow food   Special places to stay

SUFFOLK, NORFOLK & NORTHAMPTONSHIRE

Slow travel

1. Denver Windmill
2. Church of St Mary the Virgin
3. Ecotech Environmental Centre
4. Great Massingham Walk
5. Norfolk Lavender
6. Blakeney Coast
7. Mundesley
8. Fairhaven Woodland and Water Garden
9. Shawsgate Vineyard
10. The Angles Way
11. Southwold
12. Snape Maltings
13. Sutton Hoo
14. Pin Mill
15. Bridge Cottage
16. River Stour Boating
17. Clare
18. Groton Wood
19. Brecks Countryside Project
20. Wadenhoe
21. The Prebendal Manor House
22. Nene Valley Railway

Slow food

1. Iceni Brewery
2. Abbey Farm Organics
3. Cookies Crab Shop
4. Samphire
5. Norfolk Cider Company & Norfolk Apple Juice
6. Golden Triangle Farmers' Market
7. Beccles Farmers' Market
8. Emmett's Stores
9. Eat Anglia
10. Aldeburgh Beach
11. Butley Orford Oysterage
12. High House Fruit Farm, Sudbourne
13. Goslings Farm
14. Jimmy's Farm
15. Hollow Trees Farm Shop
16. Sudbury Farmers' Market
17. Oundle Farmers' Market
18. New Lodge Farm

Special places to stay

162. Milden Hall
166. The Old Methodist Chapel
170. Sandpit Farm
174. Fritton House Hotel
178. Strattons
182. Bridge Cottage

Slow travel

① Denver Windmill
Downham Market (01366 384009)
Lovingly restored working mill with guided tour, visitor center, tearoom and bakery.
www.denvermill.co.uk

② Church of St Mary the Virgin
Houghton on the Hill (01760 440470)
Personal guided tours by church warden Bob Davey MBE, who has devoted fourteen years to the rescue and revival of this remote hilltop church. It's as loved by visitors as by locals. Remarkable wall paintings go back to Saxon times.

③ Ecotech Environmental Centre
Swaffham (01760 726100)
Wind turbine tours with fantastic views. Organic garden, shop and café.
www.ecotech.org.uk

④ Great Massingham Walk
Easy two-hour walk along the long-distance Peddars Way. Begin at the

pretty village of Great Massingham, with its four large ponds on four greens. Tuck into fine seasonal food at the recently revived Dabbling Duck. The paths of the Peddars Way make it suitable for those of limited mobility. Much is open to cyclists, too.
www.walkingworld.com

⑤ Norfolk Lavender
Heacham (01485 570384)
Lavender farm of over 120 acres with tours and shop. In 1932 three men and a boy did the planting in eighteen days for a total cost of £15. Discover the secrets of distilling.
www.norfolklavender.co.uk

⑥ Blakeney Coast
Beans Boat Trips (01263 740038)
Pick up a boat from Blakeney or Morston Quay to Blakeney Point to see seals basking on the sands; if you're lucky they'll swim right by you. An Area of Outstanding Natural Beauty, a haven for migratory birds and wildlife.
www.beansboattrips.co.uk

⑦ Mundesley
Follow the cliff top path for breezes and views of the vibrant beach huts below. When the tide's out there's a sandy beach for safe swimming, tidal pools for toddlers and a beachside

café. Don't miss the beautifully restored Stow Windmill close by.

⑧ Fairhaven Woodland and Water Garden
South Walsham (01603 270449)
Over three miles of walks, a 950-year-old King Oak and fifteen rustic bridges in organically managed woodland within fifty-three hectares. Come for candelabra primulas in May, brilliant colors in autumn, winter views of the Broads. Dogs love it.
www.fairhavengarden.co.uk

⑨ Shawsgate Vineyard
Framlingham (01728 724060)
Vineyard tours, "Experience Days," abundant wildlife. Free DIY tours and wine-tasting, too—information sheet and map provided so you don't get lost. Twelve varieties of wine are produced here.
www.shawsgate.co.uk

⑩ The Angles Way
Follow the river through lovely Somerleyton, stopping at the Duke's Head for lunch, then on to the estate (see page 174) and the Angles Way. Windmills, river, open skies, two memorials, one isolated church and the village of Lound.
www.walkingworld.com

14 Pin Mill
Delightfully untouristy sailing village on the Orwell estuary, with popular ex-smugglers' pub the Butt & Oyster. Behind, a woodland path leads to a bizarre shantytown of houseboats.
www.suffolkcam.co.uk

19 Brecks Countryside Project
Thetford (01842 765400)
Miles of heathland, forest and farmland with chalk streams, meres, pingos and neolithic mines, known as the Grimes Graves. Numerous cycling, walking and horse trails.
www.brecks.org

11 Southwold
A timeless, stylish seaside town with beach huts and lots to do. Boating, fishing, art galleries, museums, restaurants and a seven-mile walk with watery views to Walberswick. Catch the one-man summer ferry back.
www.visitsouthwold.co.uk

15 Bridge Cottage
Flatford (01206 298260)
Serene walk along the river Stour from Dedham to Flatford Mill brings you to the site of Constable's *The Haywain* —and tea and cakes at thatched, 16th-century Bridge Cottage.
www.nationaltrust.org.uk

20 Wadenhoe
A village of attractive stone buildings and a rich history. The parish church has a 12th-century saddleback tower and its six bells are said to be the most musical in the country.

12 Snape Maltings
Snape (01728 688305)
A collection of 19th-century maltings on the banks of the River Alde, with shops, galleries, places to eat. Home to the celebrated Aldeburgh Music Festival.
www.snapemaltings.co.uk

16 River Stour Boating
Bures St Mary (01787 375377)
Guided summertime canoe trips from Sudbury to Cattawade.
www.riverstourtboating.org.uk

21 The Prebendal Manor House
Nassington (01780 782575)
It dates from the early 13th century and the site includes medieval fish ponds and archaeological evidence of one of King Cnut's royal timber halls. Lovely recreated medieval gardens and archaeological excavations.
www.prebendal-manor.co.uk

13 Sutton Hoo
Woodbridge (01394 389700)
"Page one of English history"—the low, grassy burial ground of the Anglo-Saxon kings of East Anglia, discovered in 1939.
www.suttonhoo.org

17 Clare
Charming historic market town. Delicious seasonal-produce lunches and champagne teas at Café Clare.
www.cafeclare.co.uk

22 Nene Valley Railway
Stibbington (01780 784444)
Steam railway running for seven-and-a-half miles between Yarwell Junction and Peterborough. Cross the river Nene on a girder bridge, drop off at Ferry Meadows Country Park, learn to drive a full-sized steam locomotive.
www.nvr.org.uk

18 Groton Wood
Ancient woodland, enchanting walks: bluebells, nightingales, toads, newts.
www.suffolkwildlife.co.uk

Slow food

1 Iceni Brewery
Ickburgh (01842 878922)
Call to arrange a brewery tour;
sniff the malt, rub the hops, taste
the beers.
www.icenibrewery.co.uk

2 Abbey Farm Organics
Flitcham (01485 609094)
Growing over fifty different organic
crops, selling locally and through a
box scheme. Public bird hide open
every day; who would guess
six percent of the world's pink-
footed geese visit Abbey Farm?
www.abbeyfarm.co.uk

3 Cookies Crab Shop
Salthouse (01263 740352)
More than just a shellfish shop: as
well as seafood straight from the
boats there are soups, salads and
sandwiches—to take away or eat in.
www.cookies.shopkeepers.co.uk

4 Samphire
Aylsham (01263 734464)
A treasure in the grounds of Blickling
Hall (National Trust-owned), run with
passion by Nell Montgomery. Breads,
brownies, smoked mackerel,
vegetables in season, perfect pies
laced with onion marmalade.
www.samphireshop.co.uk

5 Norfolk Cider Company
Hoveton (01603 783040)
Cider is made here from culinary and
dessert, not cider, apples—quite
different from the cider of the West
Country. More like an apple wine
and a little stronger at 7.5 percent.
Pop in for a free tasting.
www.norfolkcider.co.uk

6 Golden Triangle Farmers' Market
Earlham House Shopping Centre,
Norwich (01603 250000)
Second Sunday of the month.
www.thegreengrocers.co.uk

7 Beccles Farmers' Market
Beccles Heliport (01502 476240)
First and third Saturday of the month.

8 Emmett's Stores
Peasenhall (01728 747717)
Old-fashioned grocer's shop and
smoke house. Pick up some Black
Suffolk ham—dark, sticky, delicious.
www.emmettsham.co.uk

9 Eat Anglia
Earl Soham (01728 685557)
Deli and café with local and organic
food, wines, beers and gift shop. Earl
Soham brewery handily next door.
www.eatanglia.co.uk

10 Aldeburgh Beach
Twice a day the boards announce
the catch—crab, lobster, haddock,
sole, skate.

11 Butley Orford Oysterage
Orford (01394 450277)
Orford oysters—and salmon,
prawns and sprats from their
own smokehouse. In the no-frills
restaurant, smoked cod's roe comes
with thin slices of hot white toast.
www.butleyorfordoysterage.co.uk

12 High House Fruit Farm
Sudbourne (01394 450450)
Buy or pick your own.
www.high-house.co.uk

13 Goslings Farm
Trimley St Martin (01394 273361)
The biggest Pick Your Own in the
country. The undercover strawberries
are table-top grown (no bending!).
Bees are imported as pollinators,
dummy owls discourage birds.
www.goslingsfarm.co.uk

14 Jimmy's Farm
Wherstead (0870 950 0210)
Ramshackle rare-breed pig farm and
shop with woodland trail, winter
weekend sausage barbecues, pig-
keeping courses and farmers' market
the first Saturday of the month.
www.essexpigcompany.com

15 Hollow Trees Farm Shop
Semer (01449 741247)
From beets to basil they grow it all,
in fields divided by high hedges to
encourage wildlife. New farm trails,
coffee shop, wooden hill fort and
animals to feed.
www.hollowtrees.co.uk

16 Sudbury Farmers' Market
St Peter's, Market Hill
(01787 372331)
Last Friday of the month.

17 Oundle Farmers' Market
(01832 272055)
Market Place, second Saturday of
the month.

18 New Lodge Farm
Bulwick (01780 450493)
Café and shop run by a family that
has been here since 1870. Local
cakes, and their own superb Aberdeen
Angus beef. Open Saturday only.

Pubs & inns

St Peter's Hall

South Elmham, Bungay, Suffolk
The 13th-century moated manor, St Peter's, thrives, brewing and bottling its exemplary range of bitters, fruit ales and porters. Take the brewery tour or eat and drink like kings in the medieval hall. 01986 782288 www.stpetersbrewery.co.uk

King's Head

Gorams Mill Lane, Laxfield, Suffolk
One of Suffolk's treasures and little has changed in a hundred years: it creaks with character. Menus change daily; the simple parlor is dominated by a high-backed settle in front of an open fire. Oh, and there's no bar. 01986 798395

The Queens Head

The Street, Bramfield, Suffolk
Mark Corcoran's menus make reassuring reading and at least half the ingredients will be organic and local. A raftered bar; bantams and bower in the garden. 01986 784214 www.queensheadbramfield.co.uk

White Hart

Helmingham Road, Otley, Suffolk
Lynda saved the pub five days before it was to be sold as a house; now it is the free-spirited hub of the village. Anything goes here and food sourcing is impeccable. 01473 890312 www.thewhitehartotley.co.uk

Wildebeest Arms

Norwich Road, Norwich, Norfolk
One of the best-loved dining pubs in Norfolk. The 19th-century building may look no great shakes, but the atmosphere is special. There are rich yellow walls, oak beams, flowers on tables, a winter fire. 01508 492497

The Lord Nelson

Burnham Thorpe, Norfolk
It hasn't changed a great deal in 400 years: ancient benches and settles, worn brick, tile floors, good food and a serving hatch instead of a bar distinguish this marvelous place. 01328 738241 www.nelsonslocal.co.uk

The Anchor

The Street, Morston, Holt, Norfolk
All a village pub should be, it's a warren of intimate, loved and lived-in rooms, each with its own story to tell. Morston mussels and Blakeney crab draw in locals and visitors and you can book a seal trip while you sup. 01263 741392

The Cock

Hemingford Grey, Cambridgeshire
The young, enterprising licensees stripped the 17th-century pub back to its original simplicity. Airy restaurant serves pub classics and the chef makes his own sausages; beams and settles in the bar. 01480 463609 www.cambscuisine.com

Hole in the Wall

Little Wilbraham, Cambridgeshire
Hiding down a hundred lanes, it's clear the pub and its timbered bar is well-loved. Enjoy the country-style restaurant at the back; blackboard menu, much organic. 01223 812282 www.the-holeinthewall.com

Milden Hall

SUFFOLK

Juliet, up in Suffolk giving a talk to the Suffolk Preservation Society on rural studies, spotted "this gorgeous man." Being, as we will see, something of a dynamo, she went home and told friends she had met the man she was going to marry. "He plants trees and walks mountains (Himalayas at the time). He's made for me."

They have, together, created a remarkable and beautiful place—to stay, to learn, to get married, and just to be.

Christopher carries the burden and privilege of being a Hawkins farmer, with 500 acres and over 300 years of family history. It is rare to find such continuity on the land, and even rarer to find such commitment to using it with sensitivity and environmental awareness. Some of the farm is of unimproved and improved hay meadows and wetland, but they grow wheat, winter barley, sugar beet, field beans and oilseed rape. Pigs and bantams, too, play their part. Christopher, Juliet and their daughters—Holly, Ruby Tiger and Daisy—have all created ponds, planted trees, restored barns, planted hedges and carried out bird, moth and butterfly surveys. Good news pours forth from the farm: they now have over one hundred species of moth, seven of bats, and seven ponds of which six have great crested newts.

After the great storm of 1987, when the country lost trees in prodigious numbers, the Hawkinses collected seeds and replanted thousands. So they deserve the increase in wildlife and they are keen to share their enthusiasms and experience with farmers and others around them. As an independent farm conservation adviser, Juliet has spent twenty-five years working with local farmers and advising them on green issues. She also works closely with the Suffolk Wildlife Trust. There is still lots to do but she feels the tide has turned—hundreds of miles of hedgerow have been planted and traditionally coppiced, parish boundaries restored, ponds de-silted and wildflower meadows brought back into sensitive management after a post-war era of very intensive farming.

Juliet also teaches natural history. School parties come and go and they run a summer wildlife camp for local children. She provides copious suggestions to visitors on how to enjoy the farm: pond-dipping, leaf-sewing, lantern-making, even tree-hugging. There are tutor-led sessions on environmental themes such as "water," and a fleet of bikes for people to borrow. If you are staying for a while, you will be encouraged to abandon your car and enjoy the peace. You can borrow maps, helmets with your bikes, follow nature trails or planned walks taking in churches, nature reserves, villages and pubs.

Juliet and Christopher have devised several car-free days: in and around the gloriously medieval Lavenham; biking around Boxford; a day in Bury St Edmunds; a boat trip down the River Stour. You can walk the Milden-Lavenham-Milden walk, along generous footpaths through meadows and past poplar plantations, dropping in on church and pub on the way.

This is a fine county. Flat it may be, but by no means featureless. It is, rather, "gently rolling at a low level," with some of England's loveliest villages—such as Kersey, which is little more than one street dipping down to a duck-strutting ford and up again, between houses of pink and plaster, timber and wattle-and-daub, soft red brick and thatch. How have these Suffolk villages escaped the ravages of our age? Perhaps because Suffolk was a backwater for so long, only recently the victim of cosmopolitan interest.

Of all the pleasures that the Hall can bring, the most immediately impressive and magnificent is the great barn. Almost cathedral-like in its Tudor splendor, it is an aisled barn built in the 1500s probably by the famous Spring family, rich clothiers from Lavenham. There are two Tudor-style four-posters at one end, two trundle beds under these and eight boxed beds along the sides of the barn. Down the center is an oak banqueting table seating up to fifty people plus room for up to eighty more, and there is still room for dancing. Most of the beds are of Suffolk oak, like the barn itself, so you have a ravishing oaken display reaching from the ground to a methodically tangled web of oaken trusses and beams soaring and arching overhead. One's first sight of it all is heart-stopping. "We saved the barn to save the farm. Keeping the integrity of the building seems to have helped turn the farm around too. People fall in love with it—it's very popular for family gatherings, gangs of friends, young and old, retreats and weddings."

The opportunities for keeping everyone happy at Milden seem limitless, with the three B&B rooms (you can breakfast in the barn if you are part of a larger group), the self-catering barn, in all sleeping 28+ and, even, a camping meadow for extras of the same group.

The house is down a long farm drive yet only three miles from Lavenham. It is, unsurprisingly, beautiful—the front "Georgianised" in typical Suffolk style. But there are exposed beams elsewhere on the outside walls and linen-fold panelling within. The bedrooms, ranging from big to vast, have spectacular views across ancient wildflower meadows and the

walled garden. One is called the Adams Room, remodeled in the Adam style in 1770 as an upstairs ladies' sitting room and with an elegant fireplace and early woodwork. A fine staircase leads up to the room; a tapestry adds to the sense of history.

The room was used in the 1800s by eight spinsters who spent their leisure time sewing and spinning. This was a county grown rich on wool, much helped by the Flemish weavers who came over to take part and whose architectural influence can be seen in the gabled Dutch roofs scattered throughout the county. The Gallery Room has walls festooned with antique maps and prints. The bookcases reach between the walls, laden with books. The smaller Becker Room is named after Harry Becker, the Suffolk painter of rural scenes at the turn of the 20th century. The scenes through the windows lend authority to his pencil drawings, etchings and watercolors on the walls. The rooms share a big bathroom and there's an extra guest bathroom, lined with family photographs, downstairs.

You eat your breakfast in a vast room surrounded by tapestries, paintings and family pictures. Breakfast is delicious: bacon from their own Tamworths and Gloucester Old Spots; eggs from their wandering, tatterdemalion collection of farmyard chickens; wild blewits, parasols and inkcaps from mushroom-foraging in the fields; jams from garden and hedge fruits, marmalade from a neighbor, bread from Lavenham.

The Hall is heated by a wood-burner using wood coppiced from the hedgerows. Guests are encouraged to be intelligent about energy use, perhaps by pulling on a sweater rather than turning the heating up. After hundreds of years of the Hawkins family's care, Milden Hall is taking on a new life of its own and setting standards for all of us to follow.

Juliet & Christopher Hawkins

Milden Hall,
Milden, Lavenham, CO10 9NY

- 3 rooms. S/C for 22+. Celebrations for up to 130.
- £60–£80. Singles from £40. Ask about the barn.
- 01787 247235
- hawkins@thehall-milden.co.uk
- www.thehall-milden.co.uk

The Old Methodist Chapel

SUFFOLK

It is a special delight, when writing about England, to learn of the web of history connecting one village to another. Every old stone tells a story. Here, for example, in the little-known village of Yoxford, is a great house called Cockfield Hall. It has gone largely unnoticed, yet Lady Katherine Grey, the unfortunate sister of Lady Jane Grey, was imprisoned here, having committed the old crime of marrying without permission. Most of England's womenfolk would be under house arrest now had things not moved on. Katherine moved on, upon her death, to Salisbury Cathedral where she lies with her husband under a magnificent memorial.

Born in Canada, Jackum has close connections with Suffolk; she went to school here. "This place was still a church when I grew up seven miles away. My sister-in-law used to worship here." When she and David saw The Old Methodist Chapel for sale, they could hardly believe their luck. They'd been looking for a big old chapel to live in, in order to have a space in which to play loud music—along with David's harmonium. The building was in fine structural condition, with a new roof, so they put up the essential bookshelves—added a bathroom and other minor necessities—and moved in. Books are their life and their history.

David is a Londoner, born in Holland Park Avenue, brought up in Highgate. His father was a psychiatrist and his mother an actress—Eileen Way, one of the early "Doctor Who" faces. David started

in publishing early, as an executive trainee with Pergamon Press, then went on to Evans Brothers where he met Jackum, an editorial assistant who put herself up for writing a book aimed at young people with learning difficulties. After they married in 1973, Jackum wanted to return to her native Canada, to Montreal. It was an exciting time to be there—"and the food was very good"—but England drew them back. David worked for Penguin for nine years; Jackum worked freelance as a picture editor. But eventually the pace of London life got to them and Jackum vowed that she would leave and work in the country. Almost immediately she was offered two Thai cookbooks to write and set off for Bangkok to research. So the move to the country awaited her return. The delight for her was to be able to move to Suffolk with a new writing career in the bag.

Doing B&B was not part of the original plan. But somehow the notion grew, and they have been able to do it without major intrusions into their own peace and space. They have had lovely people to stay and feel that, thanks to their guests, they are now able to lead a slower and more satisfying life. "Opting out has worked! We are now joined at the hip, living in one big room and working together. Curiously, it seems to be OK. I like sitting in this 'house,' writing. It is a beautiful space and it still amazes me. I walk in and still wonder at it."

They are enthusiastically green, and very keen on where they get their food from; for example, you'll

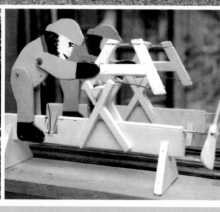

be served free-range Peasenhall bacon at breakfast. There are plenty of like-minded people in the area—artists, musicians, writers, actors, craftspeople. "Our quality of life has gone up enormously since we have been here. We wouldn't change our lives for anything. It's not about money. We are getting by in a very pleasant way. When we are free and the sun shines, we take to the beach. We live for the day."

One associates a Methodist chapel with sound social idealism and earnest, morally upright worshippers rather than with delightful living spaces. But Jackum and David have managed the transformation brilliantly. You enter the main "chapel," their living area, with the kitchen where the altar was and the sleeping area above. It's a large open space stuffed with books and objects collected on their travels, slightly chaotic, wonderfully lived-in, fun and relaxed. The guest bedrooms are at the back and have their own entrances. The double room once housed the minister's horse and trap; now it's a sunny space with its own little walled terrace backed by woods. You eat breakfast in your own eating area/conservatory. There are videos and music in your rooms, and books and flowers in every corner. The chapel itself has a fascinating Victorian air-conditioning system, the air entering through four vents on the walls and being drawn up and out through the roof. It works, and is energy-free.

Weeks spent here would not be wasted. Southwold, a town that came close to winning the Guardian Seaside Town competition for its much-loved, genteel charms, is only a few miles away. It has a splendid new pier upon which you can perambulate and play old-fashioned pier games, or sip a cuppa (tea) while gazing along the coast to Dunwich, the lost city, and beyond. There's a lighthouse, a brewery—Adnams—that gives the town much of its commercial life, beach huts behind a shingle beach and a delightful layout that includes several little "town greens." You can walk south to Walberswick, crossing a little bridge or taking a rowing ferry to get there. More pubs, a village green, a long beach and sand dunes, marshes full of birds, and an eccentric, ramshackle collection of boats, yachts and craft. There is Minsmere, the

country's best-known bird reserve, and Aldeburgh, known throughout the world for its music festival based at the Snape Maltings; you would be unlucky not to catch a concert or recital there. The "Cathedral of the Marshes," Blythburgh Church, is only a couple of miles inland, a magnificent

> "When we are free and the sun shines, we take to the beach. We live for the day"

example of the "flushed" flint style of church building and of carved bench ends. One shows a man held down in the stocks with a metal collar round his neck—for antisocial behavior, no doubt. If only someone had put Oliver Cromwell's troops in the stocks when they stabled their horses in the church and took pot shots at the carved angels on the nave's ceiling. Yoxford is a pretty little village, a long street with some interesting shops and very pretty houses. One has some delicate "pargetting" on its façade, an East Anglian creation of plastered decoration on outside walls.

Jackum and David are provocative examples of "going slow," having dropped out and then straight back in, gradually and successfully. They can be found at their writing desks as part of a co-operative team of writers working on a new publishing series. The team is scattered, but that no longer matters. For writers, at least, a quiet rural existence has always been possible. The internet has now made it even more so.

Jackum & David Brown
The Old Methodist Chapel,
High Street, Yoxford, IP17 3EU
- 2 rooms.
- £75-£90. Singles £50-£65.
- 01728 668333
- browns@chapelsuffolk.co.uk
- www.chapelsuffolk.co.uk

Sandpit Farm

SUFFOLK

Susie and Mark drove up to the house, stepped out of the car and immediately fell in love with Sandpit Farm. It is, indeed, idyllic —and in a water-meadow setting that brings in countless visitors on the wing. Kingfishers, mallard and moorhens splash, paddle and strut. Tawny owls too, and barn owls, and the birds that they have domesticated: six hens, a proud cockerel and three guinea fowl. These highly amusing (and, dare we say it, delicious) birds perch on the garden gate. "Hear no evil, see no evil, speak no evil" Susie calls them.

There is a quiet satisfaction about people who have chosen to live in Suffolk, or indeed in Norfolk. They have discovered something special. Part of the secret is the people. "Of all the people in the world I have worked with," wrote John Seymour, "I have found the East Anglian the most utterly reliable. When the seams of the world begin to crack I'll bet some East Anglian somewhere will pull a pipeful of shag out of his mouth, spit, say: 'Blast if that ain't a rummun!' put his pipe back and carry on hoeing his sugar beet."

Mark and Susie love it here and have thrown themselves gaily into local life. The houses and farms of Bruisyard run either side of the meandering river Alde, surrounded by undulating fields and ancient woodland.

There is no pub, school or village shop now but there is the ancient church of St Peter's, with a round Saxon tower and Norman vestiges. It is thought to have been built to watch for raiders sailing inland from the North Sea.

The good news is that there are very few second homes so the locals are still here, though the sale of farms goes on apace, as elsewhere. This particular farmhouse and buildings, however, have survived in fine fettle: not split up and with the black weatherboarding and mellow red brick very much as they were. There are the old stables, once used for Suffolk Punches—those great equine engines of the land. There is a handsome old Dutch barn, home now to carefully saved wood and bricks awaiting their next incarnation. An old Ferguson tractor, made in 1947 and painted a vivid and unusual red, is still in active service, most often with Susie at the wheel.

The house, although large, has a charming cottage atmosphere: some beams, a huge old fireplace, garden flowers, family pictures and china. There are two attractive bedrooms, one a double with 18th-century hand-painted beds and a trompe l'oeil door painted to look like a bookcase; the other has lovely views over the orchard and

gardens. Quilted bedspreads, hand-stencils, feather pillows; Susie takes great care of her guests. The dining room has a big antique table with red-check tablecloth, and a bureau with family photos in frames, a familiar but comforting English scene. "Everything in the house is to do with flowers, hens and the family." Breakfast is cooked on the Aga then served in the dining room, or in the garden overlooking the "moat." (Nobody knows the distant history of the house, so the assumption that this lovely old brick-lined pond is part of an old moat rests unchallenged.) If you are staying awhile, you can find a quiet corner of the garden for reading. There are, too, footpath maps for walkers and a guest sitting room to return to, with a wood-burning stove and shelves of books.

The move to live here was not a major life change for Mark and Susie, who fled London twenty years ago; Mark knew the area from weekend visits and Susie's mother lived in Suffolk. Susie considers herself to be "very green—verging on potty [crazy] green". Having begun motherhood with cloth diapers—and a commitment to keep using them!—she has become greener since living in the country. Dead trees are logged for the fires and the chippings used for mulching and to create paths in the productive vegetable garden. Susie is a member of the flourishing Suffolk Smallholders Association; her sister is a conservation farmer in Northamptonshire and a member of the Slow Food movement. The family were brought up in Yorkshire so take easily to country life, having paddled in streams and caught minnows as children. It was the perfect childhood. No traffic, noise, pollution. "We were free to play in the great outdoors, and I have never forgotten the lessons I learned. I still love the smell of nettles!"

Food produced locally is a central part of the diet here. Susie buys "Marybelle" milk and superb yogurts supplied by a local farm. Eggs come from Susie's reduced-by-foxes flock of hens, though she is no longer allowed to sell them; modern regulations have snuffed that out. The jam comes from fruits in the garden and hedgerows, the meat from a local farmer, and there is a farmers' market nearby. Every year now there is an Aldeburgh Food and Drink Festival at

the Snape Maltings and Lady Cranbrook is the president, an ardent and much-feted anti-supermarket campaigner. So there is hope for the Suffolk farming community.

Several miles inland, this part of Suffolk—narrow-laned and light-dappled—is easy to grow fond of, especially on a summer's day. It feels unspoiled, still peopled with those who made it what it is. Yet it feels connected with the coast, for the river that slips lazily through the meadows just two fields away is the Alde, which widens out among the marshes at Snape, where the famous Maltings are and to which commercial barges would sail right up until the 1950s.

Here is where you will find the wry, unsmiling humor—a tendency to underplay and understate everything. "Well, now's the time to laarn!" shouted the old Suffolk barge skipper to his mate when the latter fell overboard yelling that he couldn't swim. "And I bet the old boy pulled him out of the water without even taking his pipe out of his mouth," wrote John Seymour.

Close to Bruisyard is the marvelous church of Dennington, and then the little old market town of Framlingham, a rich reward for curious travelers who leave the coast to explore inland. The castle is still mightily impressive, even if there is little left other than the walls and the earthworks beyond them. It was built with oolithic stone from Northamptonshire, floated up the River Ore—now just a trickle. That must have been a slow process, yet the achievement was immense.

You can see the stars from Sandpit Farm, and revel in the peace, the silence not even broken by the noise of a car.

Susie Marshall

Sandpit Farm,
Bruisyard, Saxmundham, IP17 2EB
- 2 rooms.
- £65–£80. Singles from £45.
- 01728 663445
- smarshall@aldevalleybreaks.co.uk
- www.aldevalleybreaks.co.uk

Fritton House Hotel

NORFOLK

East Anglia is a region richly littered with Halls, almost 600 of them. It is thought that for some reason Suffolk, as long ago as the Domesday Book, had more free yeomen-farmers than other counties and they were able to enclose their land and build fine houses earlier than most. Even more interestingly, there are about the same number of moated houses—not least because of the clay soil. Most of them are hidden from view and delightful to discover. There are also several estate villages, such as the one built at Somerleyton, for estate workers. It was usually the sign of a utopian vision of sorts, or perhaps of a touch of landowners' social conscience, but produced some fascinating results.

The cottages on the Somerleyton estate were built to show "rare attention to the comfort and morality of peasant families." It remains a model community: a village street leading down to shops, post office and pub, with a village green holding the space and the village school holding the community together. The Crossleys subsidize the post office and stores and are fighting to keep the school open. "Without it the village would lose a huge amount— fete, school plays etc."

Locals say that smugglers and sea traders navigated

through to the lake from the North Sea and on to the river Waveney and beyond.

Somerleyton Hall has its origins as a Viking settlement and a Saxon manor. Later it became a fine Jacobean manor. Five generations ago it was bought by the Crossley family and rebuilt in early Victorian, neo-Elizabethan style: carved stonework, state rooms, massive pretensions, and unique wood paneling by Grinling Gibbons.

It is now Hugh's family home —and responsibility. The gardens are vast and many come to admire the maze and the sunken lavender garden and greenhouses built by Joseph Paxton—it was he who built Crystal Palace. The lake is even vaster—and seen during the last war as such a fine potential landing site for seaplanes that steel cables were strung across the lake to deter them.

The interesting aspect of Hugh's project here is its role as an example of what can be done with such great estates in the modern age. They can be sold off to the highest bidder, turned over to single-minded developers, farmed on an industrial scale, dumbed-down into tourist attractions and—in a host of other ways—wrenched from their real potential.

Hugh farms 2,400 acres and is going more and more into

livestock, set on creating a pedigree Welsh Black herd of cattle. (He has Welsh roots and is loyal to them. He also likes the meat.) The few cows he has live on the marsh, adding a touch of exotica to the scenery. Happily, there is an abattoir nearby in Bungay—a critically important element of a sound local food system.

Hugh once ran a restaurant in London—Dish-Dash. It was a fairly typical start for an Eton-educated scion of a big estate, but his father moved out of the house and he took over, surprised to find himself now having to lead a slower life.

From that point to full adoption of the philosophy of Slow is nevertheless a long journey—illustrated, and even led, by the gestation period of a cow. It takes time to produce the calves that will eventually end up on the table.

"We bought our first ten Welsh Black beef cattle back in 2004 and three calves arrived the following spring. Now, eighteen months on they are only just getting onto the menu. That's a long wait.

"Living with the land is bound to be slow. It is about seasonality and accepting that things don't always go your way." But he is bullish about driving farming into a new era. He is getting off to a running start with his plans for organic farming and to be 70% self-sufficient in meat and vegetables by 2009. Ideally he would be producing enough to stock the village shops, too. He also has plans to become an energy producer, perhaps with a heat-pump in the lake—a principle well established long ago by the London Festival Hall, which drew its heat from the Thames for many years.

Hugh laughs, though, when recounting how an old farm manager said to him "call it what you like—green, eco, it's just like farming always used to be!"

The hotel is another expression of Hugh's modernizing enthusiasms. Thanks to the influence of manager Sarah Winterton it is friendly and relaxed and its brasserie serves fresh, local and seasonal food. There is a fecund vegetable garden, which "moves the chefs nearer to the produce." It has really motivated them, apparently, and a full-time gardener will soon be supplying greater quantities to the hotel kitchen. "I grew up with a kitchen garden at home, but the link

between garden and kitchen isn't obvious to all. There are not many Hugh Fearnley-Whittingstalls out there."

There are eight stylish bedrooms and one family suite, all named after long-standing estate tenants. One, "Sid and Audrey," has a vast bathroom under exposed beams, a double sink and an ornate full-length mirror. Another room, the "Walter Musset," has in its bathroom what is known as the G&T stool upon which one sits in the evening to admire the view.

The drawing room has an open brick fireplace and a framed photo of the Honourable Hugh as an attendant to the Queen; it is a classically English room, with family photos on bureaus and tables, comfortable sofas, newspapers and books, a big old rug on the wooden floor and Wedgewood blue walls.

Right next-door is the Fritton Country Park, a huge success since it was created by Hugh's father along lines suggested by the Historic Houses Association. There is a wooden adventure playground, a maze and paths and "wellie trails" running down to the lake on which you may row or fish. Once it was a duck decoy, where flocks of wild duck would be decoyed into funneled netting by flocks of tame ones, and—curiously—a small white dog, and sent off to Smithfield and elsewhere.

Fritton is, of course, close to the famous Norfolk Broads—that unexpected network of rivers and waterways about which still lingers a primeval magic. One can hire a boat from Fritton and drift aimlessly through the Fens. East Anglia has always felt slow. An old lady in a village near Stowmarket told a friend that her son had emigrated to Canada. "Did he go by boat or did he fly?" asked the friend. "I don't know," said the mother, "but he took the bus to Ipswich."

Sarah Winterton

Fritton House Hotel, Church Lane, Fritton, NR31 9HA
- 9 rooms.
- £130-£180. Singles from £90.
- Lunch from £8. Dinner, 3 courses, from £27.
- 01493 484008
- frittonhouse@somerleyton.co.uk
- www.frittonhouse.co.uk

Strattons

NORFOLK

If a prize were awarded to the British hotel with the smallest ecological footprint per guest, Strattons would probably win it. They weigh their total business and domestic waste, for Heavens sake! Eighteen years ago they wrote their first environmental policy and have rewritten it every year. That in itself should win a prize, for hardly any were written that long ago and of those written since, most have been put away on a high shelf and forgotten. Their policy is a living and breathing part of their work; it changes and flexes to satisfy its demanding owners. The staff are steeped in it and as a result the hotel has won numerous awards, including a Queen's Award.

Let us begin with that most elegant of subjects, waste: they halved their output of it by 2006. They have a special recycling room where they sort, for example, magazines for the old people's home, the doctors' waiting rooms and the library; wax is used to make new candles or firelighters; newspapers make firebricks or are shredded for animal bedding.

Shutters keep the winter heat in; light bulbs are mostly low energy; new rooms have a master switch that automatically shuts down all the lights and devices at once. Miniature toiletry bottles and bar soaps

have been replaced with liquid dispensers, with 97% less plastic going to landfill.

The list of housekeeping commitments goes on, and spills outside: there are bat boxes, bird boxes and ponds in the garden to encourage wildlife. Inside, the graceful mermaid mosaic running along the back of the bath in the Portico Room is made from kitchen waste, including shells and broken crockery. Strattons is a fine example of the range and depth of the whole subject of sustainability.

It is definitely not merely a question of recycling and changing light bulbs.

Where did all this begin? Why are some people more engaged with their environment than others? Both Vanessa and Les have parents who grew up in the war years and who drummed a sense of thrift into their children. "If you leave the room, turn the light off..." after a childhood of being ticked off, most people have learned that such small things matter— turning taps off when brushing teeth, not running a deep bath. The challenge for hotel owners is to create a coherent policy out of instinctive responses; Strattons' staff do not leave the coffee machine on all day.

Another challenge, of course, is to run the hotel with fun and originality, rather than an

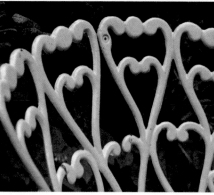

overbearing sense of ecological correctness. Being "chic" is harder, but for Les and Vanessa, who met at art college, a stylish mix of old and new comes naturally. There's a touch of panache in every corner and the rooms are constantly reinventing themselves. A creative zest is at work here. The Venetian Room—perfect for honeymooners—has a high old Italian-style bed, zebra-print rugs and silver globe lights.

The bathroom is tiled in black slate, the mirror is ornate and engraved. The view is more pastoral than exotic, over the secluded and peaceful garden, with its roaming bantams and recycled metal sculptures, tables and benches. The Seagull Room creates yet another mood, all sea and sand colors, with slatted wooden blinds and a faux-fur bedspread. The Opium Suite is in a separate building across the lawn with a big double bath at the foot of the bed so that you can fall, blissfully, from one into the other. All rooms have wind-up radios, all have a book full of cycle routes and walks, and there's a 10% discount for those arriving by bus or train.

The Brecks is the name for this inland region that straddles South Norfolk and North Suffolk, its distinctive landscape created by the last Ice Age. The light sandy soil made cultivation easy ("breck" means "land for temporary cultivation"), and encouraged early settlement. Sheep in the medieval period were most prized for their manure, used to enrich the soil; later they were run on the open heathland and great wealth was generated for the wool industry.

A hundred years ago this was a depressed area; rabbits abounded and 83,000 had to be killed before the Forestry Commission could replant just 6,000 acres in the 1920s. The planting continued, and the Brecks were transformed by forests—rather than rabbits. It is a richly interesting area and the Scotts are determined that their guests get to know it rather than rush headlong towards the Norfolk coast. There are heaths, farmland and forests, and those mysterious little "meres" which fill and empty without known cause. Swaffham is an interesting Regency town. County families would go there for the season and so too would the clergy.

Strattons itself is an interesting building. It probably began as a malting barn then became a villa in the 18th century, with a couple of added wings. Perhaps it was a sort of Palladian weekend retreat for a Norwich family; many such villas were built around Norwich and London. The Scotts bought it in 1990 and had to rip out the nylon carpets and woodchip wallpaper. "It was like a beautiful old lady over whose face someone had smeared too much lipstick." They had always loved doing up old houses and one day, after a dinner party in their last house, someone frivolously suggested that they charge people for coming. So they looked for somewhere larger to do just that.

Vanessa grew up in a large household with hordes of visiting friends and two grandmothers who were good cooks, always baking and making country food. "I was always welcome to bring friends home and was never fazed by putting meals together." Here, in the candlelit restaurant, the food is mostly local, all organic—nettle and barley broth, slow-cooked leg of Papworth lamb, rhubarb and ginger crème brûlée. Les talks you through the cheeseboard with panache, and breakfast (toasted stilton, goat's cheese omelette) is scrumptious and original.

Strattons is about as Slow as can be, combining good practice with a profound understanding of the philosophy of slow living. They love supporting other local businesses; to do anything else would feel alien. They enjoy encouraging local artists too, as such people often are as useless at promoting themselves as they are brilliant at their art. "We have to put money back into the community to keep it alive." Soon they will take their enthusiasms into doing up the old print workshop down the drive—to be as inspiringly green as all the rest.

Vanessa & Les Scott
Strattons, 4 Ash Close, Swaffham, PE37 7NH
- 10 rooms. £150-£175. Singles from £120. Suites from £200.
- Dinner, 4 courses, £40.
- 01760 723845
- enquiries@strattonshotel.com
- www.strattonshotel.com

Bridge Cottage

NORTHAMPTONSHIRE

"I'm a mix of Marjorie Proops, Delia Smith and Florence Nightingale—agony aunt, cook, nurse. All three roles have come in handy in the last eighteen months. You get it all here."

Judy, involved with farming all her life, is now living with Rod in Bridge Cottage, a revived "cottage" on the edge of the village of Woodnewton. They fell first for the setting: for the beautiful views over open country, and the brook at the bottom of the garden. The cottage is not a stately home or even a farmhouse, but they have successfully turned a modern bungalow into a home full of light, sloping ceilings and unexpected character.

The platform and summer house down by the brook are a wonderful escape. You can sit there sipping a drink and taking in the wildlife: kingfishers, red kites, swans, herons, moorhens, and cattle grazing in the fields beyond. Red kites have been reintroduced into the local woods and are breeding well. They can often be seen gliding over the garden, whistling as they go and flaunting their two-meter wingspan. Judy will lend you the binoculars.

Judy cares beautifully for her visitors, and bubbles over with enthusiasm for doing B&B. But she bubbles over with frustration sometimes too—at

the plight of British farming and agriculture in general.

"The last ten years have battered agriculture. My son, and many of my friends' sons, aren't going into farming—there is so little future. Farmers are not appreciated and food is taken for granted. People shop in supermarkets with no thought about where their food comes from.

"Food should not be complicated. Good, English, honest food is not difficult to produce, not difficult to supply. But the paperwork is something else. Farmers are being driven out of business because of bureaucracy.

"People who would prefer to spend their time producing good food and managing their farms are spending days and days filling out forms and trying to keep politics at bay.

"The dairy farmer is getting about 16p per liter of milk. Supermarkets are selling it for about 90p. Who is getting the rest? Out of that 16p the farmer has to feed the animals and produce milk economically.

"I do feel passionately about how the government ignores British agriculture. In ten years' time they may look back and say they wish they had looked after the country-side more. Who cuts all the hedges, clears the dykes and

maintains the fields and woodlands? I feel the fabric will disappear and England will become a theme park."

Most of us live within our "comfort zone"—understandably. Judy takes us by the hand and opens our eyes.

"I was brought up on a farm in Lincolnshire, a tomboy, happiest on the farm. I rode horses. My bones are in the countryside! And, after twenty

> "In this world of instant access to everything, all most people want to do at the end of the day is to feel at peace"

years as a farmer's wife bringing up three children, I've learnt to appreciate the value and goodness of locally produced food.

"The less chemical intervention the better. I'm all for free-range hens, sheep and cattle that have eaten out at grass; I'm all for animals having a decent life. But sometimes, financially, it just doesn't stack up. I used to run a farm secretarial agency—every animal needs a passport and every field needs a form!

"Local producers are being told to take the fat out of everything; people want lean meat. But the fat gives it its flavor. So here we are buying all these weird and wonderful sausages—chorizo, garlic etc. They may have their place, but who wants to go to work on that?"

Judy's feelings about sourcing good local food are as strong as those about farming. There is a large farmers' market in Oundle once a month and a good farm shop at Bulwick run by Simon and Sarah Singlehurst of New Lodge Farm. She gets her bacon and sausages from the village butcher, J & R G Mould of Nassington. "We are very strong on farmers' markets here, and there are still family bakeries and butchers. I like to fish around for high-quality foods. I don't do evening meals as there are so many lovely pubs in the area—a good one in every village."

Her new career is no real surprise. She did hotel and catering at college and worked in hotels in her early twenties. She has since done catering for weddings.

"Catering is in my blood. Here I am, three kids and a lot of catering later... Rod helps out with breakfast if I ever go away. Local girls also help to clean—they're fantastic. Business people like the family atmosphere, to talk to a human

being who minds how they feel, to get a shirt ironed, to have old-fashioned sausages for breakfast."

On the Cambridgeshire and Northamptonshire borders, Bridge Cottage is surrounded by gentle countryside, soft stone villages, and good pubs. Most people are unaware of the delights of this area. Judy's own little stream is known as Willow Brook, flowing into the Nene. Lovely walks start from the door, through woods and across fields to Southwick, Bulwick, Apethorpe, Nassington. You can stroll to Fotheringay and see the remains of the castle where Mary Queen of Scots was held captive before her trial. There are maps to borrow, cycle paths to explore and, at Rutland Water, bikes to hire.

This area is sometimes known as "the Cotswolds of Middle England," four market towns forming the Golden Square: Oundle, Uppingham, Oakham and Stamford. Stamford is a magnificent town, a day's ride from London in the 18th century, well equipped with coaching houses, stabling and related trades. It was a prosperous town with many merchants and lawyers, still has fine medieval and Georgian buildings and was happily by-passed by Victorian industrialization. Stamford was designated England's first conservation area in 1967 and many people still live in the center because it is so lovely. Nearby is Burghley House, one of England's grandest surviving Elizabethan houses, home too to the famous Horse Trails, and Oakham, county town of Rutland, a fine market town with castle, market place, butter cross and stocks, and the famous old school.

Judy is born to B&B: a natural at meeting people and making them feel at home.

"They are glad to arrive but are usually stressed and it's very pleasurable to see them unwind. They arrive on Friday night and by Saturday they are sitting in the conservatory or by the stream. I don't make people leave on the dot of 10am, especially on a Sunday. They can sit and read the papers, have another cup of coffee. We're not a hotel, open all hours, but there is a balance to be had.

"In this world of mobile phones, instant access to everything, all most people want at the end of the day is to feel at peace. I hope that I can produce that in a fun way, and to the best of my ability."

Judy Colebrook
Bridge Cottage
Oundle Road, Woodnewton, Peterborough, PE8 5EG
- 3 rooms.
- From £70. Singles £38.
- 01780 470779
- enquiries@bridgecottage.net
- www.bridgecottage.net

[WARWICKSHIRE, OXFORDSHIRE & GLOUCESTERSHIRE]

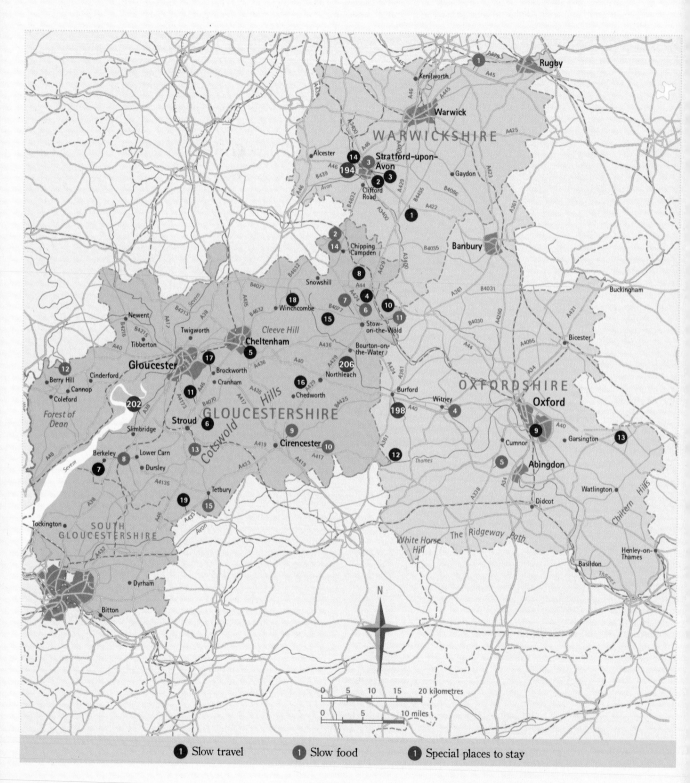

Slow travel   Slow food   Special places to stay

[WARWICKSHIRE, OXFORDSHIRE & GLOUCESTERSHIRE]

Slow travel

1. Compton Verney Gallery & House
2. Clifford Chambers Village
3. Avon Boating Company
4. Bourton House
5. Sandford Parks Lido
6. Slad village
7. Deer Park at Berkeley Castle
8. Kelmscott Manor
9. Oxford Colleges
10. Chastleton House
11. Painswick Rococo Garden
12. Oxfordshire Cycleway
13. The Swan
14. Montpelier Gallery
15. Cotswold Farm Park
16. Chedworth Roman Villa
17. Coopers Hill Cheese Rolling
18. Gloucestershire & Warwickshire Railway
19. Westonbirt Arboretum

Slow food

1. Ryton Organic Gardens
2. Mickleton Nurseries
3. Stratford Farmers Market
4. Witney Farmers' Market
5. Bothy Vineyard
6. Longborough Farm Pick Your Own
7. Donnington Brewery
8. Puddleditch Produce
9. Abbey Home Farm
10. Fairford Country Market
11. Daylesford Organic
12. Ragman's Farm
13. Hobbs House Bakery
14. Le Petit Croissant
15. The Chef's Table

Special places to stay

194. Cross o' th' Hill Farm
198. Burford House
202. Frampton Court
206. Clapton Manor

Slow travel

1 Compton Verney Gallery & House
Compton Verney (01926 645500)
Art galleries, tea room, top-notch
architecture (this is a Grade-I listed
Adam house)—a cornucopia of
treats saw this super house
nominated for a Godiva-sponsored
Award for Best Tourist Attraction.
www.comptonverney.org.uk

2 Clifford Chambers Village
Starting point: CV37 8HP,
Cross o' the Hill Farm.
Wander from Stratford outskirts
along the River Stour, through
Atherstone to this historic village,
said to be the real birthplace of
Shakespeare. Lutyens-moated
Manor House, peaceful picnic spot.
Church Cottage is home to the
Hosking Houses Trust, an arts
charity with a writer-in-residence.

3 Avon Boating Company
Stratford (01789 267073)
Hire rowing boats, pleasure punts,
canoes, even a Venetian gondola
and, if you're feeling nervous,
experienced watermen.
www.avon-boating.co.uk

4 Bourton House
Bourton-on-the-Hill (01386 700754)
A designer garden in a showpiece
village. Open regularly in summer
for delicious lunches and (now-

famous) afternoon teas. The garden
has won the HHA/Christies Garden
of the Year Award.
www.bourtonhouse.com

5 Sandford Parks Lido
Cheltenham (01242 524430)
A surprise in elegant Regency
Cheltenham is the newly restored
Lido. See the living archive
exhibition and join a tour to
understand the history of the pool.
Local triathlon athletes train here
and theater groups perform.
www.sandfordparkslido.org.uk

6 Slad village
Laurie Lee's memoirs of a Cotswold
childhood, *Cider with Rosie*, were
set in Slad, his home village, and
setting of the former clothmaking
center in a deep valley that has
enchanted many. Lee described the
valley setting... "greener and more
decently lush than is decent to the
general herbaceous smugness of
the English countryside".

7 Deer Park at Berkeley Castle
Berkeley (01453 810332)
Edward II was murdered here
and Elizabeth I played bowls. The
castle, lived in by the same family
for 900 years, rattles with gripping
history but head off to the nearby

Deer park for a sense of space,
views of the Severn and... hundreds
of deer.
www.berkeley-castle.com

8 Kelmscott Manor
Kelmscott (01367 252486)
A Grade-I listed Tudor farmhouse,
William Morris, the father of the
Arts & Crafts Movement, co-leased
this with Dante Rossetti as a
summer residence. He considered
the house a mark of true crafts-
manship, saying "it's as if it has
grown out of the soil." House,
garden, shop, restaurant.
www.kelmscottmanor.co.uk

9 Oxford Colleges
Oxford (01865 276150)
Oxford can be overwhelming for
those hoping to dip in for a brief
sightsee. Better to earmark just a
couple of destinations. Merton
College has a wonderful medieval
library, housing the first edition of
The Canterbury Tales and has the
oldest buildings of all the colleges
and a beautiful garden. Christ
Church Cathedral has been the
Cathedral of the city since 1546.
Choral evensong from 6:00pm,
Monday to Saturday during term
time. Music, art and drama events.
are also hosted here.
www.chch.ox.ac.uk

10 Chastleton House

Chastleton (01608 674355)
A Jacobean house that, until the early 1990s, was owned and lived in continuously for 400 years by one family. It's an *au naturel* National Trust house with things left largely untouched. Refreshingly, there are no ropes or barriers preventing closer inspection of the family's treasures.
www.nationaltrust.org.uk

11 Painswick Rococo Garden

Painswick (01452 813204)
A folly-dotted, flamboyant paean to English garden design. The unique 18th-century gardens feature winding woodland walks and charming contemporary buildings.
www.rococogarden.co.uk

12 Oxfordshire Cycleway

Chipping Norton (01608 642667)
Route 5 of the National Cycle Network runs from Birmingham through Woodstock to Oxford and ends in Banbury. Within is the Oxfordshire Cycleway. Easyriders organizes trips: "We don't go too far or too fast." If that sounds like your kind of riding, outings are on the third Sunday of the month, mostly from Chipping Norton Town Hall at 10:30am. Contact Jill Reynolds on number above.

13 The Swan

Tetsworth (01844 281777)
Room after room of antiques, collectibles, vintage clothing and things you don't need yet feel you must have. Voted the Best Antiques Center in the country—an award given for good reason.
www.theswan.co.uk

14 Montpelier Gallery

Stratford-upon-Avon (01789 261161)
Contemporary designers in silver/glass/ceramics and a good exhibition area.
www.montpeliergallery.com

15 Cotswold Farm Park

Guiting Power (01451 850307)
Soay sheep, bristly pigs with striped piglets and other medieval breeds at a special farmyard on Bemborough Farm. Lambing end March to early May, shearing end May to early July, milking from early May, farm safari rides all year.
www.cotswoldfarmpark.co.uk

16 Chedworth Roman Villa

Yanworth (01242 890256)
One of the largest Roman villa sites in Britain, discovered by a game-keeper in 1864, built beside its own spring. Elaborately mosaicked bath houses, on-site museum and picnics in wooded valley.
www.chedworthromanvilla.com

17 Coopers Hill Cheese Rolling

Brockworth
End of May ritual in celebration of the right of the people to graze their sheep on this extremely steep hill. Participation comes with a strict health warning! Not one for Health & Safety aficionados.
www.cheese-rolling.co.uk

18 Gloucestershire & Warwickshire Railway

Toddington (01242 621405)
Steam railway chuffs its way through north Cotswolds on a thirteen-mile (one hour) round trip most days in summer.
www.gwsr.com

19 Westonbirt Arboretum

Westonbirt (01666 880220)
Hide and seek paradise with umbrella-shaped maples and tall thick bamboos—there are over 16,000 varieties of tree. The pavilion-style visitor center and café are popular. Best to avoid autumn weekends. Trees are bathed in light for Christmas illuminations.
www.forestry.gov.uk/westonbirt

Slow food

1 Ryton Organic Gardens
Ryton-on-Dunsmore (02476 303517)
The Soil Association awarded Garden
Organic the "Best Organic Restaurant
in Britain" award. The big shop,
garden center and organic café are
open daily. The Organic Garden
covers ten acres and includes the
UK's first public biodynamic garden.
www.gardenorganic.org.uk

2 Mickleton Nurseries
Mickleton (01386 438690)
Excellent homemade cakes and
home-grown fruits to buy. Open
summer only.

3 Stratford Farmers Market
Stratford-upon-Avon
First and third Saturday of the
month. 9am-2pm.
www.warwickshirefarmersmarkets.co.uk

4 Witney Farmers' Market
On the third Wednesday of the
month in the Market Place.
www.witney.net

5 Bothy Vineyard
Frilford Heath (01865 390067)
Roger and Dorothea Fisher have
been making wine in the Vale of the
White Horse for thirty years; their
methods date back to medieval
times. Visit the vines and the vats
and take home your favorite.
www.bothy-vineyard.co.uk

6 Longborough Farm Pick Your Own
Moreton-in-Marsh (01451 830469)
All the season's fruits and a farm
shop stuffed with local produce.
Good cheeses, too.
www.longboroughfarmshop.com

7 Donnington Brewery
Stow-on-the-Wold (01451 830603)
Traditional beers brewed by this
family since 1865 at a 17th-century
mill. The only imported ingredient is
the small amount of sugar used and
the water is from their own spring.
www.familybrewers.co.uk

8 Puddleditch Produce
Berkeley Heath (01453 810816)
Winner of the "Taste of the West"
award for its cakes, jams, chutneys
and cheese, the Vale of Berkeley
farm is run by Lindsay and
Chris Morgan.
www.puddleditchfarm.co.uk

9 Abbey Home Farm
Cirencester (01285 640441)
Cattle, sheep, pigs, farm shop,
trails, organic groceries, babycare,
linen and skincare. There are
bushcraft courses, an eco-camp
and a café, too.
www.theorganicfarmshop.co.uk

10 Fairford Country Market
Fairford (01285 810616)
Country Markets are co-operatives
and individuals come to sell their
own home-made baked goods,
preserves, eggs and honey, garden
produce and crafts. Every
Wednesday 9am-11am.
www.fairford.org/CountryMarket

11 Daylesford Organic
Kingham (01608 731700)
Tea-tasting on certain weekends,
popular restaurant with
exceptionally good cakes.
www.daylesfordorganic.com

12 Ragman's Farm
Lydbrook (01594 860244)
A farm run on permaculture
principles. Courses are held on
sustainable land use, cider making,
perry tasting and willow structures.
Buy a mushroom log so you can
harvest your own crop.
www.ragmans.co.uk

13 Hobbs House Bakery
Nailsworth (01594 860244)
Stock up for the best picnic ever—
sandwiches made with some of the
finest bread you'll find anywhere
and Pieminister Pies. Much of what
is on sale is award-winning. Café
and generally a great buzz.
www.hobbshousebakery.co.uk

14 Le Petit Croissant
Chipping Campden (01789 292333)
Set up in 1994 by Janick Fievet, now
run by Andrew and Fiona Ryder. At
this exceptional bakers you'll find
everything you need for a picnic.
www.lepetitcroissant.com

15 The Chef's Table
Tetbury (01666 504466)
A café, bistro and deli where you can
find that elusive ingredient, buy the
finest fish and cheese and be inspired
by the vision of Michael Bedford,
formerly chef at the Michelin-starred
Trouble House Inn.
www.troublehouse.co.uk

Pubs & inns

The Case is Altered

Five Ways, Hatton, Warwickshire
No music, no food, no kids—but a vintage bar billiards machine fuelled by sixpences, pork scratchings and expertly-kept beer. The bar is so small you can't help but join in the chat. A treasure.
01926 484206

The Castle Inn

Edgehill, Banbury, Warwickshire
From the octagonal tower; views sweep to the Malvern Hills. Civil War maps on lounge bar walls, traditional English food and perfect pints of Old Hooky.
01295 670255
www.thecastle-edgehill.com

Bell Inn

Welford-on-Avon, Warwickshire
Off the black-and-white timbered high street, rich oak beams and settles, Persian rugs, stone floors, glowing fires—and suppliers listed on the back of every menu. 01789 750353
www.thebellwelford.co.uk

The Crooked Billet

Stoke Row Village, Oxfordshire
The rusticity of the pub charms all who manage to find it. Beams, inglenooks, books, baskets, mirrors, atmospheric candlelight and French/Italian food supremely well sourced. 01491 681048
www.thecrookedbillet.co.uk

The Five Horseshoes

Maidensgrove, Oxfordshire
Arrive early for the best seat in the garden and the finest view in Oxfordshire. Wood-burner and cushioned settles in the bar, and good home cooking.
01491 641282
www.thefivehorseshoes.co.uk

Olde Reindeer Inn

Banbury, Oxfordshire
Magnificent panelling in the pub where Oliver Cromwell held court. Country wines rival the local Hook Norton ale and there's lovely steak and ale pie. Logs in the carved 17th-century fireplace in winter. 01295 264031

Five Mile House

Duntisbourne Abbots, Glos
Bare boards, two curving settles, newspapers and cribbage. Dive into the pick of the day's produce, relish the well-kept ales. Outside: serene views to the valley below. 01285 821432
www.fivemilehouse.co.uk

Ostrich Inn

Newland, Gloucestershire
In a pretty village, a genuine old pub with a great buzz, loved by beer drinkers and foodies alike. 1940s jazz, a walled garden —and bathrooms at the back guarded by Alfie, the pub pooch. 01594 833260
www.theostrichinn.com

The Boat Inn

Ashleworth Quay, Gloucestershire
An ale lover's paradise on the banks of the Severn that has been in the family for about 400 years. Settle back with a pint of Beowulf in the gleaming front parlor— or Weston's cider and a freshly filled roll.
01452 700272 www.boat-inn.co.uk

Cross o' th' Hill Farm

WARWICKSHIRE

You can see Stratford's Holy Trinity Church, where Shakespeare lies buried, framed by an avenue of chestnut trees across the fields. (The Roundheads camped on these fields, when the Black Death occupied the town.) In just twelve minutes you can walk into town, over the river and to the theater along gentle paths.

There is an unhurried feel to Cross o' th' Hill. Theater lovers stay here, both from this country and abroad—"they are surprised and delighted that they can do all the parking and pre-theater stuff here, then take a stress-free stroll into town."

But there are many reasons to come; Shakespeare can't take all the limelight. Decima's art, for example, is on the walls. Her father was good at drawing and at the age of two she wanted to be a famous artist. She made it to the art college in Liverpool but then "events" took over, as they often do. Cyril Connolly said there is no more somber enemy of good art than a pram in the hall, so she has done well to keep painting after raising two sons.

Half of art, apparently, is knowing when to stop, but drawing and painting is in her blood: "I've always got it going on in my head." A deep fascination with, and enjoyment of, people is also her birthright. Her mother did B&B when the

family moved to Warwickshire long ago, and Decima would help look after guests. Actor Sam Wanamaker, who was the driving force behind the creation of the Globe Theatre in London, used to stay all summer, with daughter Zoe—now a star herself and the Quidditch in the Harry Potter films. She also comes from a long line of Welsh farmers who would do B&B to make ends meet; they'd look across the mountain for cyclists from Birmingham, then lure them in with the smell of bilberry jam. At the time they earned 1 shilling 9 pence a night—and twice that amount for selling a sheep. Little has changed. Farmers still earn a pittance from their sheep.

The house has 150 acres of pastureland and is approached via a splendid avenue of chestnut trees. The farm dates back to the 15th century but was rebuilt, solidly and with fine architectural detail, in 1860. The rear is older, and gets smaller the further one retreats to the back.

Decima's father bought the farm in 1959, moving from Wales ("unusual for a Welshman; he was ambitious!"). Decima and David moved into the stables first and took over when her parents retired.

The farm would originally have been pretty self-sufficient, with greenhouses, soft fruit orchards, vegetable gardens and

hop meadows. Now they grow their own zucchini, arugula and tomatoes, apricots, peaches, raspberries, red gooseberries (the most delicious), apples, pears, plums, greengages, walnuts, hazelnuts and mint—the mint they put in iced water instead of much-traveled lemons.

They source their other food locally: milk and bacon delivered by the Broadway farmer who rears it;

> "In winter they hesitate to buy flowers for the air miles that come with them and decorate with ivy or clematis"

eggs from local houses in Chipping Campden; bread from a wonderful bakery. Visitors have praised their light English breakfasts and wonderful fruit smoothies: "leaving us feeling full and refreshed, not heavy or greasy."

In summer the house is filled with sweet peas and roses; in winter they hesitate to buy flowers for the air miles that come with them and decorate with wreaths of ivy or clematis and small branches.

David says, "we have always been quietly green." Insulating the house has been the first priority and the place is now remarkably cozy. They recycle so effectively that there is spare space in their bins, even with guests.

"We have been trying to make a small difference for a very long time and I do have to fight not to despair when I notice that the local Tesco doesn't have a door even in winter."

Decima's grandparents were stoic farmers in Wales, with a powerful sense of thrift and utility. She remembers one granny rubbing dirty spoons with grit to clean them, and another laying out flour bags to catch the frost; this would whiten the sacking and remove the lettering so she could then use them for making clothes.

Both grandparents kept pigs to be slaughtered and eaten at home; Decima also remembers a granny churning butter with one hand and holding the Bible with the other. "More astonishingly, she absorbed

what she was reading, for she could quote huge swathes by heart."

The hill farms and lowlands of Wales seem to have been peopled by the family—whose names were, ineluctably, Lewis and Jones. Decima has grown up with a profound sense of the importance of good soil: "My father's farm had deep, rich topsoil and there is deep soil here too. I don't really like being around the edges, on clifftops or high mountains, where I know the soil isn't deep—it sounds odd but I must just feel that it wouldn't support animals or me."

David was new to farming, but he did contract vegetable growing after studying town planning and loves his immersion in the world of growing, and architecture. He was particularly struck by the food culture in the USA, where the norm is to have a vast plate of food and eat only half of it. *The Economist* once complained that it would take a shortage of packaging material to force us to eat fresh food. Perhaps we should long for the day.

Here, just outside Stratford, you are among people who care about such things. (They also are trying hard to avoid flying off on holidays.) Bring your own ideas to add to the mix. The mood is easy, convivial, unselfconsciously stylish. Rooms, by the way, are big and minimalist—refreshingly so. There are long comfy sofas, Art Deco chandeliers and a grand dining room.

The garden is visited by woodpeckers and pheasants; it is a treat to step out through the large sash windows onto the croquet lawn, glass of wine in hand, to sit on the veranda. Or take off for one of those theaters—there are three of them out there.

Decima & David Noble
Cross o' th' Hill Farm,
Broadway Road, Stratford upon Avon, CV37 8HP
- 3 rooms.
- £78–£80. Singles £59–£60.
- 01789 204738
- decimanoble@hotmail.com
- www.crossothhillfarm.com

Burford House

OXFORDSHIRE

The mellow stone houses of Burford tumble gently down the hill on both sides of the main street towards the medieval bridge over the Windrush. The handsome street is wide, with pavements made for strolling people rather than those bent on some urgent purpose. The spire of St James's Church, at the bottom of the street, can be seen from up and down the Windrush valley. It is a beautiful town, described by the old Shell guide, in its understated way, as "of great architectural merit."

There is an interesting story attached to the church. After the last battle of the Civil War, not far away in Stow-on-the-Wold, the Parliamentary troops were offered the choice of disbanding without pay—or fighting in Ireland. A thousand of them, calling themselves the Levellers, broke away and set off to see Cromwell, hoping to press him to stick to the principles he had declared at the opening of the war. The plan went awry and Cromwell cornered them in Burford, herded them into the church, lectured them and then executed three of the leaders by firing squad.

It was a galling end to what had started, to some extent, as a war against corrupt power. And galling, no doubt, for the vicar.

Agriculture accounts for less than 0.4% of the Cotswolds'

economy today yet Burford, like so many Cotswold towns, grew rich on the proceeds of wool. There's hardly a mean dwelling in the village, and countless houses of real dignity. One of the finest belonged to Roger Warner, a Quaker who dealt in antiques and supplied much of the furniture to Williamsburg in Virginia. To this day the town, indeed the region, is known for its antique shops and galleries.

It is also proud of its hotels and pubs, with good reason.

Burford House is something of an upstart in Burford terms, barely ten years old as a hotel. But it has fitted in well. Simon and Jane have brought along a keen professionalism, for both trained in Hotel and Catering and they have created a beautiful and unusual house, part hotel and part B&B.

"We fell in love with Burford House and Burford itself when we first walked through the door in 1996. We still love it." There are eight elegant bedrooms; colors are subtle, fabrics are of high quality, beams are of oak, windows are leaded and the house is made homey by a scattering of books, albums and treasures from foreign holidays, and kittens William and Violet who continue the tradition started by the celebrated, much-loved and much-missed Jumble. There is a bright garden room

with French windows leading onto a quiet patio garden, and a second sitting room with a log fire, deep armchairs and an honesty bar—from which homemade damson gin and cranberry and quince vodkas may be sipped from cut-glass tumblers.

The Slow Food movement has far more adherents than members. Simon and Jane are among them. "We had no idea that there was now a word, "slow," to describe what we are and what we have been striving for at Burford House for ten years. We sourced local food long before everyone started banging the drum about it, and we still buy from Castles, the butchers in Burford, where they have impeccable credentials in buying from the finest local farmers. Their stuff is not cheap but it is worth it."

"Our salmon and smoked salmon come from Coln Valley Smokery just down the road near Bibury and our bread, fruit, vegetables and milk are all from the Cotswolds. Our cakes and pastries are made here." Hand-written menus promise ravishing breakfasts and tempting lunches. Simon cooks and Jane bakes and they recommend the best places for dinner.

They also have a natural way of dealing with people, one at odds with the management styles of many modern hotels. "You are only as good as your staff. One of our greatest pleasures is watching the development of our staff and being rewarded with their loyalty. Most are born and bred within a few miles of Burford and our guests delight in seeing familiar faces when they return. Rachel, for example, began doing a few hours on the potwash; nine years on and she is our Assistant Manager. Rebecca, who used to run her own B&B, has been here four years, Jayne has been here for over five, and young Scott, who also started on the potwash, for nearly five. Even our part-time staff don't want to leave, unless they go to university and begin their own journeys."

In some ways the Hentys are quirky and old-fashioned but they strive also to keep the house up to date. "Partly against our natural instincts we have bought new flat-screen televisions with integral DVD players. We hope our choice of DVDs for the library reflects our own personalities: "Breakfast at Tiffanys," "Dr Zhivago," "Last Tango in Paris." We also have wireless internet access, but this is a decidedly un-slow thing to admit and we apologize!" The Hentys also succeed in striking the perfect balance between luxury (generous white towels) and sustainability (not laundering them daily but waiting until guests ask).

There are walking maps in the bookcase and two good bicycles to lend to guests. Simon says, "we would much prefer guests to go walking or cycling rather than watch television but we can only advise and encourage. Sometimes it takes only the gentlest persuasion. Often, once we show people the routes we've devised and the lovely pubs en route where they can stop for a good lunch, they're keen!"

Some wonderful walks criss-cross the Cotswolds and there's the Oxford Cycleway to explore. The little river Windrush can be followed for miles, and takes you past Swinbrook Church where Nancy Mitford and three of her sisters are buried. Whether on foot or on a bike, it is a pleasure to amble from one village to another in this calm English landscape. To Westwell, for example, with its delightful grouping of church, rectory, barns and manor around the village green. And Eastleach, divided into Eastleach Turville and Eastleach Martin, each with an exquisite medieval church. Treat yourself, too, to the "lost village" (lost to the plague) of Widford, with its tiny 12th-century church. Return to crumpets and tea.

The Cotswolds may be peopled by the rich, it may be too close to London to escape the weekend ravages of city dwellers, too easily reached from three motorways, but it remains largely unruffled, at least on the surface. Its beauties are widespread and indestructible, reaching deep down to the tiniest cottage and up to the grandest manor. Burford is the perfect example, and Burford House works devotedly to be itself—with decency and style.

Jane & Simon Henty

Burford House,
99 High Street, Burford, OX18 4QA
* 8 rooms.
* £125-£155. Singles from £85.
* 01993 823151
* stay@burfordhouse.co.uk
* www.burfordhouse.co.uk

Frampton Court

GLOUCESTERSHIRE

"The world's gone in a circle and has now caught up with us," says Rollo. "Suddenly, what we have always done has become the popular thing." Crunching up the curved drive to Rollo and Janie Clifford's family estate, you do sense the slipping away of any urge to go fast.

At Frampton the Slow ethos is well established. The Cliffords trace their ancestry to Norman times and the estate has stayed in the family for generations, a survivor of countless threats, disasters and general vicissitudes. Jane Clifford, better known from legend as "Fair Rosamond," mistress of King Henry II, was born here ten centuries ago.

The estate has many faces: the handsome façade of Frampton Court, the flamboyant yet elegant Orangery, the rambling, laid-back style of the manor house, where the family have planted themselves, and the impressive timber-framed Wool Barn, open for tour groups and hired out for functions. Rollo is proud that women have played an important part in keeping the estate alive; his indomitable mother, Henriette, first opened the doors of the Court to guests in the 1950s.

Up the stone steps of the Grade I-listed house— a magnificent mix of Baroque and Palladian styles, built between 1730 and 1733 by the fashionable young Richard Clutterbuck—you enter an imposing hall with a grand fireplace. The eye is immediately drawn to the impressive scale, then to delightful detail such as the signature mouse carved into the

solid "mouse man" fire seat, designed by Robert Thompson at the end of the 19th century.

It is Gillian the housekeeper who looks after you here in the B&B, aided on occasion by one of the Cliffords' daughters. Either way, this is an experience like no other—a family home lived in and loved yet full of nobility and history. You may sleep in a four-poster bed cocooned in soft white spreads and a backdrop of Jacobean hangings; watercolors of flowers are scattered exquisitely through the rooms. In these rather beautiful pictures lies a tale...

One day in the 1980s, Henriette was up in the attic and came across boxes and boxes of preserved watercolors, until then lying forgotten. There were 300 of them! In the 1800s, two generations of Clifford ladies had devoted themselves to capturing on paper the intricate markings and shapes of the flowers and rare plants that surrounded Frampton— and they had the most beautiful studio. Sisters Elizabeth, Charlotte, Catherine and Mary Anne, along with their aunts, settled themselves on the first floor of their delightful "garden house"—today's Orangery —overlooking a Dutch canal. Maybe they felt inspired by the Monet-esque flotillas of water lilies or the soft citrus scents drifting up from below. Whatever it was, they were prolific watercolorists. And if Henriette hadn't browsed there that day these treasures may not have been discovered.

It is an unexpected privilege, and delight, to be able to stay and cater for oneself in this sweet,

secluded Orangery. Restored in 2002, it is both showy
and subtle—pure Strawberry Hill Gothic. The two
octagonal towers guard gleaming windows of heavy
old glass carved up into wonderful hexagonal "spy-
holes." Up the center spirals a magnificent
cantilevered staircase. Orangery and Court combined
make an unusual and beautiful place for family
celebrations; imagine leaving the motorway behind to
wash up here. As one guest wrote, "I'm so less
grumpy than I was when I arrived a week ago!"

There is more history down the road, at Berkeley
Castle, in whose keep Edward II was prisoner before
his brutal death. Sumptuous furnishings, cannons
and armory, stepped gardens and grounds with deer
make this a fascinating place for all ages to visit.
Also close by is the Wildfowl & Wetlands Trust at
Slimbridge where you may hear hummingbirds
hum in their tropical house, and offer grain—bags
are provided—to waterfowl from all around the
world. (To the surprise of most people, there are
also six types of flamingo.) It is enchanting in
spring when cygnets, goslings and ducklings
abound, and thrilling in winter when the skies are
alive with migrating birds.

Back at Frampton, with bluebells, primroses, wild
garlic, the wild scents are the work of Janie Clifford.
Her skills are deep and effortlessly green. At the
Manor, the vegetable garden is easy to manage and
well tended. Asparagus beds sit alongside manure-
rich rhubarb and the sweetest peas you'll ever taste.
She puts this down to rare heritage varieties such as
Magnum Bonum. From an early age their daughters
were brought up to say, "there's nothing so good as
home-grown."

Ancient orchards bear testament to an estate
that has remained in safe hands. Janie makes perry,
as does her son Peter, from the old pear trees; it
gets stronger as the season progresses. Gradually
over the summer the greenhouse begins to heave
with the thirty or so varieties of tomatoes she's
trying out, with room—importantly—for a lemon
tree to provide an essential ingredient in a perfect
gin and tonic. Gloucester Old Spot pigs scrump for
fallen apples—legend suggests that they got their
splattering of spots from the falling fruit. Rollo's

chickens range as freely as they like and supply eggs for breakfast. Trees are another passion of the family and the timber from the 1,500-acre estate is recycled on site into new doors and windows, along with firewood for the community and the glorious fireplaces of Frampton. Sustainability, as so often in the countryside, is second nature here.

Rollo had a particularly clever idea back in the 1970s. He set up the Frampton Wildlife & Sporting Association to bring together all the many activities that co-exist on the estate—from sailing and shooting to angling, riding and bird watching. So what was once a happy, disparate band has grown into a community, and any disagreements are settled cheerfully over a pint.

One delightful outcome is the annual Frampton Country Fair, held at the beginning of September. Rollo rides in dressed in full military regalia while son Peter dispatches a few hundred pigeon pitta. Country traditions are very much alive, employing the estate's bounty without destroying the things that make it special. So you have lambs in spring, a sleepy backwater, a rich history and the family behind it all. As for the village: pushed to describe what makes it so special, Janie says simply, "It's a dead end." The road through Frampton indeed goes nowhere, apart from the river at one end and what was the canal at the other. It just slows down, then stops. With reputedly the longest village green in England, two pubs, a post office, a cricket team and a county fair, it needs nothing else. It is a joy to visit.

Rollo & Janie Clifford

Frampton Court,
Frampton-on-Severn, GL2 7EQ
- 3 rooms. £110. Singles £85 (weekdays only).
- Dinner £24.50.
- 01452 740267
- framptoncourt@framptoncourtestate.co.uk
- www.framptoncourtestate.co.uk

Clapton Manor

GLOUCESTERSHIRE

"I never heard anyone say that they wished they had spent more time in the office." James is one of those wise and rare souls who knew when to stop; he threw in his job in the city, went on a course and became a garden designer.

His passion for horticulture brings him dual pleasures of "doing" and teaching. He is fanatical about his own land and never happier than when he is designing outdoor spaces or engaged in small tasks such as harvesting his own basil, grown from seed in old recycled wooden wine cases, for his homemade pesto. He also organizes garden tours and lectures on the history of gardens for the National Association of Decorative and Fine Arts Societies.

James has now found his métier, a slow life doing what he loves. Karin is palpably settled, too, having turned her back years ago on office jobs in order to fling herself into being a mother, wife, gardener and cook.

They are happiest at home and if they need to escape they keep things simple and go to Scotland for their holidays and walk in the hills. For most people, life is neither a spectacle nor a feast; it is a predicament. Not, it seems, for either of these two.

The Boltons' first post-city house was the gardener's cottage of John Betjeman's old house. They had just had Frederic "and," says Karin, "life was jolly right from the start. But then Frederic got meningitis when he was twenty months old and went deaf overnight. That was hard to cope with. Soon I was

pregnant again and then discovered I was having twins—Thomas and Adam. Later, Dido was born."

They moved in April 1993 to Clapton Manor and decided upon B&B to help with the costs of running their growing family. It would be misleading to suggest that running a B&B is a stress-free way of life, but at least one is in control of one's own day and space.

The mere thought of managing four children under four and a half and cooking breakfasts and dinners for guests is still enough to make even the most robust among us feel faint, but Karin took on the whole lot with brio.

"It felt like an intelligent way of making our house work for us and I have honestly found that most people walk in with a smile and you immediately know that it will all be fine."

Someone once wrote that no human being can bear others still to be in bed when he is already up. Not so in the case of Karin; she is positively happy for you to be horizontal in exquisite comfort while she labors downstairs.

"When I am cracking on with it I love it and I get a buzz out of people coming down to breakfast and proclaiming that they have had the most comfortable night's sleep of their lives."

The rooms are rambling—an eclectic, artistic mix of styles, antiques, objects from around the world, sculptures, books, rugs, warm colors and views over the hills. One room has a superb "bookcase" door to a small but perfectly formed salmon-pink bathroom. Wellies, Barbour jackets, log fires, fresh laundry... and breakfast by a vast Tudor fireplace; it is a delight to stay here.

The house is in a beautiful setting, and within its own two-acre garden. They both worked hard at the landscaping and replanting and covered the front of the house with magnolias, roses, clematis and lilac. A recurring theme is "views;" James loves working with period house gardens. There are a walled garden and lawn, a boxed-hedge rose walk, a Moorish tower garden with a mini-fortress (for the kids), an orchard, a green garden, a walled garden and a wildflower meadow with hens. Hidden to one side of the house is their dog cemetery with some enchanting sculptures of Drogo, Thompson and Snowy (James is a huge TinTin fan).

The house has a front section built in the 16th and 17th centuries and has been added to ever since. There are a handsome Tudor entrance and a great hall, mullioned windows and massive walls two-feet thick. The Tudor arch fireplace in the family drawing room is on a huge scale, handsomely setting off the flagstoned floors and 17th-century beams.

It is easy to see how they were seduced by it and they were lucky to buy at a time when they could afford to. House prices in the Cotswolds are now so high that it is hard for those born and bred here to stay and buying local produce is not always easy.

"Surprisingly there are few local shops and suppliers. 'Local' can be a bit fairyland-ish around here with stylized places that become visitor centers—you can buy produce and eat in the restaurants but they are expensive. I do wish we had food markets like you get in France."

The Boltons' approach to Slow is typical of many people in this book who have changed their lives and learned that living slowly is their way. They are naturally frugal: rejecting plastic bags, throwing out almost nothing, recycling everything recyclable. They make jam, damson gin and elderflower champagne, that pesto from their own basil, bread from flour from Wantage Mill. Flowers are chosen from the garden, and cut foreign flowers from the florist are shunned; clothes come from charity shops. "For years," says

Karin, "my children thought that Sue Ryder was a brand name!"

Bourton on the Water is one of those Cotswold villages with an impossibly pretty center, the little river Windrush slipping through the village and under several bridges, the village green lined with Cotswold limestone houses built by wealthy wool merchants in the 17th century. The houses are as handsomely caparisoned as knights dressed for a tournament. Tourists flock into Bourton to see the bridges and the model village, making it, according to the Shell guide, "not a peaceful village in summer, though some find it invigorating."

Most Cotswold villages have escaped the worst ravages of the modern era, where communities are sacrificed on the altar of commercial opportunism. Supermarkets have bought and bullied their way in, but more discreetly than elsewhere and less often. The latest invasion of the rich may preserve the buildings but may, too, wrench the heart out of the area as small traders succumb to the lure of selling. Yet survivors are notable, such as the Keelings with their Whichford Pottery, now employing thirty craftspeople. And farmers such as the Youngs at Kite's Nest near Broadway; Richard Young runs a vigorous national campaign alerting us to the dangers of the overuse of antibiotics in farming.

If Slow Living is to thrive, it will need positive activists to stop the juggernaut of modern progress— though the Slow Food movement is already dynamic in its denunciation of the use of pesticides in farming.

James and Karin's lives represent part of the solution, simply denying space for doing things the wrong way and insisting on space for happiness.

Karin & James Bolton

Clapton Manor, Clapton-on-the-Hill,
Bourton-on-the-Water, GL54 2LG

- 2 rooms.
- From £90. Singles £80.
- 01451 810202
- bandb@claptonmanor.co.uk
- www.claptonmanor.co.uk

WORCESTERSHIRE, HEREFORDSHIRE & SHROPSHIRE

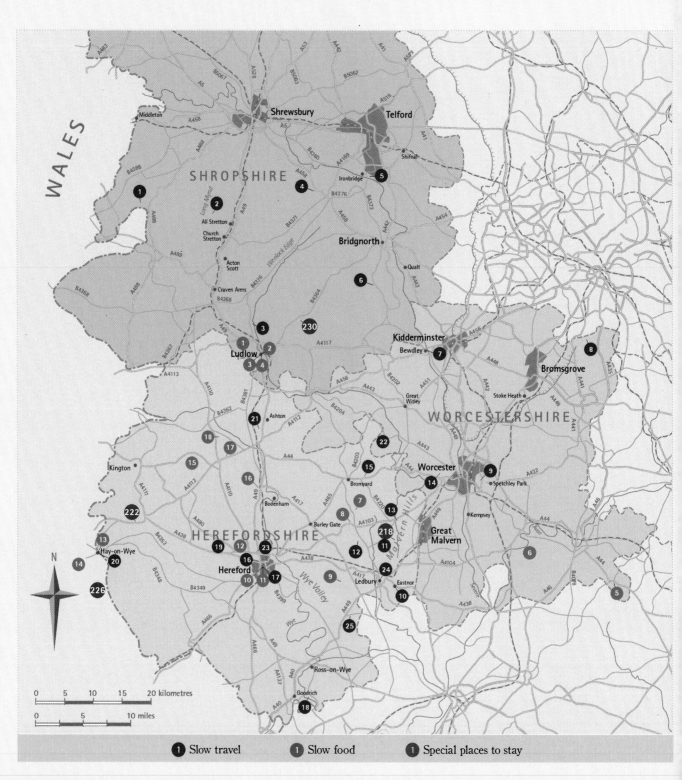

WALES

Middleton

Shrewsbury

Telford

SHROPSHIRE

Shifnal

Ironbridge 5

All Stretton

Church Stretton

Wenlock Edge

Acton Scott

Bridgnorth

Qualt

Craven Arms

6

230

Kidderminster

Bewdley 7

8

Bromsgrove

WORCESTERSHIRE

Ludlow

Ashton

21

Great Witley

Stoke Heath

18

17

22

15

15

Kington

16

Bromyard

Worcester 9

14

Spetchley Park

222

Bodenham

7

8

Burley Gate

13

Kempsey

Hay-on-Wye

19 12 23

218 11

Great Malvern

6

HEREFORDSHIRE

16

14

20

Hereford

10 11 17

Wye Valley

12

9

24

Ledbury

Eastnor

226

10

25

Wye

Ross-on-Wye

18

Goodrich

N

● Slow travel   ● Slow food   ● Special places to stay

[WORCESTERSHIRE, HEREFORDSHIRE & SHROPSHIRE]

Slow travel

1. Mitchell's Fold Stone Circle
2. Thresholds Centre
3. Moral Fibre Felt-making Mill
4. Wenlock Edge Walks
5. Blists Hill Victorian Town
6. Rays Farm Country Matters
7. The Severn Valley Railway
8. Forhill Picnic Site
9. Worcester Woods Country Park
10. Eastnor Castle
11. Beacon Hill Toposcope
12. Green Woodwork Courses
13. Blue Ginger Art Gallery
14. Elgar's Birthplace Museum
15. Brockhampton
16. The Courtyard
17. Mappa Mundi
18. River Wye Pursuits
19. The Weir
20. Hay on Wye to the Warren
21. Berrington Hall
22. Clifton-upon-Teme to Shelsley
23. Beer & Cider at the Races
24. Ledbury Cycle Route
25. Hellens

Slow food

1. Ludlow Food Centre
2. De Grey's
3. Deli on the Square
4. Wall Butchers
5. Tisanes Tearooms
6. Woollas Hall Farm
7. Frome Valley Wine
8. Bishops Frome Farmers' Market
9. Big Apple Events
10. Café @ All Saints Church
11. Mousetrap Cheese
12. Court Farm
13. Oscar's
14. River Café
15. Dunkerton Cider Company
16. Newton Court Cidery
17. Pleck Café & Farm Shop
18. Lawton Hall Herbs

Special places to stay

Slow travel

1 Mitchell's Fold Stone Circle
Chirbury (01939 232771)
Bronze Age stone circle in dramatic
moorland, once consisting of thirty
or more stones, now down to fifteen.
www.english-heritage.org.uk

2 Thresholds Centre
Picklescott (01694 751411)
Next to ancient drovers' road, a
fantastic array of art and crafts
workshops, writing courses, local
history and "horse tourism"
including overnight stabling.
www.thresholdscentre.co.uk

3 Moral Fibre Felt-making Mill
Stanton Lacy (01584 856654)
The only mill in the country dedicated
to the art of felt making, with new
wet felting machine in converted
barn. Make your own felt slippers!
www.moralfibre.uk.com

4 Wenlock Edge Walks
A. E. Housman was inspired by these
sixteen miles of limestone escarpment:
amazing panoramas, rare flowers and
remains of quarries and lime kilns.
Start from Much Wenlock.
www.walkingworld.com

5 Blists Hill Victorian Town
Madeley (01952 884391)
One of the largest open-air museums
in the UK, at Ironbridge Gorge. Spend
Victorian coins in the best sweet
shop ever, take a ride on the carousel.
www.ironbridge.org.uk

6 Rays Farm Country Matters
Billingsley (01299 841255)
Billingsley Farm animals and birds
(and owls and deer) in woodland
setting. Coffee, gift and craft shop
and fun wood carvings on a
sculpture trail.
www.raysfarm.com

7 The Severn Valley Railway
Bewdley Station (01299 403816)
Steam through sixteen miles of
gorgeous countryside and restored
stations from Bridgnorth to
Kidderminster. Keep the doors locked
as you cross the single span bridge
high above the river.
www.svr.co.uk.

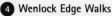

8 Forhill Picnic Site
(Countryside Service: 01562 710025)
On the North Worcestershire Path,
on the minor road Redditch to
Kings Norton, one mile west of
Wythall. Ancient hedges,
butterflies, wildflowers, woody
copses, hilltop views.

9 Worcester Woods Country Park
Worcester (01905 766493)
Acres of oak woodland, wildflower
meadows and two circular walks.
www.ramblers.org.uk

10 Eastnor Castle
Ledbury (01531 633160)
Built as a mock Welsh Borders
fortress by Earl Somers in 1812.
Come for a sumptuous gothic
drawing room, halls packed full of
armor, deer park, arboretum and
lake. Also home of the Big Chill
Festival in August, when the fields
fill with lovers of folk, jazz, dub,
club and world music.
www.eastnorcastle.com

11 Beacon Hill Toposcope
Lickey Hills Country Park
Originally built in 1923 and 298m
above sea level, it allows you views
on a clear day over seven counties.
www.malvern-hills.co.uk

12 Green Woodwork Courses
Bosbury (01531 640125)
Weekend to nine-day courses
with Gudrun Leitz, beginning with
cleaving wood from a freshly felled
tree through to making hedgerow
chairs and stools.
www.greenwoodwork.co.uk

**13 Blue Ginger Art Gallery &
Coffee Shop**
Stiffords Bridge, Malvern
(01886 880240)
Glass, ceramics and textiles in
the grounds of a 16th-century
farmhouse, plus food tastings,
fairtrade teas and coffees, lunches
and snacks.
www.blue-ginger.com

14 Elgar's Birthplace Museum
Lower Broadheath (01905 333 224)
Cottage and museum where manuscripts, music scores, letters, concert programs and photographs illustrate the musical life of the creator of "Land of Hope and Glory."
www.elgarmuseum.org

15 Brockhampton
Bringsty (01885 482077)
Enchanting medieval moated manor house, crooked gatehouse and ruined Norman chapel. Spot wooden sculptures on a walk through the parkland and woods.
www.nationaltrust.org.uk

16 The Courtyard
Hereford (0870 1122330)
Cool café bar for morning pastries, lunchtime drinks and tapas, evening suppers, at Herefordshire's Centre for the Arts. Theater, film, art, comedy, workshops and classes.
www.courtyard.org.uk

17 Mappa Mundi
Hereford Cathedral (01432 374200)
Housed in the magnificent cathedral. See how 13th-century cartographers perceived the world —the six-foot parchment includes a Norwegian on skis accompanied by a bear!
www.herefordcathedral.org

18 River Wye Pursuits
Ross on Wye (01600 891199)
Shoot the rapids, paddle the river. Hire a canoe or book in for a course: rappelling, climbing and caving too. Avoid the summer motor boats plying tourists up and down the river at Symonds Yat.
www.wye-pursuits.co.uk

19 The Weir
Swainshill (01981 590509)
Informal 1920s riverside garden with exquisite views towards the River Wye and the Black Mountains. Heaps of daffodils in spring.
www.nationaltrust.org.uk

20 Hay on Wye to the Warren
Walk down the river path by St Mary's Church to this beautiful beach for a barbecue and a swim— with or against the current. Watch the kayaks negotiate the rapids.
www.paddlesandpedals.co.uk

21 Berrington Hall
Near Leominster (01568 615721)
The austere 18th-century exterior hides an interior rich in treasures— plus dairy, laundry, butler's pantry and stables. Park landscaped by Capability Brown.
www.nationaltrust.org.uk

22 Clifton-upon-Teme to Shelsley
Easy two-and-a-half hour walk through the heart of England, from Clifton via Ham Bridge to Shelsey. Gorgeous views of the Malverns.
www.walkingworld.com

23 Beer & Cider at the Races
Hereford Racecourse
(01432 273560)
On a summer Sunday in late October, what better than to combine the thrill of the races with the best of Herefordshire cider.
www.hereford-racecourse.co.uk

24 Ledbury Cycle Route
Ledbury (01531 633433)
See, hear and sniff the countryside, and visit some of the county's cider producers on the twenty-mile Ledbury route. Cycle hire from Saddlebound.
www.saddleboundcycles.co.uk

25 Hellens
Much Marcle (01531 660504)
Gorgeous, privately owned manor house, open to visitors in summer. Outside you'll find a rare octagonal dovecote, a walled knot garden and an avenue of Hellens Early pears planted in 1710 to commemorate the coronation of Queen Anne.
www.hellensmanor.com

Slow food

1 Ludlow Food Centre
Bromfield (01584 856000)
Spanking new local-foods center and café confirms Ludlow's reputation as England's foodie capital.
www.ludlowfoodcentre.co.uk

2 De Grey's
Ludlow (01584 872764)
An army of waitresses in black uniforms and starched caps ferry florentines, tartlettes, eccles cakes, buns, iced fancies, cream puffs and moist sponges to well-dressed tables.
www.degreys.co.uk

3 Deli on the Square
Ludlow (01584 877353)
Over 140 varieties of cheeses, mustards, vinegars, hampers—and "Garden" cake steeped in prunes, figs, walnuts and damson gin.
www.delionthesquare.co.uk.

4 Wall Butchers
Ludlow (01588 672308)
Ham from rare-breed Middle Whites from Charlie and Simon's tiny shop—not to be confused with its larger sausage-making namesake.
www.wallsbutchers.co.uk

5 Tisanes Tearooms
Broadway (01386 853296)
Soups, sandwiches, curds, jellies, cakes and scones in showpiece Cotswolds town, plus thirty teas and infusions.
www.tisanes-tearooms.co.uk

6 Woollas Hall Farm
Eckington, Pershore (01386 750267)
Free-range fallow venison raised on Bredon Hill and sold at the estate.

7 Frome Valley Wine
Bishops Frome (01885 490768)
Taste the wines, tour the vineyards. They also sell Jo Hilditch's stylish crème de cassis, made with Herefordshire blackcurrants.
www.fromewine.co.uk

8 Bishops Frome Farmers' Market
Bishop's Frome (01531 640323)
The Hop Pocket, second Saturday and fourth Thursday of the month.

9 Big Apple Events
(01531 670544)
Events amongst the orchards in Putley (May for the blossom) and Much Marcle (October for the harvest).
www.bigapple.org.ukw

10 Café @ All Saints Church
Hereford (01432 370415)
Relying on a network of fantastic local producers the menu changes according to the seasons; apple juices (Katy, Greensleeves, Worcester Pearmain) come from Jus Apples.

11 Mousetrap Cheese
Hereford (01568 720307)
Quaint little cheese shop two steps from the cathedral. From Pleck Farm comes Little Hereford—like Wensleydale without the tartness.

12 Court Farm
Tillington (01432 760271)
Pick your own in a lovely setting May to end of October, then take tea. Farm animals, play area, maize maze, carp-stocked lakes, even mountain boarding (gear provided).
www.courtfarmleisure.co.uk

13 Oscar's
Hay on Wye (01497 821193)
Grab-a-table-if-you-can bistro in the center of England's secondhand bookshop capital. Coffees, teas, lovely fresh food, some vegan, much organic.

14 River Café
Glasbury Bridge (01497 847007)
Wholesome soups and packed lunches for a day on the Wye; kayaks and canoes alongside. Watch the river from the deck, or a sofa.
www.wyevalleycanoes.co.uk

15 Dunkerton Cider Company
Pembridge (01544 388653)
Pressed by a 1930s mill; rare apples include Foxwhelp (sharp), Kingston Black (bittersharp) and Court Royal (sweet). Perries, too.
www.dunkertons.co.uk

16 Newton Court Cidery
Newton (01432 260621)
Tom and Paul Stephens make organic cider from some of the oldest trees in the country and perry from pears including Dead Boy, Mumblehead and Merrylegs. Taste and buy.

17 Pleck Café & Farm Shop
Monkland (01568 720307)
Watch cheeses made by hand, then tuck into Herefordshire ploughman's and homemade cakes.
www.mousetrapcheese.co.uk

18 Lawton Hall Herbs
Eardisland (01568 709215)
Nursery of culinary, aromatic and medicinal herbs and wildflowers.
www.lawtonhall.co.uk

Pubs & inns

The Talbot

Knightwick, Worcestershire

It's run by two chef-owner sisters dedicated to self-sufficiency. Hops are grown right here and produce comes from the farmers' market they host on the second Sunday of every month. 01886 821235 www.the-talbot.co.uk

The Lough Pool Inn

Sellack, Ross-on-Wye, Herefordshire

A cozy fire, a glowing bar, head-ducking beams and a refreshingly unshowy dining room—solid tables, comfortable chairs— in which to enjoy daily-changing dishes. A relaxed and civilized place to be. 01989 730236 www.loughpoolinn.co.uk

The Pandy Inn

Dorstone, Herefordshire

Inside are heavy beams, well-worn flags, much smoke-stained stone, a vast oak lintel over the old fire grate and an intimate dining room beyond the red velvet curtain. Great garden for kids. 01981 550273 www.pandyinn.co.uk

Carpenter's Arms

Walterstone, Herefordshire

A marvelous chapel-side pub in the middle of nowhere, with great views to Hay Bluff. Vera has been serving up good home cooking and Breconshire Golden Valley from the corner hatch for twenty years. 01873 890353

The Wellington

Wellington, Hereford, Herefordshire

Banquettes around the fire and a chef who's a stickler for seasonality. Visiting celebrities like Franco Taruschio have left their mark. Be sure to book if you want to eat. 01432 830367 www.wellingtonpub.co.uk

Crown Country Inn

Munslow, Craven Arms, Shropshire

Locals gather for a chat and a pint of Cleric's Cure at dark polished tables in a winter-cozy, log-stoved bar. Chef Richard is passionate about local produce. 01584 841205 www.crowncountryinn.co.uk

Fighting Cocks

High Street, Stottesdon, Shropshire

On the lane to get here, you pass the farm that supplies the excellent meat. Sandra Jeffries wears multiple hats: jolly landlady, enthusiastic chef, manager of the great little shop next door. Unpretentious, genuine. 01746 718270

All Nations

Coalport Road, Madeley, Shropshire

Old photographs of Ironbridge strew the walls, secondhand paperbacks ask to be taken home (charity donations accepted) and dogs doze. It's a friendly ex-miners' ale house: catch it before it's gone. 01952 585747

Pheasant Inn

Linley Brook, Bridgnorth, Shropshire

Simon and Liz Reed run this single-handedly yet always find time to chat. There's no piped music and everything shines. Walkers and locals love it for a quiet pint and good food. 01746 762260 www.the-pheasant-inn.co.uk

Old Country Farm

WORCESTERSHIRE

A nightingale sings in distant woods, tawny owls duet and the night sky is liquid black, devoid of light pollution. Ella Quincy has a deep-rooted passion for the environment, and her years of commitment to Old Country Farm's eco-system have made her home and her land a haven for wildlife.

In the 1930s, her father learned about farming here. It was a primitive existence with no running water and no electricity. He loved it—as does Ella now. Her father adored trees, and bucked the trend of digging up orchards by replanting apple and pear trees in the 1940s, and keeping his hedgerows. In recent years, Ella's efforts on the 220-acre farm have been bolstered by help and advice from the Countryside Stewardship Scheme, and her "green" schemes keep growing.

Unexpected visitors have flown in. On trees, the threshing barn and even on the cider house wall, a variety of homes have been constructed: owls, tits and nuthatches have taken up residence near the house, and in the woods one hundred bat boxes have been nailed up and inhabited—sometimes by opportunist dormice.

From the gleaming gatehead table you spy swallows and spotted flycatchers, and a rogue squirrel stealing from the laden bird table. Afterwards, borrow a

pair of wellies, waiting by the door in many sizes, and walk out to meet the wildlife. Across the extensive lawns, your first encounter is likely to be with a family of ducks greeting you noisily from the pond.

In spring, the lawns take on a pre-Raphaelite air, delicately brushed with crocuses and cyclamens, aconites and snow-drops. Patches are then left to grow tall and wild with sorrel, cowslips and wild daffodils—and shorn for hay in the summer months. Goldcrests lurk in the juniper tree, robins in the weeping pear and tree creepers in the giant redwood.

Ducking through a natural arch, you find yourself in a secret world—a meditative garden with ferns and purple and white foxgloves. Just beyond are "Gog" and "Magog," two slumbering stone heads encircled by wild flowers. Styled on two Roman emperors, these heads were rejected from "The Broad"—the ceremonial heart of the Oxford colleges—and bought by a don who retired to Worcestershire, then procured at auction by Ella's father and hauled back on tractor and trailer to their final resting place.

Against the dusky pink, mineral-painted walls of the house is a place of pilgrimage for horticulturalists. Ella's mother, Helen Ballard, had a reputation

for breeding hellebores; here in the north border her original stock plants flourish—a hugely important collection. "Her intention was to get flowers that stood up and looked at you, with clear colors and big, bowl-shaped flowers," says Ella. "She started in the Sixties, knowing nothing about genetics, and taught herself."

Ella moved back to the 15th-century family home when her father died and her mother needed help, and stayed here with her two young children. The farm and family took up most of her time, but as the children flew the nest Ella decided to open up her remote and tranquil home to guests. "I thought B&B would be fun," she says.

But in many ways, Ella takes her B&B very seriously. She holds a hard-won Green Business award and relies on environmentally friendly products, from paraben-free shampoos to magnetic wash-balls. With careful research and planning, she's had a WET (wetland ecosystem) sewage system built—an impressive network of six ponds dug into the clay: these harbor millions of helpful microbes, create a pond teeming with wildlife, and prevent waste entering the water system.

Ella is an ardent believer in organic food and farming. She attended one of the first courses in organic farming in the country, grows her own vegetables and avidly supports her local suppliers. She reckons they need all the help they can get, and should "sell" themselves more. The county has so much to offer—her breakfast table is brimful of local juices, rustic breads, cheeses and Malvern organic sausages.

Two generous aunts left Ella some much-loved furniture and paintings, which make this a welcoming home. "There were lots of tables," she recalls. "All very useful now!" In one of the rustic, low-ceilinged bedrooms, her aunt's intricate patchwork quilt brightens the bed, while her battered old suitcase speaks of grand European tours.

Guests seem to unwind on arrival. One wrote: "my mother and I went to this very peaceful place in the summer. It was so relaxing—the countryside very beautiful, the bedrooms and bathrooms (one en suite) gorgeous, the visitors' kitchen and sitting room so well equipped, and the organic breakfasts great." You can stay all day, or walk to the top of the Malverns

from the door, and there are a couple of bikes and helmets to borrow.

Inheriting a little of the family free spirit, Ella has embarked on the first of many potential endeavors. "It's not all solemn and heavy—that's why I'm building a lighthouse in Herefordshire!" The Lighthouse is her stunning green oak build, set in traditional apple orchards with views to the Malvern Hills. "I wanted it to have abundant light, open space and a music room with Steinway piano and guitar."

The frame is sustainable oak, the roof lined with solar photovoltaic panels, the heating charged by a tiny, efficient boiler, and the outside walls clad in slow-grown larch.

Her hope is that musicians, artists and anyone looking for peace and inspiration will use it. Eventually, she may choose to live there herself. Ella's own love of music is deep-rooted. Having studied it at university, her passion is listening to live music and playing herself; she prefers that to having it simply as a background. Many evenings before dinner, a trio of merry ladies gathers in the drawing room for musical evenings; Elgar's great-niece plays violin.

Ella feels she has learnt a great deal through "coming home" and finding much-needed time and space. "Slow is about being in the moment, not worrying about external pressures. I try to listen to my intuition, to follow the path my spirit chooses for me. If I'd done everything rationally I wouldn't have achieved what I have so far." Ella also believes she's gathered endless support and wisdom from the many and varied people that come to stay. "There are many who stay who bring their own insights into what grows, organically, in this place. Some keep coming back."

Ella Grace Quincy

Old Country Farm,
Mathon, Malvern, WR13 5PS
- 3 rooms.
- £60-£90. Singles £35-£55.
- 01886 880867
- ella@oldcountryhouse.co.uk
- www.oldcountryhouse.co.uk

Winforton Court

HEREFORDSHIRE

There are Sheep's Nose and Cat's Head, created in the 1600s, and a hardy little Bullace too—a cross between a damson and a plum that is "great for jam," according to Jackie. Those first two apple varieties are just some of Jackie's recent planting in her walled fruit garden. She has put in pear trees, greengages, red dessert gooseberries, fig and even olive trees in pots, and, of course, Hereford strawberries. The whole area is rich in produce, a land truly of fruit and honey; Jackie is one of many growers who are bravely hanging on to old varieties and ways of growing.

"In Herefordshire the fruit trees stand with their lime-washed trunks in long grass. The air is drowsy with the pungency of summer fields; and over hedges the traveller sees men and women tossing up the yellow hay and tossing down the yellow beer and the pale gold cider. The pickers are busy in the fruit trees; in the lovely Wye Valley is a rich greenness of scenery that is unforgettably England."

H. V. Morton wrote these lines in the 1920s, soon after which 3,700 miles of hedgerows in Herefordshire were lost, in the name of agricultural efficiency. Now, of course, the government offers grants for hedge planting.

This magnificently timbered house was once the center of an 800-acre estate, with fields, orchards, vineyards and hop gardens spilling down to the river

Wye. Time and events nibbled at the edges of the estate, but it was still being farmed forty years ago. Jackie came here in 1995, to a somewhat bleak house and bare garden. Her previous cottage yielded the cuttings that she has used to restore this fine garden, and willing friends have given her the plants she has needed to create a series of beautiful garden rooms, in perfect keeping with the place.

Hereford is a naturally Slow county, part of that blessed duo (Herefordshire & Shropshire) that was declared by the Council for the Preservation of Rural England to be one of only two tranquil areas left in the country. The other was north Exmoor. Both are, among other things, largely free from light pollution and traffic noise; it is a sad reflection that the rest of the country has been condemned to both, with the surprising complicity of its inhabitants. (Witness the ease with which aircraft overfly even the smartest areas of London, over a largely uncomplaining public.) Herefordshire is far enough from motorways to be beyond reach of most of the pillagers and plunderers of our time.

When Jackie, husband Steve and family moved here from East Sussex, the villagers—who quaintly described them as "from away"—wondered: "Why have you moved so far?" Local people still tend to stay put rather than travel much, and have time for each other. But their history is less kind: Romans, Saxons and Normans fought here against the Welsh, as did several English kings trying to subdue them.

(Welsh simply means "foreign" to the Saxon intruders.) Hereford itself was once the capital of the Saxon kingdom of West Mercia. One of their kings, Offa, built the famous 240-kilometer dyke to denote the boundary with Wales and to help keep them out.

Winforton Court, too, has been a little bruised by events, which is what gives it much of its dignity. Mentioned in the Domesday Book, the original longhouse fell victim to sieges and uprisings in the 1400s, before being rebuilt in the 1500s. It was Crown property in the reign of Henry VIII. The village had no courtroom at the time and the local assize courts were held there. Each room has its story. The room where visitors have breakfast, for example, was the courtroom where the dreadful Judge Jeffreys condemned many a man to be hanged after the Duke of Monmouth's Rebellion. Exquisite, almost 500-year-old painting has been uncovered on some of the walls, and on beams too. There are carpenters' marks carved into the heavy beams of the Long Gallery, as was the custom, and scorch marks made by wayward rush lights or candles hundreds of years ago fleck the dense old oak in the handsome four-poster bedroom. The bed itself was made in Tudor style from reclaimed wood, a minor triumph by local craftsmen.

The great and weighty front door may have come from Eardisley Castle, which once stood nearby. Its little wicket door is still held by ancient butterfly hinges. Every year the summer visitors swoop in from far away places, swallows and house martins nesting at the front and swifts at the back. Five summers ago a pair of swallows chose to live in an old wicker basket in the porch, and added a mud extension. Four eggs hatched and the porch light was left off for them all summer.

Soon after moving in Jackie found what looked like a small gravestone under the old horse-chestnut tree. Thoughts of the infamous hanging judge crossed her mind, but it turned out to be one of a row of twelve standing stones marking the way for drovers; it supposedly sits on a ley line. It is a special treat to stay in a house so drenched in history, and to stretch your imagination back through the centuries. People return, for fishing, family reunions, winter escapes and the Hay Festival, now one of the main literary

events of an English early summer. They are allowed to make the house their own with Jackie "there when needed," comforted and charmed by hearty breakfasts, sherry in the rooms, a deep claw-footed bath, a roaring fire in the drawing room.

Jackie's breakfasts are as far from the packaged-jam-and-butter norm as you can get. She gathers blue and brown "painted" eggs from her neighbors, honey from a man in Winforton who has kept bees for thirty years, and most of what she doesn't grow herself she finds in Mary's farmshop-caravan up the road. "Mary always has a smile and we catch up on local news. I never go in quickly because it is enjoyable to shop there."

Architecturally Herefordshire is a beautiful county; the Black & White Village Trail is a clockwise meander through the finest "black and white" villages of its northwest corner. Most of these houses date from the 16th and 17th centuries and all are limewashed and timber framed, though the decoration is a surprisingly recent one. Now the fashion is changing again, as fashions do: some houses are revealing the natural color of the weathered wood, while the panels are limewashed not white but in soft earth tones.

The Sun Inn is three minutes' walk away and serves local food of the best kind, as well as Owd Bull from the local brewery. And there are walks from the door: twenty minutes down the bridle path and you're by the river Wye. "Driving back along the old toll road from Hay I have seen red kites. How many people can say the same thing? And the stars are bright in Winforton. It only has one lamp post." Jackie has found her slow haven.

Jackie Kingdon

Winforton Court,
Winforton, HR3 6EA

- 3 rooms.
- £75–£95. Singles from £60.
- 01544 328498
- www.winfortoncourt.co.uk

Ty-mynydd

HEREFORDSHIRE

Up in the hills, on the borders of Wales, there are people restoring the old stone walls and putting heart back into the countryside.

John is one of them. He took to building walls and damning streams with stones when he was just eight; his brother, a carpenter, gave him twenty yards of stonewall to build when he was fourteen. That was it; he left school to build dry stone walls. The walling soon led him to farms that needed him, then to buying and doing up houses and selling them on, then, finally, to this: "I had a hankering to run my own farm." He lived on his own up here, busy, active, outdoors in all weathers, content... but alone. So he sent his photograph in to Country Living magazine's The Farmer Wants a Wife campaign. About seventy candidates replied; Niki's letter, declaring that she would be quite happy sitting in front of a fire with a glass of wine ("mind you, we've never done it!") won him over.

They have taken with passion to this remote mountainside place, strewn with grazing sheep and raw, green views. Up here, you feel you are on top of the world. These are the Black Hills, brought to us by Bruce Chatwin in his novel *On the Black Hill*—a bleak tale of two brothers on an isolated farm. The Victorian vicar, Francis Kilvert, whose diaries have become worldwide classics, also walked these hills and coaxed them into the affections of millions. But they remain largely empty, a demanding yet beautiful corner of Britain where England and Wales meet in gentle amity.

Niki wrote a letter to us about this book; it says more about their lives than we could.

"Our lives, along with our organic farm and B&B here in the Black Mountains, run along "slow" principles. Our animals graze freely (cows, sheep and Oxford Sandy and Black pigs) over acres of ancient organic pastureland, with hardly any human intervention. They live and grow at their own natural pace, calving and lambing where they choose. Being organic, they are fed no artificial foodstuffs at all. When the time comes to slaughter, the animals undergo a thirty-minute drive (minimum stress) to a local abattoir/butchers.

"Our meat is then hung and matured for a month and believe me, it is worth the wait. Our eggs are supplied by my chickens, so B&B guests, at breakfast, get to sample produce born and raised on the fields they view from their window."

The farm is a joint effort between Niki and John. Stonemasonry is still his first trade, and he is sympathetically restoring an old 17th-century farmhouse in the historic Llanthony valley nearby. John's dry stone walling can be seen around the farm; keen to pass on the craft, he is considering running weekend courses sometime in the future.

"People come mainly from London and Bristol to chill out and get back in touch with the rhythms of nature and it is so lovely to get feedback from our guests, especially the ones with young children who have run wild, safe and free. Last summer John took

two guests' boys out on a sheep-rounding exercise
and showed them how to work the dogs, Floss, Susie
and Bracken. Their parents are eager to come back

> "The vegetable patch up the
> hill is bursting with wholesome
> stuff and very often gets
> invaded by fat hens"

again this year. That tells us that we are successfully
sharing our way of life with others; what more do you
really need? Good fresh local food, healthy clean
mountain air and lots of space."

Add unspoiled views and stunning sunsets and
you have the perfect life.

These 130 acres of unspoiled pasture and woods
with the Blaendigeddi brook running through are
free for guests to explore. Follow the bridleway, once
an old road, through the land and down the valley
into the village of Llanigon, and, if you are feeling fit,
on to Hay on Wye. In Hay (six miles as the crow flies)
are pubs, restaurants, cafés and secondhand
bookshops by the score. And in May and June Hay
hosts the celebrated Festival of Literature & Arts,
described by Bill Clinton, memorably, as "the
Woodstock of the mind."

It was Niki who wanted to do it all organically, in
spite of organic farming being a relatively unusual
concept at the time. Breakfasts here are delicious and
the only item that has to travel to the table is the
milk; bread is homemade, by hand not machine. The
water is from their own spring and tastes as only
spring water can. The vegetable patch up the hill is
bursting with wholesome stuff and very often gets
invaded by fat hens—not so much free range as all
over the place.

She and John are also undergoing an agro-
environmental scheme (Tir Gofal) which enables
them to rejuvenate old hedgerows and fence off an
ancient bluebell wood from the grazing animals,
something that hasn't been done for nearly a
century. Now beautiful carpets of bluebells appear
every spring.

"People are fascinated by our lifestyle, and sit and stare out of the window at breakfast time—not talking, just winding down and taking it all in." At night, Niki lights candles in the windows and by the door so you can find your way in; but linger a while to watch the bats. You'll sleep well—the only sound is sheep—in two sweetly restful bedrooms on the ground floor, with proper eiderdowns, shared country bathroom and green views.

It is not always easy, especially in winter, and there's no extra money for holidays. But they feel that the faster the world gets, the slower they want to go; it is so much more enriching and fulfilling. And it is a life only dreamed about when as a lass from the industrial North East, armed with an English degree and all her belongings crammed into a Nissan Micra, Niki turned up at this Welsh mountain farm on a freezing March day.

That is the sort of energy and enthusiasm that changes lives—and places. At the end of the long, bumpy track, the once-dull bungalow, cheaply built and with aluminum windows and hardboard doors, has been transformed by John's vision. When he first came here, there was little birdsong. Now the farm is filled with it, house martins swooping over the fields and into the nests under the eaves. The collies are real characters, including the unstoppable Floss with only three legs. The children, Daniel, five, and Madeline, three, are sweet natured and at home in the winter mud and muck.

Altogether, the family and their farm are enough to persuade the most hardened urbanites out of their rural "denial." John and Niki are the architects of their own lives; it may be hard work but they avoid much that overwhelms the rest of us.

Niki Spenceley

Ty-mynydd,
Llanigon, Hay-on-Wye, HR3 5RJ
* 2 doubles.
* From £70. Singles £50.
* 01497 821593
* nikibarber@tiscali.co.uk
* www.tymynydd.co.uk

Timberstone Bed & Breakfast

SHROPSHIRE

Alex and Tracey met in the wine trade and then fell for a pair of derelict cottages. He had been a carpenter and water sports enthusiast; she had worked with a Michelin chef, Shaun Hill of the Merchant House in Ludlow. She was also a passionate traveler and had taught and worked with charities in Ghana and Belize. At Timberstone they have woven their enthusiasms together, during gaps between travels, into a whole that embraces everyone, somehow providing space for other people to be themselves.

"When we bought the house at auction, we felt as though we had signed up to live in the middle of nowhere. Ludlow wasn't famous then," says Tracey, "and it certainly hadn't achieved gastronomic or Slow status. Now we find ourselves just five miles away from the mecca for fresh food and passionate retailers. Best of all, there are no McDonalds or shopping malls."

Ludlow is now recognized as the Slow Food capital of the UK, it has also achieved Slow City and Fairtrade status. The town with over 500 listed buildings hosts a famous annual food extravaganza, supports scores of artisan producers, superb butchers, enlightened retailers and a monthly farmers' market.

Tracey and Alex grow their own fruit and have chickens

and whatever else they need they get from local suppliers. Jams and bread are homemade, and food integrity can be measured in egg-meters rather than food miles. The wine list is interesting—as you'd expect—the gin with your tonic is organic and Tracey's food is likely to be delicious; they will start serving dinner once the new dining room is ready. Chicken-liver parfait to start with, local lamb roasted with buttery asparagus, and blackberry and apple crumble to finish. Or perhaps Stinking Bishop cheese and homemade ice cream.

They are brilliant hosts, for whom nothing is too much trouble. The interest in doing things well reaches into other corners of their lives. There is heat and hot water from a sustainable source, wood-burners too, a compost heap, energy-efficient light bulbs and other ecological devices. "You have to put your money where your mouth is," says Tracey. Stacked outside are logs for the fire: hawthorn and other wood taken from the hedgerows. Alex enjoys his foraging and chopping the way other men enjoy their computers—probably more. The inside of the house is as lovely as the outside, with touches of carefully considered luxury in curtains and quilts. There is a

large family room upstairs in the top of one of the old cottages, a handsome bathroom with a huge tub and a walk-in shower lined with Welsh slate. Children revel in the coziness of the separate bedroom in the eaves. At the other end of the house is a fine double room. And there are numerous touches that might bring a smile to your face: charming old country pieces, books tucked into unexpected places, handles and catches devised by craftsmen, an Indian kilim on aged oak boards, a straw hat on a whitewashed wall.

Tracey's Chicken Liver Pâté

Serve with toasted bread, a few mixed leaves and some tomato chili jam or red onion marmalade.

500g (1lb) fresh chicken livers
1 large spanish onion, roughly chopped
250g (8oz) butter
1 clove of garlic, chopped
1-2 rashers rindless bacon, chopped
1 bay leaf and some mixed herbs
Glug of red wine, slug of port, dash of brandy

• Cut out any tough bits in the chicken livers, wash and pat dry
• Gently fry onion in a little of the butter then add garlic and bacon and stir
• Add livers and bay leaf and fry until livers are pink.
• Add herbs, red wine, port and brandy and cook, stirring, for a further 3-4 minutes
• Remove from heat, add half the butter and allow it to melt, then cool slightly and blitz in a food processor
• Pour into one shallow dish or ramekins. Place in fridge to set. Once cool, melt remaining butter and pour a little over each of the dishes to make airtight

Wending your way down the wooden walkway to the bottom of the garden you come across the retreat—part Balinese, part English seaside hut and built around the four hop poles that Alex secured into the ground in an act of random but symbolic determination. The retreat has no TV, just a big bed, a tiny kitchen and a bathroom. It is the family's favorite place, for there you can catch the morning sun on

one side and the evening sun on another. Pour your wine, light the little barbeque and watch the sun go down. For them it is their "going away" place.

Tracey's suggestions for the slow life are simple... Choose to see the glass half-full, plant something you can harvest, take a country walk, do a good deed every day, think of five things that make you smile, take a few deep breaths and exhale slowly, take the time to cook a proper meal, sit down at the table to eat as a family, switch off the TV, drink good wine, put on some music and dance!

At the far end of the garden is a little pavilion, where Tracey—now a trained Bowen Technique therapist and reflexologist—can minister unto her visitors. (The Bowen technique involves light moving of hands over muscles, devised to aid men in Australia returning home with war injuries.) There is also an infrared sauna, whose health benefits include detoxification and weight loss.

Jack and Alfie, the two little boys, bring the place to extra life. They have a play area with sandpit and evolving treehouse, and boundless enthusiasm. What is even more special is that they readily sweep visiting children into their circle of friendship.

Hotels and B&Bs are not always free and easy with their wellies, bikes and binoculars. Tracey and Alex are, and, though you may relax in the garden with a good book, there is more to do in this area than an army of visitors could absorb—castles, gardens, hill walks, the races and Ironbridge Gorge.

In the shadow of Clee Hill, you can take off straight from the door in almost any direction on foot, up hedge-rowed lanes fringed with cow parsley.

"This is the life style we have chosen. We wouldn't be welcoming people into our home if we didn't love it." That is Tracey talking, but they both feel it.

Tracey Baylis

Timberstone B&B,
Clee Stanton, Ludlow, SY8 3EL
• 3 rooms. £60-£80. Singles £30-£40.
• Dinner, 3 courses, £22; 4 courses, £26. Licensed.
• 01584 823519
• enquiry@timberstoneludlow.co.uk
• www.timberstoneludlow.co.uk

[YORKSHIRE, CUMBRIA & NORTHUMBERLAND]

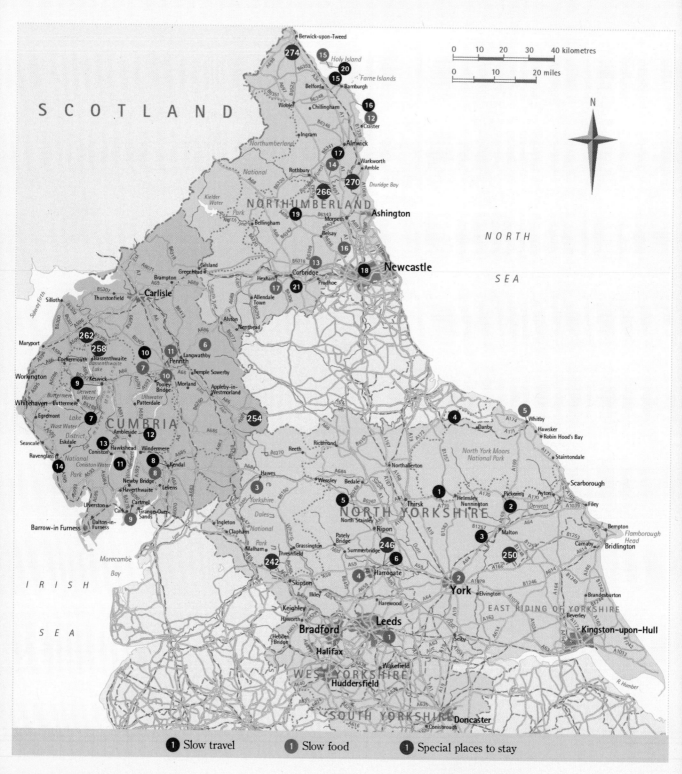

SCOTLAND

Berwick-upon-Tweed

274

15 Holy Island
20
15 Farne Islands

Belford
Bamburgh

Wooler
Chillingham
16
12
Craster

NORTH

SEA

Ingram
Northumberland
Alnwick
17
14
Warkworth
Amble

National
Rothbury
270
Druridge Bay

Kielder
Water
Park
NORTHUMBERLAND
266
Ashington

19
Morpeth
Belsay

Bellingham
16

Gilsland
13
Greenhead
Corbridge
18
Newcastle

Brampton
Hexham
17
21
Prudhoe

Carlisle
Thurstonfield
Allendale
Town

Alston
Nenthead

Maryport
262
258
Langwathby
6

Cockermouth
10
11
Penrith

Workington
Keswick
7
Temple Sowerby

Whitehaven
Buttermere
9
Morland
Appleby-in-
Westmorland

CUMBRIA
Pooley
Bridge
Patterdale

Egremont
7
Lake

Seascale
Ambleside
12
District
254

Eskdale
13
Windermere
Reeth
Richmond

Ravenglass
14
Coniston
Hawkshead
11
Kendal
Northallerton

National
Coniston Water
8
Wensley
Bedale

Park
Newby Bridge
8
Levens

Ulverston
Haverthwaite
Cartmel
Hawes
3
Yorkshire

Barrow-in Furness
Dalton-in-
Furness
9
Grange-Over-
Sands
Dales

4
Danby
Whitby
5

North York Moors
National Park
Hawsker
Robin Hood's Bay
Staintondale

Helmsley
Nunnington
Pickering
2
Ayton
Scarborough
Filey

1
Thirsk

North Stainley
3
Malton
Bempton
Flamborough
Head

Ripon
5
Camaby
Bridlington

Pately
Bridge
Summerbridge
246
6
250

Ingleton
Grassington
Harrogate
4
2
York
Brandesburton

Clapham
Malham
Threshfield
A59
Elvington

Morecambe
Bay
242
Skipton
Harewood
EAST RIDING OF YORKSHIRE
Beverley

IRISH
Ilkley
Kingston-upon-Hull

SEA
Keighley
Bradford
Leeds
1
Selby

Haworth
Hebden
Bridge
Halifax

WEST YORKSHIRE
Wakefield

Huddersfield

SOUTH YORKSHIRE
Doncaster
Conisbrough

1 Slow travel   1 Slow food   1 Special places to stay

NORTH YORKSHIRE

YORKSHIRE, CUMBRIA & NORTHUMBERLAND

Slow travel

1. Walk from Rievaulx Abbey to Byland Abbey
2. North Yorkshire Moors Railway
3. Castle Howard
4. Roseberry Topping
5. Masham Sheep Fair
6. Knaresborough
7. Galleny Force
8. Abbot Hall Art Gallery
9. Theatre by the Lake
10. Greystoke Cycle Café
11. Brantwood
12. Jesus Church
13. Swallows & Amazons Cruise
14. Ravenglass & Eskdale Railway
15. Bamburgh Beach & Castle
16. The Farne Islands
17. The Alnwick Garden
18. The Biscuit Factory
19. Elsdon
20. Holy Island
21. Corbridge

Slow food

1. E Oldroyd & Sons
2. York Food Festival
3. Wensleydale Creamery
4. Betty's Café Tearooms
5. Mister Chips
6. The Village Bakery
7. Dalemain Marmalade Festival
8. Low Sizergh Barn
9. Cartmel Village Shop
10. Pooley Bridge Farmers' Market
11. Cumbrian Food Tour
12. L Robson & Sons Ltd
13. Brocksbushes Farm
14. Corner Shop
15. St Aidan's Winery
16. The Northumberland Cheese Company Ltd
17. Hexham Farmers' Market

Special places to stay

- 242 The Angel Inn
- 246 Gallon House
- 250 Manor Farm
- 254 Augill Castle
- 258 Willow Cottage
- 262 High Houses
- 266 Thistleyhaugh
- 270 Eshott Hall
- 274 West Coates

Slow travel

1 Walk from Rievaulx Abbey to Byland Abbey
Two ruined and magnificent abbeys on the North York Moors with an atmospheric six-and-a-half mile walk between them. Reward yourself by stopping off at the Abbey Inn (01347 868204) fifty paces from Byland's door.
www.english-heritage.org.uk

2 North Yorkshire Moors Railway
(01751 472508)
From Pickering to Whitby and back again, steaming your way through the ruggedly beautiful North York Moors. August is heather heaven.
www.nymr.co.uk

3 Castle Howard
Near Malton (01653 648444)
There's a divertingly lovely farm shop with all manner of regional food and drink—and the Palladian Castle and gardens are captivating, too.
www.castlehoward.co.uk

4 Roseberry Topping
Newton-under-Roseberry
(01642 328901)
320m high and worth every puff for the 360 degree view from the summit—to Whitby and the sea one way, the Yorkshire Dales t'other.

5 Masham Sheep Fair
In September in this pretty market town, featuring a cast of thousands. Gambling types might fancy a flutter on the 200 yard sweepstake when woolly racers sprint to the post lured by buckets of feed.
www.visitmasham.com

6 Knaresborough
Hire boats in yet another pretty market town and wend your way up the river Nidd, marveling at the castle and the spectacular viaduct on the way. Buy some toffees at Farrah's on Market Place—it's housed in what was the oldest chemist's shop in England, established in 1720.
www.knaresborough.co.uk

7 Galleny Force
Wild swimming in the tumbling Galleny at the head of Borrowdale. Two fairy glen pools, with silver birches and ferns, frame a stunning Lakeland scene.

8 Abbot Hall Art Gallery
Kendal (01539 722464)
Entrancing Georgian house on the banks of the river Kent with an impressive program of temporary exhibitions alongside a permanent collection.
www.abbothall.org.uk

9 Theatre by the Lake
Keswick (017687 74411)
A great program of events year round but the summer season is the highlight—and you're on the spectacular edge of Derwent Water.
www.theatrebythelake.com

10 Greystoke Cycle Café
Greystoke (01768 483984)
A lovely garden for lunch or tea—much organic. Book a massage too: 01768 899851. Outside opening hours is a "cyclists barn" replete with towels, blankets, drinks and flapjacks (honesty box). Brilliant for cold wet bikers.
www.greystokecyclecafe.co.uk

11 Brantwood
Coniston (015394 41396)
The Lakeside home of the Victorian writer, artist, thinker and early conservationist John Ruskin, now a lively center of arts. Acres of gardens with spectacular views cling to the rocky slopes—fabulous.
www.brantwood.org.uk

12 Jesus Church
Troutbeck
A place for quiet contemplation.
The east window, designed by
Edward Burne-Jones with additions
by Ford Maddox Brown and William
Morris, is inspiring.

13 Swallows & Amazons Cruise
Coniston Water (015394 36216)
All aboard the solar-electric
launch for a watery exploration of
the places that inspired Arthur
Ransome to write his classic
children's book.
www.conistonlaunch.co.uk

14 Ravenglass & Eskdale Railway
(01229 717171)
Aka the La'al Ratty: an entertaining
and scenic seven-mile steam train
journey (open to the elements in
summer) from Ravenglass, the
Lakes' only coastal village, to
Dalegarth.
www.ravenglass-railway.co.uk

15 Bamburgh Beach & Castle
A vast, big-skies beach overlooked
by an equally impressive castle
(01668 214515) perched on an
outcrop. The Grace Darling Museum
(01668 214910) is in Bamburgh, too.
www.bamburghcastle.com

16 The Farne Islands
Billy Shiel's family have been taking
visitors from Seahouses to the
Farne Islands since 1918. You'll
spot an astonishing array of wildlife
as you cruise, with gray seals and
puffins galore.
www.farne-islands.com

17 The Alnwick Garden
Alnwick (01665 511350)
Forget about decking and quick
fixes as you wander the Duchess of
Northumberland's visionary
creation. This is gardening on a
grand scale.
www.alnwickgarden.com

18 The Biscuit Factory
Newcastle Upon Tyne
(0191 261 1103)
Britain's biggest original art store
with two floors of exhibition space
and two of artists' studios. You can
arrange art hire, too. Lunch smartly
at the buzzing Brasserie Black Door
(0191 260 5411).
www.thebiscuitfactory.com

19 Elsdon
Walk down a long, lonely road
between Elson and Cambo high in
the Redesdale hills, shiver at the
hangman's gibbet on the way.
Elsdon's small 14th-century church
is said to be haunted. If you're
here at the end of August try the
village fete for some more down-
to-earth fun.

20 Holy Island
(01670 533037)
Hugely atmospheric tidal island
reached via a causeway (watch for
closing times!), credited with being
the birthplace of Christianity.
Lindisfarne Castle was transformed
by Lutyens into an Edwardian
holiday home, with a walled garden
designed by Gertrude Jekyll. Plus:
renovated upturned boats that allow
you to experience the interior of a
19th-century herring drifter.
www.lindisfarne.org.uk

21 Corbridge
Corbridge has long been regarded
as a great place for idling away
the day shopping. Don't miss
Re-found Objects (01434 634567;
closed Mondays): it's beautifully
laid out and sells recycled,
reclaimed and rescued objects of
usefulness and beauty.
www.re-foundobjects.com

Slow food

1 E Oldroyd & Sons
Rothwell (0113 2822245)
Forced rhubarb is grown in dark sheds and picked by candlelight—find out more on a tour with Janet Oldroyd Hulme, High Priestess of Rhubarb.
www.yorkshirerhubarb.co.uk

2 York Food Festival
York (01904 466687)
September markets, cooking workshops, tutored tastings and all manner of events.
www.yorkfoodfestival.com

3 Wensleydale Creamery
Hawes (01969 667664)
Say cheese or even taste cheese—restaurant, shop and viewing gallery. Wallace and Gromit's favorite cheese has been made in Wensleydale since 1150.
www.wensleydale.co.uk

4 Betty's Café Tearooms
Harrogate (01423 877300)
An institution and rightly so. Elegance, afternoon tea and the infamous Warm Yorkshire Fat Rascals.
www.bettys.co.uk

5 Mister Chips
Whitby (01947 604683)
One can only wonder at Captain Cook's wanderlust when he was apprenticed in wonderful Whitby. Tuck into proper fish and chips.
www.misterchipswhitby.co.uk

6 The Village Bakery
Melmerby (01768 898437)
Breads baked at this pioneering bakery are based on the motto "time equals flavor," a slow maxim if ever there was one. A restaurant with a gallery above and a shop.
www.village-bakery.com

7 Dalemain Marmalade Festival
Dalemain (017684 86450)
February fun and marmalade—an obvious mix.
www.marmaladefestival.com

8 Low Sizergh Barn
Kendal (015395 6042)
A farm shop, a trail that's part of the Soil Association's organic farm network, and craft gallery. Time your cup in the tearoom right and you can watch the cows being milked.
www.lowsizerghbarn.co.uk

9 Cartmel Village Shop
Cartmel (015395 36280)
Another must-visit for foodies—and for sticky toffee pudding addicts.
www.stickytoffeepudding.co.uk

10 Pooley Bridge Farmers' Market
By the river Eamont on the last Sunday of the month, April–September, 10:30am–2:30pm.
www.ortonfarmers.co.uk

11 Cumbrian Food Tour
(01900 881356)
Get chauffeur-driven around the Lake District by local-food champion Annette Gibbons.
www.cumbriaonaplate.co.uk

12 L Robson & Sons Ltd
Craster (01665 57622)
The smoking ban doesn't apply at this world famous smokery, home to the legendary kipper... Wonderful harborside restaurant for lunch and supper. Call for opening times.
www.kipper.co.uk

13 Brocksbushes Farm
Corbridge (01434 633100)
May your basket overflow with strawberries, raspberries, tayberries and more at this gorgeously situated pick-your-own farm. Cream teas too.
www.brocksbushes.co.uk

14 Corner Shop
Longframlington (01665 570241)
A proper village shop with a true gentleman at the helm; David Carr stocks everything his community could wish for.

15 St Aidan's Winery
Holy Island (01289 389230)
Mead is reputed to be one of the world's oldest alcoholic drinks and it's an aphrodisiac. Still made on the island.
www.lindisfarne-mead.co.uk

16 The Northumberland Cheese Company Ltd
Blagdon (01670 789798)
Award-winning producers with shop and café serving curd tarts, cheese scones and more.
www.northumberland-cheese.co.uk

17 Hexham Farmers' Market
Hexham (07963 426932)
Second and fourth Saturday of the month, 9am–1:30pm, in the Market Place with the abbey as backdrop. Universally acclaimed.
www.hexhamfarmersmarket.co.uk

Pubs & inns

White Horse Inn (Nellies)

22 Hengate, Beverley, Yorkshire
Wonderfully atmospheric: gas-lit passages, small rooms, old quarry tiles, smoke-stained walls and open fires. Locals love the place, the straightforward food and its prices. 01482 861973 www.e-hq.co.uk/nellies

The Star Inn

Harome, Helmsley, Yorkshire
Andrew and Jacquie arrived in 1996 and the Michelin star in 2002. There's a bar with a Sunday papers-and-pint feel, a coffee loft, and a deli. Exceptional. 01439 770397 www.thestaratharome.co.uk

The Birch Hall

Beck Hole, Goathland, Yorkshire
Two small bars with a shop in between, unaltered for seventy years. The Big Bar has been beautifully repapered and has a little fire, darts, dominoes, and service from a hatch: baps, beer cake and pies. 01947 896245 www.beckhole.info

The Appletree

Marton, Kirkbymoorside, Yorkshire
Menus reflect the seasons and change every day... Herbs from the garden, fruits from the orchard, farm-reared meats. Bliss in summer to relax on the orchard patio. Log fires and candles in winter. 01751 431457 www.appletreeinn.co.uk

Old Crown

Hesket Newmarket, Cumbria
Owned by a cooperative of 147 souls, it is the focal point of the community, even supporting the post office whose postmistress repays in puddings and pies. Ask about brewery tours. 01697 478288 www.theoldcrownpub.co.uk

The Langstrath Country Inn

Stonethwaite, Borrowdale, Cumbria
A popular refuelling stop on the Cumbrian Way and the Coast to Coast path. Vertical timbers create cozy stable-like corners, a fire adds warmth. Great local food. 01768 777239 www.thelangstrath.com

Kirkstile Inn

Loweswater, Cockermouth, Cumbria
Hard to imagine a more glorious setting—the inn is tucked in among the fells, next to a church and a stream. The whole place is authentic, traditional, delightful—including the sticky toffee pudding. 01900 85219 www.kirkstile.com

Dipton Mill

Hexham, Northumberland
A ten-minute drive out of town along a rollercoaster road, it squats in a deep hollow next to a brook. Tiny and traditional, the inn is the brewery tap for Hexhamshire Brewery. Ploughman's and a rare choice of cheeses. 01434 606577

The Feathers Inn

Hedley on the Hill, Northumberland
It is a rare treat west of Newcastle to find such an authentic little place. Four cask beers and food—Greek beef casserole, tortillas and croustades, ginger pudding—home-cooked, fresh and flavorful. 01661 843607

Angel Inn

YORKSHIRE

There is a tiny restaurant in Montpellier, France, run by a woman who somehow does all the cooking and much of the serving. The food takes ages to arrive, but this matters not a jot because it is very, very good. More to the point, "Service Lente" is stated clearly on the menu.

Denis and Juliet used the same little trick long ago, with "This is not a fast food outlet, so please be patient—all food is cooked to order." Juliet speaks with passion about their own, untitled campaign for people to take their food slowly.

"Denis died a few years ago but people called him the 'Godfather of the Gastropub.' (He scorned the name!). He always had a dream that he could serve good food in a pub. Everyone at the time was promoting fast food. It was all gammon and eggs and scampi and chips—'fast' from freezer to fryer. We broke the mold a bit. We stopped serving chips over twenty years ago."

Juliet met Denis in Preston in 1968 when he was the manager of a coaching inn. First they worked in Dublin and then Bristol, where Denis spent ten years at The Grand Hotel and The Grand Spa (now the Avon Gorge) as overall general manager. "Denis helped organize the Bristol World Wine Fair in 1978. I didn't quite realize how much

flair and vision he had." They had a good life in Bristol but being Lancastrians, eventually came up here, Juliet's mother selling her house and moving in with them so that they could buy the old place. "We bought it at auction, and lived upstairs with the children for eight years."

Their vision was to run an English country inn full of nooks, crannies, beams, crackling fires and delicious food. That vision has become a legend. The Angel, an old drovers' inn standing in the middle of a hamlet surrounded by lush grazing land with Rylstone Fell rising behind, has it all. It is a freehouse, so buys its beer where it chooses. The local Black Sheep is on handpump, as is Timothy Taylors, brewing beer at Keighley since 1858. From the start Denis imported wines too, mainly from Burgundy. And the Angel was probably one of the first pubs in the country to serve champagne by the glass.

Juliet's full-blooded support for Denis and his enthusiasms has been remarkable. "Denis had the food, wine and people skills, while I was a really good 'gofer.'" But it is thanks to her that all the ancient trimmings—the mullioned windows, the oak-paneled bar, the working range— are so beautifully looked after, and that the bedrooms, peacefully in the barn over the

road, are so luxurious. After a day trekking the moors what bliss to come back to lashings of hot water and a comfortable big bed, complimentary chocolates, comfy robes, fat white towels, space to lounge in—and chess!

It is Juliet who is the founder of the recently inaugurated Chocolate Festival, but the Angel has been putting on special events for years. During

> "Everything is cooked individually in little skillets: we've always been slow and would never rush a thing"

September's Seafood Festival, stylish seafood platters spill over with lobster, crab, langoustines, oysters, prawns, smoked salmon, mussels and scallops; at the summer barbecue you get Dales spit-roast lamb with live jazz. There are Winter Warmers in the bar and Supper by the Fire with English pies and stews, sponges and crumbles. The bar is informal, the restaurant is smart and people travel miles for Bruce Elsworth's cooking: black pudding with spiced apple compote, roasted mallard breast with thyme mash, seared brill with langoustine purée, Granny Smith

crumble cheesecake. The pub also does an "Inn Focus" newsletter for the public: news and views, events and local suppliers.

"I've tried to build on what Denis has done, not to change it radically but to give it a fresh look. At first I didn't want anything to change, but now we are redesigning our menus—with four distinct seasons."

The rustic Wine Cave across the road adds another, unusual, touch. It is Pascal's baby. "The Angel has been importing wines from small producers for fifteen years. We get our house wine from Georges Blanc in Burgundy. Dad even bought a cottage in Burgundy, he loved it so much. I came back into the business five years ago after training at Oddbins and in 2002 I did a wine-making course. Grape picking is the hardest job I have ever done. Dad said, 'Son, it's the only honest job you've done in your life!'

"I am a Burgundy specialist and run professional wine tastings for up to eight people at lunchtimes. People come from far and wide. There is nothing here that you would find in a supermarket and there aren't many places like this in the country. Many Burgundy producers are small and don't use chemicals, apart from, perhaps, copper sulfate spray."

Juliet and Denis were way ahead of their time in many ways. They banned smoking years ago, long before banning it became a political necessity. They

were also devoted to local and organic sourcing before it became the thing to do. "We have always done this. You can't be completely organic, but we do what we can. We changed over to organic salmon a while ago; it's paler and it's lovely. We do our best. Our co-director's father was farming in this area, and he knows all the farmers, so is at home with them. The idea of buying local is instinctive to him, not a marketing ploy."

The food is modern British, with influence from France and Italy. Sunday lunch is delicious and traditional, and has an award-winning Yorkshire pudding. They also do Little Angel menus for children.

Slow? You'll not find pork chops and potatoes "boiled in the bag" here. On the contrary, everything is cooked individually in little skillets. "We've always been slow and would never rush a thing. It demands care and attention—and a lot of your time. Why on earth would you want to eat fast food?"

If you need further encouragement to stay at the Angel, this is wonderful countryside, within the Yorkshire Dales National Park, "James Herriot country" as the Tourist Board calls it. The glorious up-hill-and-down-dale drive to get here is part of the charm. There are supreme limestone landscapes with valleys, crags, peaks and caves, and moorland criss-crossed by drystone walls and dotted with

sheep and field barns. There's walking, cycling, pony trekking, caving, fishing—and fell-running for the heroic. With wind in your rucksack you can walk the Pennine Way from here and the Coast to Coast Walk too, not to mention the Dales Way. There are short family cycling routes and the rigorous 210-kilometer Yorkshire Dales Cycle Way.

If you are moved to be a tourist, and it would be entirely understandable, you have Skipton Castle, Bolton Priory, Fountains Abbey; and the handsome market towns of Grassington, Malham, Ingleton, Kettlewell, Skipton and Settle. Charles Kingsley, who wrote *The Water Babies*, was a frequent visitor to Malham Tarn and wrote part of the book here. J. B. Priestley loved the Southern Dales, too, and is buried in Hubberholme Church. You are in good company.

Juliet Watkins

The Angel Inn,
Hetton, Skipton, BD23 6LT
- 2 doubles, 3 suites. £130-£155. Suites £155-£180.
- Bar meals from £5.75. Dinner from £25.
- 01756 730263
- info@angelhetton.co.uk
- www.angelhetton.co.uk

Gallon House

YORKSHIRE

This is Ronda—or England's best attempt at it. The Spanish town is famously, and defensively, perched on the edge of a stupendous gorge with views far to the south and east. Knaresborough once needed defending too, though not against the Moors, and its 14th-century castle is still magnificent. Views of it from the house are wonderful.

The river Nidd, in the gorge far below, curls round a sandstone cliff; from Gallon House you are poised above it all. The Nidd joins the Ouse, already fed by the Ure and the Swale, and later, with the Wharfe, Aire, Derwent and Trent, becomes the Humber—a veritable cascade of names and rivers.

This is the Vale of York, lush and fertile, an ancient passageway for Romans, Cavaliers and pursuing Roundheads and, no doubt, scootering skinheads, with a limestone ridge that has offered up the handsome stone for many a fine building, including York Minster.

Sue, a Knaresborough girl, was working at the famous tea shop, Betty's, in Harrogate, and needed a chef to train the staff. "Along came the gorgeous, immaculate Rick—pristine and in his whites. He was charming and an instant hit with everyone. Soon after that we started going out together." That was eleven years ago. The couple married just after moving into Gallon House, then went on honeymoon and when they returned wondered what on earth they had done. The place was awash with pink and avocado bathroom suites—all a bit "Bavarian."

So their achievements are remarkable, and should help qualify Knaresborough as a new gastro mecca.

They have turned a grim old guest house, built in 1835, into an eccentric-looking yet contemporary B&B that somehow manages to pulse with both energy and calm. They named it Gallon House after John Gallon who owned the flax mill below, reached by steep Gallon Steps from the back of the house, a challenging climb and very good exercise. The mill is a reminder that Knaresborough was vigorously prosperous, as are the Georgian houses that dominate the narrow streets and alleys. The town is not unlike Durham, with its impressive railway viaduct that once, impossibly, brought the vulgar steam engine and its tourist hordes to a sleepy town. The station is just a minute from Gallon House, so you need no car. The pace of life in the house will take you over, followed by the food, Rick's special passion. He used to own and run restaurants, but now much prefers this less hectic pace.

Breakfasts have come a long way since A. P. Herbert's "Breakfast Ballad:"

Give me a little ham and egg,
And let me be alone I beg,
Give me my tea, hot, sweet and weak,
Bring me the Times and do not speak.

The Gallon's guests are less curmudgeonly about breakfast conversation, and eat more exotically. Rick, for example, will give you fruit compote in cinnamon syrup with homemade muesli, followed by grilled Whitby kippers or a bacon muffin, or scrambled eggs and smoked salmon. If you are undaunted by serious excess you can have a traditional Yorkshire breakfast instead, with black pudding, made by Rick. "Cooking is generally quite simple. It only looks complicated." For dinner, after a glass of sherry, you may eat caramelized onion and tomato tart, herb-encrusted chicken breasts in basil sauce, seasonal vegetables

"Cooking comes from the heart and soul; it has to have love in it"

and a light summer pudding; such things are the tip of an impressive culinary iceberg. Rick has spent thirty-six years as a chef, and is remarkably fit. Apparently a hard-working chef can easily do seven miles in a day, careering about in the kitchen. He is also a keen cyclist, one of the John O' Groats-to-Land's End brethren and a committed supporter of Sustrans, the cycling charity that has done so much to restore our confidence in cycling as a viable means of transport—as well as a slow path to happiness.

Rick's father was a farmer but he went to catering college rather than back to the farm, preparing animals for the table, not raising them. He learned his craft at the Imperial Hotel in Torquay, the Box Tree in Ilkley, and later in Florida. His family owned brasseries and hotels in Harrogate before he left to come here, where life is slower and within his control.

Time spent gently trawling the local markets and farm suppliers is well spent. "I grew interested in Slow Food about four years ago, hearing about it on the radio. I totally subscribe to its principles, and it is now very much a low carbon footprint movement too. Cooking comes from the heart and soul; it has to have love in it." His does, and finding good ingredients is all part of it. This is a far cry from the 1980s, when restaurants vied with each other to introduce the most exotic ingredients out of season and by the fastest means. Sue points out another

aspect of Slow living: the willingness to work with other people. She would love to run courses on this very subject—and probably will. She is a determined woman, with Yorkshire grit as well as charm.

They have done colorful and comfortable things to the house's interior. In your snug room with a view (of castle or river) you will find a bottle of Black Sheep Ale from Masham, Yorkshire Tea and Taylor's roast coffee, along with Harrogate Spa water (Harrogate is ten minutes away by train). The conservatory is bright and sunny, with views over the gorge and river, a tiled floor to echo the creams and terracottas of the hall, big pots and plants and a table for tea. There is a Cornish harbor scene by John Malby (with moving boat parts), and if you have lost touch with the *National Geographic* magazine you can drift back through thirty years' worth of them. The sitting room has a huge fireplace decked out with candles, original oak paneling and irresistible sofas.

If you are here in August you will witness the Knaresborough Feva, a colorful festival of entertainment and visual arts. Sue and Rick organize themed evenings: up to twenty-four locals feasting in the conservatory and dining room. They enjoy being involved, so much so that Rick has volunteered to be a fireman. Guests no doubt hope that he is not called out while cooking their dinner.

Knaresborough has one last claim to fame: Mother Shipton, England's most famous prophetess who lived at the time of Henry VIII and foretold the attempted invasion by, and subsequent defeat of, the Spanish Armada in 1588. She also gave forewarning, Samuel Pepys tells us, of the Great Fire of London, but must have been ignored.

Sue & Rick Hodgson

Gallon House,
47 Kirkgate, Knaresborough, HG5 8BZ
- 3 rooms. £110. Singles £85.
- Dinner, 3 courses, £27.50.
- 01423 862102
- gallon-house@ntlworld.com
- www.gallon-house.co.uk

Manor Farm

YORKSHIRE

"A farm is an irregular patch of nettles bounded by short-term debt, containing a fool and his wife who didn't know enough to stay in the city."

The humorist S. J. Perelman was a New Yorker and therefore as far from farming as one can get, but he knew how tough it could be. The attitude of most city dwellers is perhaps similar; the last few decades have seen, in the UK and elsewhere, a growing divide between city and countryside and so many rural disasters—BSE, Foot and Mouth, Bird Flu —that farmers are seen more as producers than husbanders. The world of agriculture hardly knows which way to turn: organic, bio-fuels, intensive, extensive, smaller, bigger? Yet behind the headlines are farmers who, whatever the politics of the day, derive huge satisfaction from their work and from looking after their animals as they would like to be looked after.

Enter stage left the delightful Gilda and Charles, the voice here being Gilda's.

"As one of the declining number of mixed family farms in England, we hold on to the important values of farming: looking after our animals with respect, and caring for our farmland in a way that serves the stock and preserves the landscape at the same time.

"I have not shopped at a supermarket for four years and take pride in supporting other farmers who have had to diversify. Businesses like our own battle against a world of red tape, a badly informed public and a planet that is changing too fast, with sad and frightening results.

"Our farm is not, technically, organic but other things in the equation are just as important, such as sourcing food and other products locally and thus supporting other small businesses." All the bread— and the deliciously crunchy muesli—comes from a mill and bakery attached to the family-run Carr House Farm nearby.

Thixendale, where all this happens, was described in 1951 as "perhaps the most isolated village in the Yorkshire Wolds—approachable through steep-sided valleys that are impassible in snow." Snow is more rare and roads are fairer now, but the village is no less remote and beautiful, in spite of being half an hour from York by car and an easy ride to the coast. From the late 18th century to 1941 it was part of the Sledmere Estate. Sir Christopher Sykes created the farm holdings in 1795, and the Manor Farm (rebuilt in 1843) was one of them. The double bedroom was probably the farm foreman's; the outer room, where two high wooden beds and a green velvet sofa lie, would have housed up to twelve laborers!

The village was built of chalk and flint and now has a shop, a pub and a post office-cum-tearoom that sells puncture repair kits to passing cyclists, of whom there are many. There are, too, good local food suppliers and a farmers' market once a month.

The community is alive and kicking in an age when many are on their last legs. It is, insists Gilda, absolutely unnecessary to go to a supermarket, given all the above and the variety of family-run shops still surviving in Malton, just to the north.

This is a tenanted farm. There are 800 acres, 300 of them suitable only for sheep and the rest arable (wheat, barley, oil seed rape) or given over to beef cattle. It is "in the middle of nowhere but not far from anywhere," in a gentle landscape and alive with animals of all sorts. It was tenanted by Charles's family before he took it over and Gilda came in on a wave of enthusiasm at having "found my farmer husband."

Charles's father's family had come from Lincolnshire to the farm; Charles went to agricultural college and came back, taking up hunting as many farmers do. One day out hunting, Gilda was having trouble with a rearing horse and she dropped her gloves. Charles got off to pick them up and hand them to her. They married three years later.

They lived first in a cottage in the village, producing the twins—Emma and Charlotte—and moved to Manor Farm in 1987 when Charles's parents decided to move into the village. Emma works from home and Charlotte works at Ascot Racecourse.

The house is beautifully decorated and furnished, for Gilda has a way with fabrics and colors. She makes her own cushions, upholsters, makes dresses and mends anything that is torn or broken. Low-ceilinged bedrooms are stuffed with color; there are old armchairs and thick rugs, books and rose china. The guest bathroom has a deep old bath, its water heated by the Aga. In the large cozy kitchen jolly plates line the dresser, hams hang from curing hooks and a collie dozes.

Gilda might have been a vet; she breeds thoroughbred horses and nurtures those too old to hunt or race. This love is shared with her daughters, who have always ridden; in the kitchen, seven silver cups line up on the dresser. The four collies herd the geese as happily as they do the sheep; the hens are Buff Orpingtons and Marrans. Gilda uses antibiotics as a last resort, uses poultices on lame horses and is angry about the closure of the local abattoir and the resulting long journeys for animals.

Her enthusiasms spill over into the garden. She and Charles have created it on a blank canvas, dug it all by hand and allowed it to become an obsession. It is a mix of formal and "fluffy," eccentric and delightful, bursting with sculptures and surprises. It is blessedly non-dependent on garden centers. They buy all their plants from a local nursery run by a lady who has become a friend, and swap cuttings with others. Their garden opens to the National Garden Scheme every March (for the hellebores) and July.

"When I first heard of the book "Go Slow" I thought of my Aga," says Gilda. "We eat things that people would throw out—cuts of meat that need slow cooking, especially in the winter.

"There's peace and quiet here, and walking from the door; my own company doesn't bother me, as long as I have animals. And the guests! They are always lovely people that I am happy to host; I would have some back as friends."

For many readers of country magazines, Gilda and Charles may just be living a familiar Aga-centered, horsy life in the country—a touch privileged, perhaps, even a bit lucky. But there is a different perspective: they have created their own luck with hard work, unfashionable thrift, real skills, toughness ("why turn on the heating for ourselves when we can wear another layer?"), and an underlying philosophy of self-reliance. They are instinctively Slow. "Everything here has a story. We pray we can keep farming just as we are. So many little farms are disappearing—it is so sad.

"Farmhouses are sold off with a few acres and the land is sold separately. What good is a million pounds? I wouldn't swap this for anything." This is not self-centered renunciation, nor a retreat into the hectic comforts of our era. It is life-affirming.

Gilda & Charles Brader

Manor Farm, Thixendale, Malton, YO17 9TG
- 2 rooms. From £70.
  Singles £35.
- Packed lunch £7.50.
- 01377 288315
- info@manorfarmthixendale.co.uk
- www.manorfarmthixendale.co.uk

Augill Castle

CUMBRIA

It is wild and beautiful here. Rising to the east are the Pennines, the long and mighty ridge that is the backbone of the north, and just to the southeast spreads the Yorkshire Dales National Park.

From the windows of Augill Castle the hills beckon gently. Less gently brood the great hills, nearly 3,000 feet high, of Cross Fell and Great Dunn Fell to the north. This is the green Eden Valley, an anglers' and walkers' paradise, dotted with Swaledale sheep and stone villages, criss-crossed by dry stone walls. In the heart of it is Appleby-in-Westmorland, the "place of the apple tree," dominated by the great castle built by the Normans and famous throughout the land for its June Gypsy Fair.

Augill looks like a perfectly formed, small, turreted castle but is really a beautifully restored Victorian gentleman's folly. (Aware that the only follies we regret in life are those we never committed, the English have a curious affection for them.) It was reputedly built in the 1840s by John Bagot Pearson who lived at Park House, nearby. Bagot fell out with his sibling and moved to higher ground whence he could look down on his family home from a house that was bigger and better. This extraordinary creation was the result, a "castle" built and

decorated in the neo-Gothic style. Later in the century Doctor Abercrombie, surgeon to Queen Victoria, moved in.

By the time Simon and Wendy saw Augill in the 1990s it had lain empty for four years. "We were still running a restaurant in London when I saw the castle in the back of Country Living. We had an offer on a house in Chiswick but the castle was the same price. Simon said, 'don't be ridiculous,' and put the details in the bin. I said, 'let's just go for the weekend.'

"We had nothing to lose. We have a deep sense that life is short, each of us having lost a parent when we were young, and we believe that you get just one chance. Turning the corner of the lane and getting our first view of the castle was awe-inspiring. We were in our late twenties, and we sat there thinking, 'Who do we think we are. Can we do this?' We wrote a long list of all the things that would probably be wrong, so we could walk away—heating, roof, that sort of thing. But they were all fine. Cosmetically, however, it was a mess."

They had no business plan, no plan of any kind. The turning point was provided by Simon's mother who sold her house, moved in with them and supported them. The idea was, simply, to do B&B and live the

good life. But in 2001 there descended upon the country, and with special cruelty upon Cumbria, the dreaded foot and mouth. Then along came 9/11 and the drying up of visits from the USA.

"Despite these events the bills got bigger and bigger and the guests got more excited, and we got excited too. We introduced house parties and weddings, and, in among it all, had two children, Oliver and Emily. Our black lab Holly joined the family in year one and, more recently, Harry the white cat.

> "Augill looks like a perfectly formed, small, turreted castle but is really a beautifully restored Victorian gentleman's folly"

"We thought we had a lot of stuff when we moved here but it filled half a room! Simon and I like to mix antiques with things from second-hand sales, junk shops, even skips. We have found old suitcases and typewriters, and lovely old leather books. The man at the tip was the ultimate recycler, he used to pass things on and we'd donate money to charity. He found an entire set of leather-bound Churchill's Wars and chairs of all kinds. He even

found a little mahogany box complete with 1920s Electrolux vacuum cleaner—untouched, and sent to the skip!"

So it's grand but intimate too and guests feel quite at home in the elegant drawing room (with honesty bar) and the music room with its tumbling curtains, well-loved antiques, old rugs on polished floors and significant African touches (Wendy once lived there). Bedrooms are historic but homey: four-posters, swagged curtains, maybe a turret wardrobe or a piano. Staff ply you with fabulous tea trays, scented hot water bottles, big pillows and massive tubs. You can banquet on weekends around a huge table in the dining room beneath a paneled ceiling of stunning blues; there are simpler suppers during the week. Breakfast is the sort that can lure an eager eater up a motorway: grilled Manx kippers, smoked salmon and scrambled eggs, poached eggs, Woodall's Cumberland sausages, porridge. Or the full works, with black pudding.

Augill slows you down and places you in some of Britain's loveliest countryside. The atmosphere is created by Simon and Wendy, who have chosen quality of experience over the modern pressure to have more, bigger, faster. They have reintroduced a wonderful kitchen garden, its raised beds encircling an ancient apple tree. They have also planted over a

thousand trees, use LPG (Limited Petroleum Gas) to heat the house, fuel open fires with wood from their own land, use low-energy bulbs, recycle as much as possible and feed their hens with kitchen waste. No longer do they use brand-name soaps and shampoos here, but natural products, handmade locally.

"We are the types to wash out the glass pots and reuse them," says Wendy. "My family lived in Nigeria, then Malawi then Kenya and we remember how nothing gets wasted. We wouldn't describe ourselves as eco-warriors but we don't like waste. We enjoy buying locally, too; Cumbria is one of the best counties for local food producers."

Simon had gone from Food Science and Technology to hotel management. "Then Dad died, so I bought a round-the-world ticket, working as I went. I returned to a job on the *Northamptonshire Evening Telegraph* as a reporter, met Wendy at a ball and we had a couple of years together, in an idyllic thatched cottage. Four days after our wedding we moved to London and bought a restaurant. It was an ailing Italian bistro in the basement of a lovely house in Mayfair. We turned it round in eighteen months and sold it on."

Wendy has clear plans for their future. "We need to spend more time with our children, and have decided to step up a gear—refit the kitchen, get in a chef to help with the weddings and parties, and step back a bit ourselves. We don't want to shut the kitchen door on guests; we'll do kids' and adults' cookery courses next year. We do children's suppers now—give them pizza dough to throw, things to make their own toppings. The families that come here often don't have time to cook together at home, and tend to eat out at weekends.

"We live a slow, privileged existence, and we believe in each other, which is essential."

The acclaimed artist Andy Goldsworthy, who sees the magic in every small thing, once lived in Brough, the next village, and created his recent Sheepfold Project there. The fascinating sheepfolds and pinfolds he made or restored can all be visited. It is not difficult to see why he was inspired by this sweet valley, squeezed between Cumbria and the Dales.

Simon & Wendy Bennett

Augill Castle,
Brough, Kirkby Stephen, CA17 4DE
- 12 rooms. £140. Singles £100.
- Dinner £20–£40.
- 01768 341937
- enquiries@stayinacastle.com
- www.stayinacastle.com

Willow Cottage

CUMBRIA

"We are going Slow for England at Willow and Barn Cottage," says Chris. To gild their lily, they came second in the Great Cumbrian Breakfast competition, so they are to be taken seriously in the home of the mighty Cumberland sausage.

The scale at Willow Cottage is miniature. Being here feels like being in a Beatrix Potter book— flagstones and rush rugs, dried flowers and pretty china, glowing lamps and antique linen, a scattering of farming implements, a collection of christening gowns. The Barn project has been a labor of love; Roy and Chris lived here for twenty-five years before the farmer sold them a second barn. They took on the conversion themselves, unable to pay for more than the occasional hour of labor, and transformed it into a self-contained space for four bed and breakfast guests. They used reclaimed wood, spare fabrics from Laura Ashley when their daughter worked there, and anything else they could get their hands on. Roy has a garage business fixing crashed cars and his practical skills have been wisely used creating, for example, a staircase from an old ship's wooden planks. Other stuff was salvaged from skips—encouraging in a throwaway culture that has merged with the everything-is-cheap economy. It is rare now to see people rummaging—from thrift rather than poverty— as they did just twenty years ago.

The backdrop to Willow Cottage is spectacular: Skiddaw rearing up behind Bassenthwaite, a "grand old mountain, an easy climb, smooth and grassy with no frightful precipices," as A. Wainwright, the great Lakes walker and writer, wrote. The lake itself glistens easily between hills and forests, undisturbed by the winds that funnel through mountain passes and across lakes elsewhere in the Lake District. The breezes are steady and gentle here, lifting the sails of the many small sailing boats. To go down to the lake with a picnic maybe and stare empty-minded across the water and to the hills is a meditation in itself. The Pheasant Inn at Bassenthwaite Lake, one of our Special Pubs, is another fine place for meditation, with a garden that looks across to Sale Fell.

Those thousands of sheep that scatter across the hills, fells and fields were once the source of great wealth, as elsewhere in England. The sheep have shaped the landscape with their grazing and are called the "nibbling gardeners" of the fells. The main breeds are Herdwick (Beatrix Potter's favorites), Rough Fell and Swaledale (the main local type), their wool coarser than that of their lowland cousins, perfect for carpet-making. Carpets from Herdwick sheep wool were recently commissioned by the National Trust in a project intended to generate extra income for their Lakeland tenant farmers who had lost so much during the Foot and Mouth outbreak.

Herdwicks are unique to the Lake District: black lambs with white eyebrows and tips to their noses, with fleeces that go brown and then gray with age.

(Perhaps we have a special empathy with them.) They are very hardy, the adults having short sturdy white legs, white heads, long grey fleeces and the hint of a smile. The males have curled horns.

After the Enclosure Acts of the 19th century, when common land was privately enclosed for the first time and with considerable ruthlessness, the dry stone walls that are such a feature of this area were built to keep in the sheep—much to our delight now. Nowadays, tups (males) of Bluefaced Leicester sheep, the ones with fine Roman noses and long legs, are bred on Swaledale ewes to create much-prized and vigorous commercial sheep, the North of England "mules." The male "gimmer" lambs from these are mated extensively with lowland Suffolk and other breeds to create good lambs for the table. *Et voilà*— you have an unexpected and potted version of the history and significance of Lake District sheep.

Neither Roy nor Chris is a sheep farmer, but they were born and raised here. They met as teenagers, and he lured her with his motorbike—an old trick that worked well in those days. Chris's father worked at the Keswick garage that Roy later joined and now runs with others. He retires this year, free at last to roam the hills and wallow in the unparalleled beauty of the Lakes. His involvement with the world now known as Slow has come gradually upon him, like the settling of snow. As is often the way, it has been through his wife that new ideas have emerged.

Chris's interest in new and healthier ways of living began in the late seventies, when she began to wonder where food came from. She remembers collecting elderberries from the lane to make cough mixture, and the children calling out "Hubble bubble, toil and trouble" as they walked through the kitchen. Then she attended a nutrition course during which Nick Jones spoke. He was responsible for Andrew Whitley, the ex-Russian correspondent for the BBC, coming to set up the now-famous Village Bakery. (In a few years he has created a reputation as one of the finest bakers in the British Isles and has won prizes galore—a fine reward for what began as a labor of love.) Nick was growing organic wheat and declared that an organic bakery was needed. He was an inspiration to Chris, giving a boost to her fledgling

green enthusiasms. She had always enjoyed home cooking—stews and dumplings—but was ripe for a deeper change, even riper after the onset of diabetes and high cholesterol.

Chris is now committed, and Roy with her: to organic food where possible and local food elsewhere; to growing as much as possible on their own allotment and in their garden; to eating seasonally and well; to using natural products and fewer chemicals; to drying nettles and mint over the Aga for tea. Their enthusiasm for their own garden is almost palpable, and they have also taken on the two village allotments across the way, with all its steep-sloped, rubble-strewn and shallow soil. They have raised beds, added fruit trees and loads of manure and created a haven for free-roaming chickens. From there they can sit and admire the hill views; and encourage their guests to do the same with a glass of wine as the sun goes down.

Sweet little bedrooms have paneled bathrooms and dreamy views. TV is delightfully absent, classical music plays and the village (with pub) is on your doorstep.

Bassenthwaite is not as tourist-stricken as much of the Lake District and has the gentle self-deprecating humor that the English enjoy so much. The highlight of the year is the great plastic duck race on the beck. One hundred and twenty ducks set off, floating vigorously for charity. Such is life here. "We are happy to go and sit on the lake shore—there is seldom need for a doctor."

Roy & Chris Beaty
Willow Cottage,
Bassenthwaite, Keswick, CA12 4QP
- 2 rooms.
- £60-£65. Singles £40-£45.
- 01768 776440
- chrisbeaty@amserve.com
- www.willowbarncottage.co.uk

High Houses

CUMBRIA

The views carry your gaze, on a good day, across the Solway Firth to Scotland. Behind you are the hills of the northern Lake District with Skiddaw to the south at over 3,000 feet. In England that is a mountain (our highest peak is Scafell Pike at 3,210 feet). This is lush, rolling, beautiful countryside, excuse enough for anyone who loves nature to journey here. High Houses is remote, and high, a brilliant escape from the urban crush, even from the crawling traffic that snarls its summer way along the passes and through the towns of the Lakes below.

Jill's grandfather bought the land in the 1940s to do mixed and hill farming. He was the first man in Cumbria to have Friesians and his son, Jill's father, was a keen hunter. Horses have played a major role in the family's life, so much so that they bred racehorses and keep in retirement a racer called The Grey Monk. You can bring your horse to stay with you; it will be stabled at the bottom of the hill. Jill's brother, Roddy, now lives in the family house, where they were raised, at the foot of the track below High Houses. Their parents live in a cottage next to the house, still on these 400 acres that they once farmed.

Not for a moment have hunting, shooting and this benign—if hard-working—country life spoiled Jill or narrowed her mind. She is easy-going and open-minded, filled with zest for life and welcoming to strangers. She bought the house in 1989 from her father. Once a yeoman's farm cottage it was now derelict: a pile of rubble where the kitchen is, and a roof that was caving in. Among the last residents had been two German prisoners-of-war. There was no electricity, no water, no bath, no taps. But there were those views and the familiarity of home.

Over seven years Jill gradually restored the house, burying a big water tank to hold the spring water, turning the hayloft into a bedroom, putting a kitchen where the carthorses had lived; it has kept its cobblestone floors. She brought in every imaginable modern comfort, including a generator for electricity, reinforcing but not undermining the integrity of the building. She has used limewash and color on the walls to bring out the best sense of texture.

It was hard work; she had little money in reserve. In 1996 she moved into one end of the house, finishing it off in 2001, just as Foot and Mouth threw hill farming into disarray. All her B&B bookings were cancelled and her brother could bring in no animals to graze his fields. It was a disaster for them, as for others. (The Government's draconian mass slaughter policy is still hotly debated; the majority view now seems to be that it was ill-conceived.) But things have gradually picked up and word has got out that this is a remarkably lovely place to stay.

It is easy to wonder at Jill's obstinacy in buying such a wreck, doing it up on her own and carving out a life in such a remote spot. But she is made of strong fiber. "I have never been a nine-to-five person; I can't cope with it. I like working for myself and don't mind funny hours.

"Being able to live at home and earn a living is just fantastic. I am totally lucky and all the people who come and stay want to be doing what I am doing."

Hot Game Salad

2 pheasant breasts
2 partridge breasts
Butter
Garlic
Ginger root
Olive oil
Lemon juice
Leaves of lettuce, parsley and arugula

• Gently heat butter, then fry breasts whole
• Add the garlic and ginger root and fry a little longer
• When the breasts are cooked (not too pink in the middle), remove and slice
• When cool, place in a bowl with the salad leaves
• Heat the olive oil and lemon juice gently, pour over leaves and meat and toss all together. Serve with roasted vegetables

One couple got married here, have returned three years in a row and will, Jill suspects, eventually do B&B themselves. But then, of course, they also learn that there is more to this life than pretty animals and views. She has to muck out the cows, provide wood for fires, cook, iron, clean. It never ends, but "I am totally into nature. It is my religion and should be everyone's. They should learn about real life. I would love to bring children out here to learn, but it isn't easy to organize it, given the size of the place and modern health and safety concerns." Her own childhood was wonderful. They rarely went on holiday; she remembers only two before she was fifteen, to Blackpool and to the Isle of Wight where granny lived.

Much of Jill's life is centered on the world of shooting and hunting, and she makes no apology. She argues the case for them well. Indeed, the Slow movement, with its commitment to bio-diversity and socio-diversity, would have little argument with Jill.

She lives and breathes nature, and her love of game is part of this. She rears hens, and George, with whom she has lived for eight years, rears partridges and pheasants for shooting. High Houses is not far from Caldbeck, where John Peel—of "D'ye ken John Peel, with his coat so grey..."—lies buried, so hunting is woven into the very fabric of country life in the area.

Jill had a varied life before settling here. She left home at eighteen, learned how to be a secretary, worked in London, Nova Scotia, Ottawa, British Columbia, then Paris. A girlfriend persuaded her to go to Scotland ("I'll teach you to cook and then we'll set up a cooking business") and that is how she learned a skill that serves her well now. She cooks the game that she and George shoot on the farm—gray partridge ("rare and delicious"), pheasant, plus snipe and whatever else turns up. But there is a fine butcher in Wigton, plus a vegetable shop to supplement her own garden output, and a bakery.

Those who are lucky enough to stay here can cheat a little: you are deep in this glorious countryside, enjoying the fruits of Jill's flair without having to make any effort. From your bed you can see Scotland on a fine day. From the old claw-footed bath in your shared bathroom you have long and magnificent views. There are bare walls, stone slabs, vast rugs, planked floors, roaring fires in inglenooks, an old Knole sofa, a painted four-poster, garden flowers, wagging Jack Russells and a thrilling stairway to the loft where the chickens roosted, now a bolthole for kids. The interior brims with stylish simplicity. Jill has found a way of combining landscape, beauty, comfort and the absence of pace. It is hardly surprising that she came home.

Miss Jill Green

High Houses, Snittlegarth, Ireby, Wigton, CA7 1HE
* 3 rooms, one with cockloft for children.
* £80. Singles £50. Whole house, self-catering, £450.
* Lunch £10-£15. Dinner £15-£25. Packed lunch £5.
* 01697 371549
* enquiries@highhouses.co.uk
* www.highhouses.co.uk

Thistleyhaugh

NORTHUMBERLAND

Deep in the heart of Northumberland, the farm flourishes. There are 300 Welsh Black and Aberdeen Angus beef cattle and 1,500 ewes gently chewing their way through the 720 acres that are Thistleyhaugh. A smattering of hens, too. To stay here and be part of this bustling family community is a privilege. If we were to derive our view of modern England from newspapers alone we would be sadly unaware that farming families such as this not only stay together and help each other out but thrive.

We are told that at best farmers are unappreciated, at worst, held in low esteem. What a delight, then, to encounter a farmer who loves his job, who is successful at it, and whose family flourishes around him. The farm has been in Henry's family for over a hundred years, and the farm has been in its current shape since 1780.

So fearful of Scottish raiders were the Northumbrians that the 18th century produced few buildings up here that were built for pure pleasure. Older history of this land reveals Saxon settlers, and then the Danes who pillaged, ravaged, plundered and then settled so much of old Northumbria. They brought a strong strain of individualism, based on land ownership, to mix with the English blood. They

resisted the feudalism that emerged elsewhere, preferring a free peasantry—though great estates flourished later. They brought, too, their customs, such as their duodecimal system of counting in twelves, rather than tens. Much of the special character of the northeast, much-loved to this day in England, is owed to the Danish mix. Anthropologists have recently found powerful DNA connections between Geordies and modern Vikings, so the mix is verified.

Henry and Enid were both Young Farmers—a solid rural beginning. They met at a car rally. Henry was working on this farm and Enid was working with her father, a butcher who also farmed. In fact, her family's farming story began even earlier than Henry's. But she moved in with Henry, into a bungalow built for them on the farm; when his parents retired, they moved into the main house.

They had three sons: Duncan, who now looks after the sheep, Angus, who cares for the cattle, and Henry, who works in London in the world of finance. He was headed that way long ago, while the other two were bent on farming. So Henry was given a private education to equip him for London, with the B&B providing the fees. (The Tourist Authority soon provided three

stars—and an insistence on trouser presses, unused to this day.) Duncan went to Kirby Agricultural College and met Zoe there, a Newcastle girl happy to roll sleeves up and help out with the B&B. Janice was lured to the farm by Angus's inability to leave it, so busy was he; she stayed to help out and is now full-time. Enid talks of these girls as "hand-picked" and

> "The family has always considered itself a guardian of the countryside"

clearly rejoices in their company. Laughter can often be heard in the kitchen, a charming surprise to those of us familiar with the language of the modern chef.

With encouragement from their vet, Angus and Duncan have converted the farm to organic methods —the beginning of what should be a long but satisfying, and profitable, journey. Hand in hand with this goes an appreciation of good food and there is no shortage of local suppliers. Best of them all is David Carr, whose fabulous little village shop in Longframlington won the Countryside Alliance's "Best Rural Retailer of the North East" in 2006. There are Craster kippers, local cheeses, and vegetables; David rises before dawn four days a week to buy them. The shop is the heart of the community and David, there since the 1970s, is much loved and respected. "If I haven't got them I'll get them. It is much better than it used to be for local suppliers round here." The "girls" at Thistleyhaugh are his best customers.

It is entirely possible, of course, for good food to be ruined once it hits the kitchen. But Zoe works an old-fashioned magic with it. For dinner, after a convivial sherry in the Garden Room or under the arbor watching the setting sun, you could be treated to zucchini and Roule cheese soup, Thistleyhaugh roast chicken and a fruit-studded pavlova. Dinner is around the big table, all guests joining the conversation; some enjoy themselves so much they arrange to meet here again, year after year. Breakfasts, too, are sumptuous. It's a handsome and comfortable Georgian farmhouse, and an easy place to mix with others. Enid is a relaxed hostess. If it's

wet, you can stay all day. "People ask if they have to dress for dinner. I laugh and tell them that, well, they need to put something on!"

The five guest rooms are awash with space, old paintings, crisp linen, bits and pieces of fine old furniture and peaceful views over the garden and the farm beyond. There are, generously, two sitting rooms for guests, with open fires, books galore and some of Enid's art collection, put together with income from her B&B. Step beyond the 700 acres and there are the Cheviots to discover. The village of Hartburn is built dramatically high above the Hart—the burn on one side, a stream on the other—and Mitford, the village of the Mitford family, is set in a wooded valley and still somehow removed from this century.

The family has always considered itself a guardian of the countryside, a far cry from the agricultural barons of East Anglia for whom land is a business asset. It is good to remember that farmers have the Herculean task of keeping England looking beautiful for us all. If they were properly rewarded for that they wouldn't have to struggle so hard to keep heads above water. However, farming remains tough, so the role played by visitors to the B&B has been crucial in giving the family the extra security needed. In return, they show a natural warmth towards visitors. "People often arrive stressed and after their second glass of wine at dinner they open up. By the time they leave they are changed people. They unravel."

The fact that the family thrives so well, working and living seven days a week under the same roof, must have much to do with this unraveling. It is interesting to reflect that many of us appear to believe that the only way for families to stay together is to live apart.

Henry & Enid Nelless

Thistleyhaugh,
Longhorsley, Morpeth, NE65 8RG
- 4 doubles, 1 twin. £75. Singles £50–£75.
- Dinner £20.
- 01665 570629
- thistleyhaugh@hotmail.com
- www.thistleyhaugh.co.uk

Eshott Hall

NORTHUMBERLAND

Ho's mother had Chinese connections, which inspired her at the last minute to name her son this way; Ho means 'good' in Manchurian. Two other names to conjure with here are Emerson Bainbridge, Ho's great, great grandfather, son of a Weardale hill farmer who went on to found the world's first department store in Newcastle, then bought Eshott Hall. Emerson's granddaughter Elise married Fred Sanderson an engineer who built Europe's first mass-produced motor car, the "Angus Sanderson," one of which was found by Ho being used as a hen house on a farm in Australia. It has since been restored.

Eshott was a massive challenge. Dry rot had taken hold of it in the war and the central part was demolished in the 1950s. This was a great era for demolition: over 250 great English houses were pulled down, burned, allowed to decay because their owners couldn't afford to keep them.

In 1996 English Heritage declared that Eshott was doomed, but Ho and Margaret determined to take over the whole place. The globally scattered partners in the estate had planned to pull the house down and build a bungalow from the stone. Over seven years they tracked all of them down and bought them out. It was a magnificent and visionary achievement, eclipsed only by their rebuilding of the "Lost Wing" and the restoration of the whole estate.

When they first moved into the house it was derelict, with moss growing on the dining room wall. They and their children camped out in it; gradually they created their own building company to do the restoration to the highest possible standards. They may have been considered mad but the result is a company that has apprentices and does superb work on other old buildings now. "We persuaded the planners to let us build twenty-two houses on the estate, many of them rented to estate workers. We wanted to bring the estate back to the life it enjoyed in Victorian times, but with a modern ecological, organic theme."

Ho and Margaret took sustainability, both ecological and economic, as their central premise. So the business began with three rooms and them doing all the work; now they have six bedrooms and run weddings and conferences. Ho was a director of the Oxford Farming Conference and a Soil Association inspector for several years, and his parents knew Lady Eve Balfour, the founder of modern organic farming. So farming organically and sustainably is a natural choice for this Soil Association registered holding. He grows wheat, barley, clover, beans and oats; the rainfall is unreliable here so they don't have dairy any more, though Ho remembers supplying the coal miners with milk during the miners' strike. "These were difficult times and there is still over 50% unemployment in the old mining communities here, so it is important to provide jobs and affordable houses. We can play our part."

They have both known how tough farming can be. For twenty years they farmed on the Home Farm, with the oldest herd of Ayrshire cows in England. "I was a proper farmer, leading a bucolic life. We lost the whole herd to Foot and Mouth and thus lost the bloodline." Then BSE came along, and milk quotas, so they abandoned dairying. Margaret was an enthusiastic farmer's wife, milking the cows, feeding the calves, keeping the chickens.

Margaret is a talented cook and, like so many other English women, depends on her Aga for slow and effective cooking. She also has an eye for luxury and style, hence the fine textiles and fittings and the all-pervading sense of serenity. "Conserve, restore and sustain" is their mantra; ceramic floors, working shutters, a rare staircase and a stained-glass window designed by the William Morris School are a few of the stunning architectural features protected by this philosophy.

Outside, a major project is the restoration of the walled garden. It now produces fruit and vegetables for the Hall's visitors and for a small local community retail business. Their chickens drop the finest eggs and their bees gather nectar from their organic crops.

Any food for guests that cannot be sourced from the estate comes from organic producers within a ten-mile radius. They have entirely embraced the Slow Food philosophy, inspired by their own experience but also their travels in Italy. "Genoa is an interesting, tough sort of place. We loved it and it is where the Slow Food ideas came from. People there are slightly more thoughtful about everything they do. In the UK we have lost small scale production— there are few fishermen and small farmers anymore— and people have forgotten how to enjoy food."

There are about forty houses on the estate and they have just formed a small (twenty-five people) Eshott Community Group to pool ideas. "We are probably going to use biodiesel, electric cars and offer a shuttle to the stations—only seven miles away. We are determined to have a wood-burning heating system for the Hall; we have stacks of wood on the estate. Soon we will have pigs, and we are restoring the Victorian fernery with old and new species."

Their sustainability plan runs across the whole business. They do the big things—sewage, for example, is dealt with naturally on the estate—and

are now beginning to take care of the smaller things, like light bulbs and energy systems. All the water comes from an underground aquifer and they plant one tree per visitor for their Eshott Hall Friends' Wood. One day they will restore the old water meadows and put livestock back on them. Sustainability is a serious matter here and they are following the ten One Planet Living principles set out by the WWF and the Bioregional Development Group that focus on zero carbon, zero waste, sustainable transport, local and sustainable materials and food, sustainable water, natural habitats and wildlife, culture and heritage, equity and fair trade and health and happiness.

The entire estate is working to protect red squirrels. You notice this as you approach the house from the village, passing a "Red Squirrel" sign before you press on through dense woodland (some redwoods and other rare trees) to emerge to the sheer surprise of the house. They work with Dr. Peter Garson at Newcastle University on red squirrels, doing trials and forming a grey squirrel exclusion zone—part of the SOS (Save Our Squirrels) campaign with Northumberland wildlife.

"If you haven't seen a family of baby red squirrels then you haven't lived!" Well, there is hope for us all, for there are now about six squirrel pairs per hectare —a huge achievement in an age when many other estates have been abandoned to the grays.

It may be hard to drag oneself away from this wonderful place but you will do so imbued with something of its ethos. Says Ho, "We try to protect our heritage in all its forms. Everything we do is for long-term, not short-term gain."

Ho & Margaret Sanderson

Eshott Hall,
Morpeth, NE65 9EN
- 6 rooms. £128. Singles £79.
- Dinner £33.
- 01670 787777
- thehall@eshott.co.uk
- www.eshotthall.co.uk

West Coates

NORTHUMBERLAND

Langoustines fresh from the sea, split and grilled with garlic and herb butter; griddled sea bass, equally fresh and local, and roasted peppers stuffed with tomatoes and anchovies; broccoli and potatoes from the garden; and then, to ensure your return, strawberry ice cream with soft fruits from the garden and locally made organic meringues.

Karen's cooking is irresistible, and her sourcing of ingredients is impeccable. Robson & Son provide Craster kippers, arguably the best in the world; the ice cream is Doddington's. Karen even runs cooking classes, small, laid-back, low-key, for adults and children in the autumn and winter.

Lindisfarne is just to the south, on Holy Island, a name that conjures more magic than most in England. From here the heartbroken monks, their priory sacked by the Danes, set out with the bones of St Cuthbert and ended, seven years later, in Durham. They laid his body there and the great cathedral built over it was dedicated to the saint and grew in stature to become the seat of Prince Bishops. So the island is soaked in history and meaning, and is close enough to Berwick to give you no excuse for not going. (The scallops from Holy Island are among Britain's best, too.)

Just to the north is Scotland, a bare three miles away. Berwick has see-sawed between Scotland and England for centuries, and it is England's gain that she lies south of the border, for she is among the finest of English coastal towns. Nicholas Pevsner described it as "A real town, with the strongest sense of enclosure... a town of red roofs on grey houses with hardly any irritating buildings anywhere." The town walls, built and rebuilt many times, are still impressive. So is the Royal Border Bridge, one of the finest railway viaducts in the world and opened by Queen Victoria and Prince Albert.

Karen's house is just ten minutes' walk away from the town center—along the river, past three bridges—so you have the best of both worlds: country and town. For comfort-seekers there is all you could ask for, not least a big indoor swimming pool and hot tub. For the eco-aware there is a sense of being in a house that works hard to do the right thing. For the food lover there are the sea and the land, and fine local producers. For the country lover there is a beautiful coastline, and, of course, the whole of Northumberland.

Karen was brought up in The Borders, twenty miles away in Scotland. Her parents farmed and had a big family. "My father was a proper shepherd and Mum

helped on the farm." She met Logan when she was sixteen and married him at twenty-two. They bought a run-down farm at Jedburgh and farmed, as a hobby, with cattle and sheep for ten years. It was a simple place, with water only from springs, but they loved it.

Karen worked in the hotel and catering business, having qualified in this in Edinburgh. The children came along—Angus, now nineteen, and Isla, seventeen—and Karen took to catering to boost her income. Then they sold up, rented a house and pondered their future for a year. One day they strolled through Berwick, saw this house for sale and fell for it. It was solidly built by a merchant in the 1870s and needed little more than redecorating; the bright glossy walls were repainted and the brown carpeting whipped away. They have been determined to keep the atmosphere of a big traditional family home, with good furniture, relaxed spaces and very fine bathrooms (avoiding profligate deluge showers). Now three elegant bedrooms with fruit, homemade cakes and fresh flowers welcome you. "The house cried out to be used as a B&B."

They are ahead, environmentally, of most of their colleagues. They are part of Green Tourism in Northumberland but initially fell out over the plastic water bottles demanded for bedrooms. "Why defeat the purpose? We do chilled water in flasks." Energy-saving light bulbs, eco-friendly cleaning products, water bottles in the cisterns to save water, changing towels only when asked.

Their purposeful recycling allows them to put out rubbish only once every two weeks—impressive for a house with three guest bedrooms. "It's all about organizing yourself, avoiding packaging, asking people what they want to eat so you don't waste food. We do it our way and enjoy it. We have always used local suppliers; local food is part of my life, the way I was brought up. Logan is in the meat industry and understands husbandry, how you look after your animals. The best quality Aberdeen Angus beef comes from our neighbors who farm Castlehills and run the farmers' Well Hung & Tender meat company." The organic eggs are particularly delicious, and make a lemon curd that has won awards—and an army of fans—for Karen.

The swimming pool, not usually supplied in "green" houses, uses non-chlorine products and the garden is a haven for wildlife, with birds bringing added life to the woody, leafy garden. "It would make such a difference if everyone did even just a little for the planet."

L. S. Lowry was fond of Berwick, visiting many times from the mid-1930s to 1975. He did more than thirty paintings and drawings here and came the year before he died. The crisp, clean air was an antidote to the polluted city and he loved drifting among the back streets. There is a Lowry Trail now. Beyond the town is a coastline of ravishing beauty, and the bird-rich Farne Islands to the south. Bamburgh's castle is one of the country's most impressive, dominating the coast from its great basalt outcrop. The village of Craster is rugged and delightful; at the turn of the century it had twenty boats supplying four kipper/herring yards. Now there is only one, but at least it survives. Hadrian's Wall is easy to reach from here: a bus ride away. Hikers can plunge into the county's interior while urbanites can hop onto the Edinburgh train... much of the railway hugs the coast and it is a memorable ride.

Karen and Logan are among the happiest of people, and one can see why. They have found a way of life that suits them, and those who come to stay. "We enjoy meeting the people that come through the door. We hardly ever do one nights—people come to relax, and to explore Northumberland." All who arrive stressed, leave revived. "One guest arrived so wound up that before breakfast I thrust a towel at him and told him to go to the pool and hot tub. He came back a new man."

One other couple were, perhaps, too relaxed, remembers Karen. "They were very tired, also pretty laid-back and they came down late to breakfast in their pajamas. And they did it again the next day!"

Karen Brown

West Coates,
30 Castle Terrace, Berwick-upon-Tweed, TD15 1NZ
- 3 rooms. £90-£100. Singles from £50.
- Dinner £35.
- 01289 309666
- karenbrownwestcoates@yahoo.com
- www.westcoates.co.uk

Slow travel

www.lowcarbontravel.com

Observer journalist Ed Gillespie is shunning the "aluminium sausage" on his no-fly Slow trip around the world. Read his blog and vicariously share in his adventures.

www.walkingworld.com

Search for any walk in the UK that takes your fancy: you'll find it here.

www.sustrans.org.uk

Superb site for cyclists from the leading sustainable transport charity. Downloadable maps of the National Cycle Network, lots of travels tips and regional guides to many areas of the UK.

www.seat61.com

The best place to find out about train travel to the continent, set up as a hobby by former railway worker Mark Smith. "Many people prefer train travel, but information can be difficult to find. I aim to help them and to INSPIRE people to do something more rewarding with their travel opportunities than getting on a globalised airliner and missing all the world has to offer."

www.raileurope.com

Book your chosen continental train ride. They say... "Eurail travel is for everyone: young and old, the frugal or the spend-happy. Because the goal of any real traveler is to experience that sense of place. Beauty is found not just in a museum or monument. It's also right outside your train window."

www.traveline.org.uk

For train, coach, ferry, underground and bus travel in the UK. Want to know how to get to Totnes on a coach and then on to your favorite beach? They guide you every step of the way—excellent, accurate and very local. If you are on the road, you can phone them, too, on 0870 608 2 608.

www.greentraveller.co.uk

An ever-expanding site set up by well-known eco-journalist Richard Hammond, author of *Green Places to Stay*. His site is packed with ideas on choosing a greener holiday, worldwide.

www.walkit.com

Walking routes between cities' attractions—want to get from Tate Modern to Tate Britain? Choose whether you want the fastest or the quietest route and download directions or a map. They started with Birmingham, London and Edinburgh and are expanding.

www.biotravel.co.uk

Biodiesel taxi service run by a team of Newquay surfers.

www.bigfriday.com

A biodiesel taxi service to help you get the hell out of London on a Friday evening. Meet at Hammersmith, strap on your board, then settle back to watch DVDs all the way to Cornwall's north coast. From £74 return.

www.river-swimming.co.uk

River and lake swimming association's website that encourages you to experience the joys of splashing about in the wild. The association is putting up a valiant fight against the health and safety lobby.

www.liftshare.com

The best of all the car-sharing websites—helps you find commuting/traveling buddies, on four wheels or two.

www.sailrail.com

An alliance of UK train operating companies and ferry companies dedicated to getting you to Ireland without a car.

Page	Property name	Nearest station	Free pick-up?	Can stay all day
20	The Gurnard's Head	Penzance/St Erth	free if someone available	yes
24	Primrose Valley Hotel	St Ives	free	yes
28	Cornish Tipi Holidays	Bodmin Parkway	no	yes
32	Hornacott	Plymouth	no	preferably not
36	Lantallack Farm	St Germans/Saltash	free if available	yes
40	Lower Norton Farmhouse	Totnes	charge for Bentley ride	yes
44	Fingals	Totnes	for a charge	yes
48	West Colwell Farm	Honiton	free	yes
52	Beara Farmhouse	Barnstaple	no	yes
56	Southcliffe Hall	Ilfracombe coach station	free on occasion	yes
68	No. 7	Taunton	possibly for a charge	yes
72	Royal Oak Inn	Taunton	no	in rooms not pub
76	Parsonage Farm	Taunton	for a small charge	yes
80	Church Cottage	Bridgwater	yes	yes
84	Harptree Court	Castle Cary/Bristol	no	yes
88	Lower Farm	Castle Cary	no	yes
92	The Bath Arms	Warminster/Westbury	no	yes
96	The Old Forge	Gillingham	no	yes
100	Frampton House	Dorchester/Yeovil	free from Dorchester	yes
104	Marren	Moreton	no	no
116	24 Fox Hill	Crystal Palace	free	maybe
120	Shoelands House	Guildford/Farnham	usually a charge	no
124	The Griffin Inn	Haywards Heath	no	yes
128	Castle Cottage	Pulborough	no	yes, for longer stays
132	Dadmans	Sittingbourne/Faversham	for a charge	yes
144	Milden Hall	Sudbury	no	B&Bs: no; S/C: yes
148	The Old Methodist Chapel	Darsham	free	yes
152	Sandpit Farm	Saxmundham	no	in gdn in summer
156	Fritton House Hotel	Haddiscoe	free if available	yes
160	Strattons	Downham Market	10% disc. for no-car guests	yes
164	Bridge Cottage	Peterborough	free	no
176	Cross o' th' Hill Farm	Stratford-upon-Avon	no	yes
180	Burford House	Charlbury	for a charge	yes
184	Frampton Court	Stonehouse	no	no
188	Clapton Manor	Moreton in Marsh	no	no
200	Old Country Farm	Colwall/Malvern	free	yes
204	Winforton Court	Hereford	no	yes
208	Ty-mynydd	Hereford	no	no
212	Timberstone B & B	Ludlow	free	yes
224	The Angel Inn	Skipton	no	yes
228	Gallon House	Knaresborough	free	yes
232	Manor Farm	Malton	free if available	no
236	Augill Castle	Kirkby Stephen	free	yes
240	Willow Cottage	Penrith/Carlisle	no	yes
244	High Houses	Penrith/Carlisle	no	no
248	Thistleyhaugh	Alnmouth/Morpeth	no	yes
252	Eshott Hall	Alnmouth/Morpeth	free for longer stays	not always
256	West Coates	Berwick-upon-Tweed	free	yes by arrangement

Place index